WONDER WOMAN

WONDER WOMAN

GODS AND GODDESSES

JOHN BYRNE

PRIMA PUBLISHING

PRIMA PUBLISHING and colophon are registered trademarks
of Prima Communications, Inc.

Library of Congress Catalog Card Number: 96-67541

ISBN: 0-7615-0483-4
97 98 99 00 01 AA 10 9 8 7 6 5 4 3 2 1
Printed in the United States of America

How to Order
Single copies may be ordered from Prima Publishing, P.O. Box 1260BK, Rocklin, CA 95677;
telephone (916) 632-4400. Quantity discounts are also available.
On your letterhead, include information concerning the intended use of the books
and the number of books you wish to purchase.

Visit us online at www.primapublishing.com

TO PAUL KUPPERBERG,
WHO KNOWS WHY

WONDER WOMAN

PROLOGUE
TWO YEARS AGO

IN the dream Rebecca Chandler
walks in darkness. So total, so absolute that it presses against her eyes,
hard and cold, trying to squash them back into their sockets.

She is fully clothed in the dream, which surprises her, since in her
nightmares—and this is very much a nightmare—she is always naked,
leaving her vulnerable and ashamed. But then, her nightmares are usually filled with punishment, torture, and humiliation. They reach into
her deepest psyche and find the hidden things that torment and drive
her, giving them form. Giving them voice and power to hurt her.

But for all the times this dream has invaded her sleep, there has
never been a sense of punishment in its earliest moments, never a feeling that she was wrong, that she was bad, that she must struggle
always to redeem herself. No, in this dream—in the strange progression
of this dream, night to night—there is more a sense of discovery, of
searching in the Stygian blackness for an answer, a reward of some
kind. In fact, she has come to realize this dream would almost be comforting, with its sameness, its lack of any sort of threat or pain, were it
not for the claustrophobic quality of the dark.

Rebecca walks through the dream slowly, arms stretched out before her, fingers spread, sifting the darkness. The floor—if it is a floor—

1

is smooth beneath her feet, and while she has never fallen in this dream, there is a distinct downward slope to the surface she walks upon that makes her feel as though she is descending. Each night—many nights now—she has had the sense this dream is carrying her down, down, deeper and deeper into the inky thickness, her final destination unknown and unknowable.

No matter how often it comes to her, Rebecca is never entirely sure how the dream will end. Assuming there is no sudden alteration of the scenario she has passed through these many nights, she will simply walk, walk, walk for what seems in the dream to be hours, days, until the darkness begins to soften. Until there appears before and around her something that is not so much light as a subtle lessening of the absolute blackness. She will begin to see, to sense shapes, forms, edges defining themselves, black on black, the merest suggestion of a wall, a corner, a doorway. Are these columns, rising around her? Is this a precipice that yawns to the side? Rebecca is never sure, no matter how many times the scene repeats itself. Although the forms seem always to be the same, always to be exactly the ones she has encountered before, she is not sure even now what they are, what they mean.

Tonight is like the others. The darkness diminishes. The forms take shape, grow solid all around her. In the way dreams have of being simultaneously different and familiar, it seems longer this time. She is walking deeper into the area defined by these phantom shapes. She wants to call it a temple, though she does not know why. There is nothing holy here, she is sure, and yet the impression of columns, of the smooth floor, the vaulted ceiling, makes her think of ancient Greece, of the Parthenon in all its unbroken splendor, of statues of Zeus, Athena, Apollo. All the false gods who ruled the minds of men before the Truth was laid bare to them.

The pattern continues to change, subtly. Rebecca feels her heart beat faster, her mouth grow dry. These are strange sensations for a dream, and not for the first time she finds herself wondering if this truly is a dream—though what else, she asks herself once more, can it possibly be? There is no reality she comprehends that could encompass this infinite place, this eternal darkness. No portion of the world she knows could ever contain these columns, this floor, this half-guessed ceiling. It must be a dream, yet if it is a dream, it is more intense than any she has ever known.

Rebecca begins to feel now an even greater certainty that she is being given a mission. A holy mission. She does not know its form just yet, but each night for the past week, perhaps as long as ten days, as the dream has played itself out before her, the notion, the conviction has grown stronger and stronger in her breast. She is being taken to see something, she is to be shown something, made to understand something. And she knows, without ever having seen it, that it will be a pagan, obscene ritual, the hideous mockery of a normal, natural act. Putting, if true, the lie to everything she believes, all she holds sacred. If she accepts, for even an instant, that what she will witness could have been, even might have been, then she has been wrong. Her entire life. The things she preaches. The Bible she believes to be the Gospel, the word of God. All wrong.

As if prompted by the strength of that understanding, this night the darkness draws farther back, and she sees that she is, indeed, in a temple built very much in the style of Athens in its glory. The blackness still seems to coil and flow around her, as though a veil were between her eyes and what she sees, but now the details are far more clear, far more absolute, and she sees that she stands at the top of a long flight of marble stairs, leading down, down, toward a shadowed landscape that evokes in her thoughts of green fields, rolling hills, and trees filled with bright birds singing.

But there is no sound, no color. Only a compulsion growing in her heart and mind to walk down those long, steep steps, to enter the wooded land—she knows instinctively that it will grow clearer, show her more of its secrets as she approaches—and walk under the arching trees, following such paths as they may allow between their gnarled trunks, until she sees . . . what?

A dark-haired woman. Rebecca comes upon her in that sudden and entirely natural way dreams have of changing, turning round the thick bole of a tree—*When did I leave the temple? When did I walk down the steps?*—but the woman does not see her. She walks by, tall, strong, dressed all in white, with her raven hair bound up around her head, her olive-hued limbs wrapped in subtly wrought gold and silver. In her arms she carries a small bundle, a shape wrapped all in silk that she holds against her bosom as a mother might hold a child.

And there is a name. Rebecca knows the stranger's name. Hippolyta.

She follows Hippolyta along the leafy path, down along a gentle hillside, under the trees, their branches filled with leaves, all the world filled, it seems, with the energy of life. Hippolyta does not seem to know she is being followed. She walks slowly, carefully, toward the edge of a bright, silvery lake that laps against the bottom of the hill.

At the lakeshore Hippolyta unwraps her small bundle. It is a statue, a model, less than two feet long, but perfect in every detail, every aspect. A newborn child, a female child, chubby faced, little fingers groping without moving at the air. Hippolyta sets aside the silks that wrapped the clay form, steps down into the water of the lake. Overhead the clear, blue sky is suddenly filled with clouds, speeding across the dome of the heavens, whirling.

Hippolyta moves a few feet offshore, kneels in the water. She holds the clay doll down before her, as if baptizing it, and her mouth moves in silent prayer. The waters begin to move, small waves rising, and large ones following fast behind. The wind begins to blow. The clouds darken overhead.

Something begins to move around Hippolyta. Watching from the shore, Rebecca cannot say what it is she sees. *Energy,* she thinks. Blobs and spots of energy that seem to dance around the kneeling woman as she rocks back and forth over the effigy in her arms. The muscles bunch and play under the smooth skin of Hippolyta's back. Her shoulders hunch. She seems suddenly racked with unimaginable pain. Squatting in the water, sweating and straining like some savage animal, as energies crackle and dance around her and the thing she cradles in her arms ripples as if with a life of its own.

It is very clear. Rebecca does not know how she knows, but the mud doll, the clay effigy, crafted so carefully by the woman called Hippolyta to mimic every detail of humanity, is the image of the female child Hippolyta so longs to call her own. And the energies that burst and burn about the thing are the gifts of beings who live beyond the world of men and women, who dare challenge the order of the Universe by calling themselves gods—and who here, this day, commit the ultimate depravity, imbuing mud and soil with the precious gift of life!

Rebecca sees all this now, in her dream. And it makes her sick, violently ill, so much so that she falls to her knees on the lakeshore, heaving, sweating, feeling as though the world she knows, the Universe she knows has been despoiled, raped, turned into something horrible and incomprehensible.

But she will not accept it because it cannot be true. It is a dream. A nightmare, a hideous mockery of life and truth. Lies spread by one in league with evil, one seeking to bring down the one True Word.

She must find a way to spread the message she draws over and over from the dream and the dark: she must find a way to utterly and totally destroy the lie, the living abomination a foolish world has chosen to call Wonder Woman.

As she wakes, sodden with sweat but safe in her own small bed, her own small room, she thinks, just for the moment that it takes for sleep to fall away from her, that she hears someone laughing.

The laughter chills her more than anything she has seen in her strange, silent dream.

CHAPTER ONE

ABOVE the shoulder of the world, the towers of Gateway City rose against the first blush of the morning sun, a galaxy of stars frozen in columns of ebony.

Diana turned, arching her supple body on the crest of the night air, banking toward the north, toward the span of rust-red bridge that hurled its steel frame over the mouth of Gateway Bay, that same inlet that gave its name to the first settlement, the great grandfather of this sprawling metropolis.

Below her the towers seemed for a moment to bend, to turn toward her as she let herself drop through the stillness of the autumn air, let the invisible fingers of the wind lift her long hair and spread it, raven wings, black on black against the sky.

The city was peaceful, quiet. On the streets below traffic moved, but no horns blared, no voices were raised, and Diana knew it was only her altitude that painted the horizon with the colors of dawn; in the deep bosom of Gateway City it was still night, still that last quiet moment before the city stirred itself to face a new day.

The towers rushed up toward her. Diana twisted again, easily, finding the currents of the air, riding upon them as unerringly as a mortal would walk a familiar path. She turned, letting her head rise, her feet drop, so that her long legs became the point of an arrow dropping into the center of the city.

There were others, Diana knew, whom a perhaps overzealous press had dubbed "super heroes," who daily, nightly went out into the cities they called their homes—Metropolis, Gotham, names out of legend and fable—to patrol the streets, to seek out those who broke the law, those who threatened the fragile stability of urban life. They saw themselves, or at any rate allowed themselves to be seen, as crimefighters, champions of truth and justice. Though she had stood with them, battled beside them, Diana did not see herself in this way. Raised on Themyscira by the last of the Amazons of old, she was a warrior, not a policeman, and she did not fly above her adopted home in search of wrongs to right, evil to undo. She soared above the towers of Gateway simply because she loved the freedom of flight, the feel of the wind against her face. Because she could.

Still, Gateway City was like all big cities, densely packed with a populace not always happy, not always content with its lot. The people moved through the arteries of steel and stone like blood through a body, carrying life, hope, power and pettiness, good and evil. And as a warrior, Diana found herself more often than not thrust into the role of peacemaker, champion, protector of those who could not protect themselves.

Tonight, it seemed, would be such an occasion.

She heard the scream of the sirens before she saw the lights flash and bounce on the steep walls of the canyon streets below her. Bending her body into the night wind, changing course, Diana brought herself above the noise and tumult.

Three police cars were in pursuit of a large armored vehicle, something she saw as a curious cross between a train engine and a tank. It crashed down the street, tearing up the pavement like rice paper, crushing cars as pedestrians bolted for the small safety of doorways along the avenue. The police pressed close in their pursuit, but they had not yet opened fire on the fleeing vehicle. Diana guessed their restraint to be twofold in its origin—the heavy armor plate of the quarry would resist anything the police might be carrying in their vehicles, and bullets fired at that armor would surely bounce, ricocheting into the bodies of the few unwary onlookers abroad in the hours before the city came fully awake.

The speed of Hermes, swiftest of all the Greek gods, drove Diana as she accelerated above the jarring scene, pushing herself in front of the hurtling tank, turning in midair so that she flew now backward, looking small and vulnerable before the behemoth.

Until she acted.

A single massive cannon thrust out of the broad, blunt snout of the vehicle, black and rough, as though the metal had been left deliberately unfinished to emphasize the evil of its purpose. This Diana seized, the metal groaning softly as her strong hands closed about it. Peering from the safety of their hiding places, a few fortunate citizens had a chance, a fleeting moment to see the muscles bunch beneath the smooth flesh of Diana's back, before the tank and its new passenger rumbled past, and Diana twisted her grip.

Like someone twisting loose a recalcitrant bottle top, Diana turned the long barrel of the cannon in its socket. Metal moaned, then screamed, then ripped like timeworn fabric, scraps of shrapnel whipping about the Amazon Princess as she wrenched the barrel from its mount.

The tank slewed sideways, massive treads grinding into the pavement, coughing chunks of asphalt that crashed and clanged against the pursuing police cars. The sudden movement was faster than one might have expected from the big vehicle, but it did not catch Diana unawares. Tossing aside the barrel of the cannon, she shifted her grip to the gaping hole her work had made in the face of the tank. She reached deep into the wound and grabbed whatever she could find, twisting, ripping, until the front of the tank began to sag and droop in a manner almost comic, looking as a result of her handiwork like a child's plastic toy left too long in the hot summer sun.

Diana planted her feet firmly on the face of the tank and pulled up and over, beginning to peel back the top turret, rivets popping, outraged metal bellowing. Her strength was said to be that of the very Earth itself, impossible to measure, to gauge, perhaps second only to the equally immeasurable strength of the Kryptonian who guarded Metropolis. The tank opened like an orange, metal rolling back to reveal a quartet of strangely garbed—and suddenly very vulnerable—men crammed together in a cockpit that might have struck Diana as intensely claustrophobic, had she not just rendered it open to the early morning air.

The men were armed. Three scrambled in the still-confining space to draw weapons, while the one hunched over the controlling mechanism shifted levers, turned wheels, and spun the big tank wildly about in the vain attempt to hurl Diana from her perch. When the failure of that maneuver became obvious even to him, the driver slammed down a heavily booted foot, crushing a pedal to the grimy metal floor, and the tank shuddered to a stop. So sudden was the halt that the foremost of the pursuing police cars slammed headlong into the rear of the armored vehicle.

The other three men raised their weapons, big, blockish things that Diana recognized as rifles only from the way the men held them. As the tank grumbled into silence the night was suddenly filled with the deafening cacophony of those rifles, spewing fire and steel from many mouths, all directed at the Amazon.

What followed was something that had more than once defied description. The eyes saw, the mind recorded, but logic refused to build a coherent picture from the image. As the guns vomited their lethal load, Diana moved with speed and fluid grace such as no words could ever fully convey save to those fortunate enough to witness it in person. The silver bracelets covering her forearms became a blur of liquid mercury, deflecting the streetlights in a galaxy of scintillations, and deflecting also the red-hot slugs that spewed from the weapons.

More than deflected them. Controlled them, directed them. The ricochets the pursuing police had feared were directed by Diana's lightning moves, so that each slug that bounced from her whirling bracelets snapped back and down, striking harmlessly in the broken pavement around the treads of the tank.

Their ammunition exhausted, the four men likewise lost both sense and logic. Having seen what Diana could do, they nonetheless broke from their confining steel and plastic nest and scrambled over the sides as if they believed their small, human speed would be sufficient to carry them away from her.

But of course it was not. Two she caught before they made it out of the ruptured cockpit. A third she brought down by the simple expedient of hurling one of her captives against the fugitive's back with sufficient force to render both unconscious.

The fourth, in that short time, had opened a respectable gap between himself and Diana. Smiling, she tossed the man she still held toward the waiting police, slipping from its place on her hip the golden, glowing lasso many had come to think of as her trademark, and with a sudden, supple turn and twist launched the shimmering cord out and down, unerringly looping about the running man, snapping back with just enough force to yank him from his feet and lift him up and back to land, astonished, in Diana's irresistible embrace.

Stepping down from the top of the tank, she offered her fourth prize to the waiting police.

"Wonder Woman . . ." The closest cop tried to find words, and failing, blushed deep and hot, his face bright red in the streetlights.

"I'm sure you can deal with these men now, officer," Diana smiled. The cop heard a faint accent in her perfect English. Greek, he suspected, since that was said to be her heritage, albeit a Greek of thousands of years past.

"Yeah," he said, and again felt foolish that he stood before a living legend—not to mention the most beautiful woman he had ever seen— unable to find sufficient mastery of his mind and tongue to do more than grunt.

Diana turned. She surveyed, quickly, the damage the monster vehicle had done and decided there was nothing there that she could fix. She stepped again into the air and hurled herself up over the towers of the city, all now salmon pink at their pinnacles as the rising sun heaved itself at last over the horizon.

Diana did not look back as the streets dropped away below her. She coiled the lasso back into a tidy loop and returned it to her side. Magically, it clung to the golden girdle that rounded her waist, no clasp, no catch to hold it in place. She flew up and over the towers, headed into the hills that rose abruptly on the city's eastern side. It was there, in one of the small, quiet communities that overlooked the city, that Diana had found a place to call her own.

The narrow streets rushed up to meet her, houses like a hundred shoeboxes set on end crowded close along the winding avenues. Windows like blind, dark eyes looked down on empty pavement, on parked cars and wrought iron railings that wound along the fronts of the houses, defining small, green garden spaces in the hollows between steep front steps.

Diana slowed her descent and once again the speed and power of flight vested in her by Hermes himself set aside the rough embrace of gravity. She paused a moment, holding herself stationary in the air, luxuriating in the morning cool on her bare skin. She felt still something of the exhilaration that had flooded her as she battled the man-made juggernaut. She had been sent into this world as an ambassador of peace, to teach the ways of love and gentle understanding that were the cherished tenets of her distant island home—but there, too, she had been trained in the martial arts, the warrior's code, and this small encounter had spoken to that part of her, making her blood sing, her heart pound. It had spoken to her innermost nature, her Amazon heritage, and she was happy to feel it, to have been able to use her great power once again in a just cause. It was one thing to preach peace, a worthy endeavor indeed, but it was something else again, something indefinable, intangible, to heed the songs a warrior sings.

Directly beneath her one house stood apart from the rest. Tall and narrow like its sisters, it held the corner of the block, and to its side, where another house might have crowded close, an empty space of land was filled with trees and shrubs, grass and wildflowers left to bloom unhampered by the regimentation of landscaping. In the steep roof a single skylight stared up at Diana, a cyclopean eye beyond which lay the small, sparse apartment she rented from her new friend and employer, Helena Sandsmark. Professor Helena Sandsmark, of the Gateway City Museum of Antiquities.

Diana let herself drift down to the skylight, opened it, and floated through into her new home. It was, in many ways, the first place she had ever really been able to call a *home,* the first since she had left the comfort and isolation of Themyscira, the hidden island that had been the only home she had known for so many years. When she had first come to the world outside Themyscira, she had lived with the woman and her daughter who had befriended her in Boston, on the other side of the continent, but that had been as a boarder in a spare bedroom in their home and not in a separate apartment of her own.

Themyscira—she could no longer bring herself to call it Paradise Island—was behind her now, set aside in the quest she had imposed upon herself to find a place in the world that had nothing to do with her life as the Princess of that fabled land. She had turned away, slowly at first, but more and more as she learned the ways of the rest of the world—"Patriarch's World," her mother had called it—and as the once-serene patterns of her life on Themyscira had broken and crumbled before her.

She was now, in all proper respects, an orphan. Her mother, Hippolyta, Queen of the Amazons, had betrayed her. A well-intentioned betrayal, true, but one that had cost Diana much, cost her the very fabric of her life, the soft cocoon of trust in which she had always lived. And more, since the same betrayal had cost the life of another Amazon, a fiery, raging woman known as Artemis, who had for a while assumed the mantle of Wonder Woman, and who died because of it.

Diana closed the window above her and settled to the floor. Around her the building was asleep, the other tenants unaware not only of her return, but the manner in which she had achieved it. She did not have, as so many others of the super hero community did, a "secret identity," an alter ego behind which she could hide her powers and abilities.

But friends conceived the name "Prince" to go after "Diana" and created a semblance of a self she could present to the rest of the world, when it became desirable to set aside, for a while at least, the burden of her role as Wonder Woman.

Wonder Woman. Diana smiled, a small, fleeting thing. There was something, still, in that name that seemed so odd, so nearly preposterous. She had not chosen it for herself, certainly, but it seemed now as much a part of her as did her real name. Diana was Wonder Woman, and Wonder Woman was Diana. If the world needed labels for those who fought for it, defended it, then she would be Wonder Woman and not Diana. It was a harmless enough thing, after all, and Diana was quick to give her preference when anyone asked; she was Diana to her friends, her colleagues, the many mortals who inhabited her life.

Diana moved easily through the darkness of the apartment, shedding the bright metal of her costume, setting aside the tiara that she still wore despite her abdication of the rank it represented. She unclasped the golden girdle that surrounded her narrow waist and supported the magic lasso, and slipped off the red and gold breastplate, the interwoven double-W emblem that had for her an altogether different meaning than the alliterative initials of her public identity. She stepped out of the star-spangled briefs, the scarlet and white boots, slipping the shimmering silver bracelets from her wrists. Unadorned as the day her mother crafted her from the native clay of Themyscira, Diana climbed between the soft, dark sheets of her narrow bed and closed her eyes.

Today was Sunday, and though the specific significance of that day held no special meaning for her, she knew it was a day of rest, and intended to take full advantage of that. She would sleep, she decided, until just before noon, and then she would rise, wash, dress, and meet Helena and Cassandra for their previously scheduled lunch. *It will be a good day*, she thought as sleep came.

Father Donald Morris closed his pale gray eyes, leaning his deeply wrinkled brow against the cool glass of the door to the hospital's Intensive Care Unit. The weight of the night pressed close upon him.

The long, vampire hours demanded at last their payment. *Teach us, good Lord,* he thought, instinctively, remembering the oath of the Jesuit order, to which he did not, himself, belong, *to serve you as you deserve; to give and not to count the cost, to fight and not to heed the wounds, to toil and not to seek for rest, to labor and not to ask for any reward save that of knowing we do your will.*

Behind him the racking sobs of little Katherine Dorrity faded into soft whimpers as the drugs slowly overwhelmed her mind and her pain.

You could have done that hours ago, Morris thought. *Why let the child suffer? Why let her cry and whimper, scream like an animal in a trap? Because her body has built a resistance to the painkillers? Because a dose sufficient to ease her suffering might end her life? Why not? Why not? She's dying. There is nothing the doctors can do. Nothing prayer can do.*

He was shocked for a moment as the idea took form in his mind. But only a moment. It was not, after all, the first time those words, that thought had tried to force its way into his brain, work its way up into his consciousness. It was merely the first time it had succeeded.

I can't do it anymore. I thought I could do it forever, for always, for as long as the children needed me. But I can't. There are too many. Too much needless pain. Too many years.

He raised a thick-fingered hand to brush away the tear rivering its way down his leathery cheek. He straightened, opened his eyes. From the reflective surface of the door an old man looked back at him, stooped, worn. Morris wondered where he came from, how he had managed to replace, so subtly, so insidiously, that handsome, straight young man who had embarked with such relish on the calling of the priesthood.

Morris closed his eyes again. *My God, my God,* he thought, *have you at last finally forsaken me?* But it was not Donald Morris who was forsaken, he knew. It was all those children, all the countless years of children, suffering, dying, bodies racked with pain they couldn't begin to understand.

How do you tell a child she's dying? Father Donald Morris asked himself, not for the first time. *How do you tell a child that the benevolent God she's been taught about, the God who made the Heavens and the Earth, the God who crafted Adam and Eve and filled the world with all the things that fly and swim and walk and crawl—how do you tell a child that same God has now directed a small portion of His infinite energy toward the creation of a cancer, a tumor, a terrible, consuming thing in that child's brain or stomach or lungs or bones?*

Morris drew a long, shuddering breath. *How do you tell a mother that her unborn child is already cancerous, that it will be born to pain and sickness, to shrivel and die before her, nothing she can do, nothing anyone can do but. . . .*

He caught the reflexive, instinctive thought, breaking it off like a dry branch on a dead tree. *Nothing to do but pray.*

Donald Morris's lips curled in a mixture of anguish and disgust that would seem totally alien to the sisters he worked with, the nurses and the doctors who ministered to the children, tending to their bodies as he tried to tend to their souls.

"Oh, Father Morris!"

He turned. It was Sister Mary Anne, the one he always thought of as "the pretty one," her dark round face and big brown eyes seeming always on the verge of exploding from the constrictions of her habit. "Yes, Sister?"

"They're showing Wonder Woman on the television," Sister Mary Anne said, her eyes wide with wonder, childlike. "Live from Gateway City. I was going to fetch Sister Mary Angelica. She always likes to see Wonder Woman. I didn't expect to find you here."

"I was with the little Dorrity girl," Morris said, hating the sound of it, the accepted phrasing that seemed so diminishing, so dehumanizing. "I believe Sister Mary Angelica is there now."

"Thank you, Father." Sister Mary Anne stepped lightly past him, her habit floating about her. He went on through the door, down the short hall to the little waiting room where he knew the TV to be.

A small group of sisters, doctors, and parents were gathered around the big, ugly color set, a donation from a patron who had never bothered to read the Sermon on the Mount.

Morris shook his head. *Such bitterness. And so suddenly!*

But he knew it was not sudden at all. It was the logical conclusion of years of grinding pain, mental and physical anguish, wearing at him, pummeling him into this last, bitter submission.

"Isn't she a wonder?" Oblivious to the redundancy, one of the Sisters stood with hands clasped to her bosom, staring with almost childlike delight at the image on the screen. "News Copter 5" declared a floating logo in the lower right of the big screen. In the center, seen through the distortion of a telephoto lens the star-spangled form of Wonder Woman moved quickly and—it would seem to Morris—easily through the task of demolishing a large and particularly ugly tank.

"She's a menace."

The words were spat into the air, hard, harsh, and Morris did not have to turn toward the speaker to know who it was. The Mother Superior, her pale face reddened with anger, her cobalt eyes narrowed to electric slits. "She is evil, corruption made flesh."

"Now you sound like that Chandler woman," one of the waiting parents said, a young man Morris knew well, lean and drawn with the torment of his child's suffering.

"I have little patience for the Evangelicals, Mr. Sweeney," the Mother Superior snapped, not taking her eyes from the image on the screen, seeming, Morris thought, to be trying to melt the screen, dissolve the offending image with her laser eyes. "But in this case I must agree. This so-called 'Wonder Woman' is an affront to all that is true and holy." She turned her eyes away from the screen long enough to see Donald Morris. "Don't you agree, Father?"

"I haven't given it much thought," Morris said. He watched now as the dancing, bouncing image showed Wonder Woman turning her captives over to uniformed police officers. "It seems as though she performs a certain needed function. Much like the other super heroes."

"Hardly like the others," Mother Superior scowled. "At least they have the proper respect to keep such differences to themselves. This 'Wonder Woman' preaches heresy and paganism."

"Oh, hardly 'preaches,' Reverend Mother." Mr. Sweeney seemed, in Morris's estimation, to be mustering all his inner strength to dispute the powerful forces contained in Mother Superior's small, stout form. "She comes from a different culture, and she talks freely about it when asked."

"She preaches heresy," Mother Superior snapped. "She teaches of the old gods, the pagan gods. She talks of them as if they are real."

"To her they are," Morris said, himself not a little afraid to risk an argument with so formidable an opponent.

Mother Superior's eyes blazed. "What has that to do with anything? All pagans believe their abominations are real. It is for us to teach the truth."

"What is truth?" Morris felt suddenly emboldened by his bitterness. "All my life I have served God and Jesus, never questioning, never doubting, yet always operating solely on faith, on the sure and certain belief that what I have been taught is true."

The color darkened in Mother Superior's cheeks, making her eyes blaze all the more. "What are you saying, Father Morris?" She used his title, he felt, as a weapon in her own arsenal, as a reminder that it was not his place to join the wrong side in this debate.

"I mean," said Father Donald Morris, picking his words carefully, understanding even as he spoke their full import, the terrible power they held, "that I have believed in and worshiped Jesus all my life, but I have never met him. Wonder Woman, it is my understanding, has had lunch with Zeus!"

One floor down from Diana, at ten o'clock that same Sunday morning, Cassandra Sandsmark sat staring at a television screen.

She knew all too well the face of the woman she saw there. Rebecca Chandler—the Reverend Rebecca Chandler, of the First Temple of the Savior's Grace. Cassandra wrinkled her button nose as the phrase passed through her mind. Her mother had always taught her tolerance and compassion for the needs and feelings of others, but in this phrase Cassandra found a pretension, a claim to superiority of spirit she found untenable.

Doubly so, as she listened to the words the slim, elegantly appointed woman spoke into the microphone before her.

"This woman has come among us as a friend and a champion," Rebecca Chandler was saying, enunciating each word carefully, modulating and controlling the stammer Cassandra knew—from magazine profiles—had vexed Rebecca since childhood. "She has presented herself as a hero, a role model. A 'super hero,' someone cast in the mold of Charlemagne, of even Jesus Christ Himself—" A pause as the thousands in her immediate audience drew a sharp breath. "But she is nothing less than the Devil's own! She is nothing less than a demon sent to lure our children from the path of Righteousness!"

"Oh, drop dead!" Cassandra thumbed the power switch on the remote control in her right hand and the image on the small screen shrank instantly to a single glowing phosphor. "The Devil's own!" *Yeah, right.* Like the woman asleep in the apartment upstairs, probably the best friend Cassie had ever had outside of her mother, could be an agent of Satan. *Get a grip, Chandler!*

"Cassie?" In her office off the living room, Helena Sandsmark leaned back in her chair to see her daughter sitting cross-legged before the silent, dark television. "Who are you talking to?"

Cassie rose, a smooth, supple movement of long, slim limbs that evoked a pang of passing jealousy in Helena. She was only thirty-five, but already she felt the encroaching stiffness brought on by too many hours behind a desk, too little exercise, too many chances to keep herself in shape sacrificed to books and learning.

"That Chandler bitch," Cassie said. "She was dumping on Diana again."

"Language," Helena said reflexively. She slid her chair back from her laden desk and stood up. "Is this what you were telling me about before? How she's attacking Diana because of her faith?"

"Yeah." Cassie crossed to the small red couch that faced the TV. Dropping heavily onto faded cushions, she inspected the remains of a peanut butter and jelly sandwich she no longer found particularly appetizing. "I mean, it's not fair, is it? Rebecca Chandler preaches all the time about God and Jesus and everything she believes, and Diana never really says *anything* about her gods. And, like, she's actually *met* Zeus and Athena and Hermes and all of them, but she doesn't go around telling everybody they should worship them or something."

Helena leaned against the frame of the door that opened between her small office and the only-slightly-larger living room. "That's difficult for some people to understand," she said. "I don't agree with Rebecca Chandler, and I certainly don't approve of her attacking Diana, but I understand how she must feel. It's perplexing for modern people to be told those old gods really exist."

"But that's the whole point," Cassie scowled. "Chandler says they *don't* exist. She says Diana is lying about all that and that she's some kind of devil sent by Satan or somebody to lie and corrupt us. Especially us kids, since so many of us think Wonder Woman is way cool."

Helena shook her head, taking off her glasses to rub the bridge of her slender nose with thumb and forefinger. "The early Christians accepted the existence of the gods their faith supplanted," she said, lapsing for a moment into the tone of voice Cassie thought of as her mother's "lecture mode." As the chief curator of the Gateway City Museum of Cultural Antiquities, Helena had an unfortunate habit— in the eyes of her teenaged daughter—of turning everything to some reference to her work. "They accepted the existence of the Greco-Roman gods," Helena now said. "They simply chose not to worship them. Eventually, they even turned some of them into the prototypes for their images of demons and goblins. Pan in particular seemed to hold a special fear and fascination for them. He became the blueprint for less sophisticated pictures of the Devil, and even gave us the word *panic*."

"You're doing it again, Mom."

Helena blinked. "Oh. Sorry." She laughed, a silvery thing belying her deliberately dowdy mode of dress and deportment. Sometimes Cassandra wished her mother would pay greater attention to her appearance. She was not unattractive, with her bright eyes and her smooth white skin, and even Cassandra had to admit that at thirty-five, she was not all that old.

"I'm sure it's nothing to worry about," Helena continued. "Diana has battled cosmic menaces and fought side by side with the greatest heroes in the world. I'm sure someone like Rebecca Chandler holds no special dread for her."

"Maybe," Cassie frowned, playing with the sticky edges of her sandwich. "But I've heard some of my friends' parents talking the same way, and Mrs. Holdeman even took me to one side and told me it was probably wrong for you to let me hang out with Diana like I do."

Helena stiffened. She had weathered much in her years as a single mother. There were always those who wanted to tell her how to raise Cassandra. Always those who looked askance at her, knowing there was not and never had been a Mr. Sandsmark. "Well, the next time she says something like that," Helena said in as even a tone as her anger allowed, "you find the most polite way you can to tell her I said to mind her own business!"

Cassie chuckled, a throaty sound that reminded Helena altogether too much of a nasty cartoon character. "I will. But right now I think I'm gonna go find something better for lunch than this sandwich."

Cassie disappeared into the kitchenette, leaving Helena to study the blank TV screen. Rebecca Chandler. Yes, it had been about two years, Helena recalled, since she came on the scene, talking only a little at first about Wonder Woman and how she was a threat to all that was good and true. Back then, Helena hardly noticed.

But back then, she had not yet met Diana, Wonder Woman. Had not come to think of her as a friend.

Helena retrieved the remote control from the rug. She turned the TV back on for a while and listened. Rebecca Chandler spoke smoothly, carefully, nothing shrill or threatening. A honey voice, a pitchman's voice. She was a pretty woman, small, fine-boned. She did not affect the big hair and garish, clownish makeup that Helena thought of as endemic to her calling. She did not cry, did not rail. She spoke calmly, clearly, and despite herself, Helena found herself thinking that Rebecca Chandler believed what she was saying, genuinely believed Diana to be some manner of hell-sent menace.

Helena turned the TV off. *Bitch,* she thought. The emotion was stronger than she would have expected, and for a moment Helena found it disturbing. She shook herself, shaking off the uncharacteristic rage before returning to her reading.

CHAPTER TWO

"**Y**ES, I am aware of this woman. She does not disturb me. Do you think I should be concerned?"

It was Monday morning. A gray sky hung low over the towers of Gateway City and threatened to drown the afternoon in one of the sudden, drenching summer storms for which the city was famous. In the office of Helena Sandsmark, in the Gateway City Museum of Cultural Antiquities, the lights were on, pushing back the gray day and throwing pools of soft yellow onto the old books, the parchments, the many curious and sometimes unidentified things that crowded the shelves lining the walls.

It was a place in which Diana, Princess of Themyscira, felt most comfortable, steeped as it was in age, in the commemoration of tradition and the value of time and tradition.

"I don't know if you should be concerned or not." Helena looked over the tops of her glasses at the beautiful young woman seated on the other side of her desk. *Diana may be Wonder Woman, may be a living Amazon, but she's still naive in so many ways, still ill prepared for the way the world, this world works.* "Rebecca Chandler has a lot of followers. Two years ago no one had heard of her; now she claims to have millions of followers. Even Cassie watches her, just so she can make fun of her. But that's the way her message gets through. People hear it, maybe begin to believe it."

Diana frowned, a small darkening of her perfect features. "I do not understand why this Chandler woman should be so offended by my very existence. I have said nothing against her faith. I understand there are many gods and goddesses, many faiths."

Helena nodded. "But it's not that simple. Rebecca Chandler would be the first, I'm sure, to say they're all the same god, all manifestations of the one true god, but she does not really believe it. Behind closed doors I'll bet she thinks her own particular interpretation of scripture is the only one that has any merit, and she hates you—well, hate may be too strong a word, but she sure doesn't *like* the fact that you represent another theology. I think if you were a member of some sort of cult, if you followed a David Koresh or Reverend Moon or any other extremist, she wouldn't feel so threatened by you. But your gods, though thought nicely dead and gone, are respected and recognized. And now you come along and not only worship Zeus and Athena and Hera and Apollo and all the rest, but have actually met them. Actually owe your existence to them!"

"Why would that trouble anyone, though?" Diana's tone and the expression in her bright blue eyes were genuinely troubled. "I understand that the God of the Christians is more obtuse, less obvious in His manifestations than Zeus. That does not trouble me. I do not dispute His existence."

Helena leaned forward, placing her slim hands flat on the worn blotter on her desktop. "Some would say, Chandler would say, that by your very existence *you* do. You've been taught tolerance, Diana, understanding. And for you, religion is, well, it's second nature, it's as easy as—I don't even know how to say it. Look, in this culture, none of us are used to dealing with the concept of real gods who walk around, talking and interacting with people. I guess the analogy that comes to mind is movie stars or baseball players or something. I've never met, oh, Sean Connery, but lots of people have, and I know he exists. It would be pointless for me to dispute that he exists. But for Rebecca Chandler it's like—well, it's like having Sean Connery exist suggests that Mel Gibson *doesn't*." She paused. "That doesn't make much sense, does it?"

"A little," Diana nodded. "You are saying that to Rebecca Chandler the fact that I have actually met Zeus somehow says Jehovah does not really exist."

"Yep. And in a way I can almost understand her. Faith is a difficult beast at best. Gods aren't supposed to walk the earth anymore. Maybe having you saying you met Zeus, that you got your powers from Hermes and Athena and Hestia and the rest, maybe that reminds Rebecca Chandler that some of those Old Testament stories are not so very far removed from the myths and legends of the Greco-Roman gods. In fact there is a distinctly Greek feeling to a whole bunch of stuff in the Old and New Testaments. Jesus smiting the fig tree and all that. Very Olympian."

Diana rose, crossing to the window to look up at the brooding sky. "This is most troublesome, Helena. I did not come to Man's world intending to tear down established religions. But when people asked me about my background, about where I came from, how I got my powers, I told them."

"Yes. And you told them that story about being molded out of clay and brought to life by your mother's prayers and the intervention of a half-dozen gods. I have to admit that makes even me feel a little queasy, and I don't have much use for religion altogether. But I can see where Rebecca Chandler would be bothered, would see it as some kind of, I don't know, some kind of mockery. God made Adam from the dust of the earth. Your mother made you from clay." Helena shrugged. "It would probably have been for the best if you'd kept that part to yourself." She smiled, ruefully. "And I am the absolute master of retroactive advice, you know."

Diana shared the smile. "I understand." She turned from the window, moving as she always did with the fluid grace of which Helena wished she might possess one tenth, one hundredth part. "Perhaps I should approach this woman, speak to her directly. I have found there are few problems that cannot be addressed by reasoned and reasonable discourse."

"Beard the lioness in her den? Very Biblical, but maybe not all that appropriate."

"Why not?"

Helena paused, considering. "I don't know. I just have a bad feeling about it. I feel like there are dominoes toppling, or maybe set to topple, and if you're not very careful you could send them all tumbling down to finish up God knows where." She frowned. "This isn't my day for particularly apt metaphors."

Diana smiled. "Perhaps not. I understand your concern, however. But I also think little can be accomplished without a direct meeting between myself and Rebecca Chandler. I believe I shall go there this afternoon. It will take me only an hour or so to fly to Chicago."

She felt him before she saw him.

It was always that way. The man's power, his sheer masculine presence seemed always to permeate a room, fill a room. She swallowed and walked into her office as if she were not afraid.

For a moment it seemed as though she might be wrong. The office was broad, bright, sparsely furnished, as Rebecca Chandler felt was only appropriate to her calling. None of the gaudy ostentation that seemed to characterize far too many who had walked this path before her. The office was set high into the sloping face of the Crystal Tower, the gleaming headquarters of the New Soldiers of Salvation, looking out over the flat blue steel of Lake Michigan. Because the Tower curved, one wall curved, and that wall was glass, smooth and clear, angled up and back, twelve feet from burgundy carpeted floor to gently sculpted ivory ceiling. Against the window stood Rebecca Chandler's desk, large but plain, polished onyx, and behind that her chair, with its high, broad back turned toward her as she entered.

That was where he was, of course. Sitting in her chair. Relishing, she was sure, the small hint of power it gave him, power over her, over her cause. She reminded herself not to say anything. She was annoyed, but she refused to show it, to give him that tiny victory.

"You're here sooner than I expected," she said. She was tired, worn out from what had turned out to be a particularly long day, yesterday, Sunday. *The day of rest is never so for those who do the Lord's work.*

"Yes," he said. The voice was deep, resonant, yet with an odd sibilance that seemed to catch some of his words, as if he were always on the verge of hissing. *Hissing,* Rebecca thought, *through bared, clenched teeth.*

He turned slowly in the chair, rising. He was tall, broad, seeming to block out all the light, almost to cover the broad expanse of window. He looked now as he had looked when she first met him, nearly two years ago. His hair was dark, but shot through with silver. His face was strong, his eyes bright in a way that was not entirely friendly. He moved with an easy grace, but with a weight, a solidity, as though a mountain walked. He wore a dark suit, a dark shirt and tie. He smiled, and his teeth were perfect, even, bright in the dark frame of his mustache and beard.

"I want you to step up your campaign," he said. "I am informed of a growing groundswell, a reaction building up from the grass roots. This is good. I believe it can be accelerated."

"I disagree." Rebecca Chandler felt a knot in the pit of her stomach. She could not explain, even to herself, what she felt for this man. A certain kind of basic, animal lust, yes. But something more. He had a casual power about him, an ease, a way of saying the least thing as though he were used to having people hang upon his every word.

"Do you?" He smiled again. "Very well, tell me what you would do. You have been wise and true in this adventure so far, Rebecca. I am prepared to listen."

"If I go too fast now," Rebecca said, crossing to take her place in the seat he had vacated, "I will start to seem shrill, overbearing. I place my references carefully, place my attacks carefully. This witch can be brought down, but not by too much force, too soon."

He shrugged his broad shoulders. "I am, as you know, a man of action. I prefer to move swiftly, quickly. But I also appreciate the subtleness of a plan, a scheme well laid and carefully executed." He sat on the inside edge of the desk, one foot on the floor, his hanging leg a hair's breadth from her knee. "I chose you carefully, Rebecca," he said, and she heard an edge of threat in his voice. She did not know how she should respond to it. "I chose you carefully, and I have been, thus far, content in that choice. But remember that it was my power, my wealth that elevated you, that paid for this—" a sweep of his big hand encompassed the office and all beyond "—and if you fail me, I can easily do the same for another who will not."

Rebecca frowned, drawing strength from the sudden, unexpected depth of her anger. "I won't fail you. Why should I? I want this too. I want the truth to eclipse the darkness. Just as you do."

He laughed, a slow, rumbling thing that she felt as a wave rolling through her belly, her loins. It evoked an elusive memory in Rebecca's mind. Something she experienced every time she heard him laugh, and yet something that continued to elude her.

"Yes I do," he said. He reached out to cover her small hand, where it rested on the desk, with his own big paw. His flesh was warm and dry, as it had been the first time they shook hands, when he introduced himself, when he made his offer. She remembered how he seemed to smile, something wry, as if at some great, hidden joke when she asked his name and he said "Stephen Ramsey." She had searched in vain for the joke ever since.

"We make a great team, Rebecca, you and I. A great team. Together we will accomplish what many have sought to accomplish, and failed. This time there will be no failure."

"This time," Rebecca thought. *Something in the way he says it. As if he's referring to himself, somehow. As if he's tried before to destroy Wonder Woman. Tried and failed.*

The intercom on her desk buzzed. Rebecca freed her hand from Stephen Ramsey's touch, reached for the switch. "Yes, Alyce?"

"M-Ms. Chandler. . . ." Her secretary's voice was choked with an emotion Rebecca could not immediately identify. It struck Rebecca that in the years they had worked together, she had never heard Alyce Ruste sound so much as flustered, much less frightened, certainly not by anything that might happen in the office. They had met almost three years ago, when Alyce had come to work part time in the Christian Science Reading Room where Ramsey had found Rebecca. Their relationship had been casual at best, but they would often talk during slow moments or on breaks from work, discussing their shared faith. Rebecca had been impressed with Alyce's devotion, and Alyce, in turn, had looked to Rebecca for her unique insights into the Scriptures. When Rebecca had left the Reading Room to devote her full time and attention to her evangelical movement, Alyce Ruste had been the first to volunteer to join her. She had, as far as Rebecca knew, no one else in her life, nothing save her faith in Jesus and her devotion to Rebecca Chandler.

"What is it, Alyce? What's wrong?"

"It's Wonder Woman," Alyce finally managed. "The lobby security people just called up. Wonder Woman is here. . . ."

Eight monitor screens showed the same image from different angles, different distances.

Rebecca Chandler stared at them, spots of light against a velvety black background. She normally kept the screens hidden behind an elegant pewter and silver world map, now drawn to one side by the touch of a button.

"Wonder Woman! Here!" Rebecca felt her pulse race, not sure what to make of the emotions that suddenly surged in her breast. *Hate? Fear? Anger?* All were present, in different quantities. More than anything else, though, she felt astonishment. Somehow, in the back of her mind, she had supposed her open attacks on Wonder Woman might, eventually, lead to some kind of confrontation. She had even played through several imaginary scenarios, mental gymnastics in which she, Rebecca Chandler, always emerged the victor. Physically she was no match for the Amazon Princess, but she had no doubt she was the intellectual superior of a woman who was, after all, little more than a savage, a primitive who had lived out the first two decades of her life on an island stuck in an age that had withered and died when Christ was born.

She looked at Wonder Woman. Unexpectedly, the Amazon was not wearing her famous star-spangled uniform. She wore instead a demure skirt and blouse ensemble that, while it could not help but show off her spectacular physique—Rebecca noted ruefully that Wonder Woman was nearly a head taller than the security personnel who surrounded her—neither did it draw unnecessary attention like the more famous outfit. Wonder Woman's ebony hair was drawn back into a loose ponytail, and her cheeks were rosy, as if she had been facing into a stiff breeze.

She flew here. Of course. Under her own power. She just stepped into the air and flew here from Gateway City. How long did it take her? Hours? Seconds?

Rebecca shuddered. *Dear Lord, what have I set myself against?*

The cameras panned automatically to follow as Wonder Woman allowed herself to be led by the small phalanx of uniformed security personnel. Rebecca noted how people turned to watch Wonder Woman as she passed, following her with their eyes if not their bodies.

And when their eyes follow, how far behind are their hearts? She could sense Wonder Woman's innate power. Rebecca studied her easy grace, the way she moved so smoothly, with such assurance. She noted the way her security people kept touching their holsters, fingering the regulation nightsticks that dangled from their belts. She was aware again of just how militaristic the uniforms of the security corps really were—Ramsey's idea, not hers—softened not at all by the subdued colors of the Army of Salvation armband each wore on his right biceps, the white SoS wrapped around a golden cross on a pale blue background. Why had she deferred to Ramsey on the matter of the uniforms?

What do they think they could do? If Wonder Woman decided to, she could rip their heads off. Literally. And no one has ever been able to shoot her. She is simply too fast.

Rebecca reached out to tap a button as Wonder Woman stepped into the private elevator that would carry her directly to her office. Four of the screens went dark, the others shifting their images to show four different views of the inside of the elevator, one from each corner of the ceiling.

She hasn't looked at a camera even once. Does she not know the cameras are there? Not know she's being watched? Or—more likely—does she not care?

"When she gets up here, do you have anything you want to say to her?"

When there was no response, Rebecca turned from the screens. "Stephen?"

But he was gone, her office empty. Rebecca became frighteningly aware of the utter absence of anything that could afford her protection from a wrathful Wonder Woman. Not that there really was anything that could have served that function. *This woman is one of the most powerful beings on Earth, very nearly the equal of Superman.*

Rebecca shuddered.

But she wasn't exactly powerless herself. She had, she realized, one weapon, one small, psychological weapon she could play, use in the hope that it would show Wonder Woman that she, Rebecca Chandler, was not afraid, not at all apprehensive at this unexpected meeting.

The elevator door opened at the far end of the office. Rebecca took several steps forward, wanting Wonder Woman to see that she was moving toward her, facing her, not backing away, not seeking refuge.

"Welcome, Diana," she said, putting emphasis on the name, hoping the absence of any formal title—no "Wonder Woman," no

"Princess"—would convey immediately that Rebecca did not consider her visitor in any way her better. "Won't you please come in and have a seat?"

"Thank you." Wonder Woman's voice was soft and smooth, and there was a trace of accent, as Rebecca had read. She crossed to the big chair facing the desk, as Rebecca indicated, as Rebecca herself moved to the bigger chair behind the desk.

They sat facing each other for a long, silent moment. Rebecca wondered if her visitor were sizing her up, taking her measure as she, Rebecca, could not help but now do with Wonder Woman.

Of course she was taller, her hair black to Rebecca's auburn, her skin darker, though not quite the Mediterranean hue Rebecca expected. She was fuller figured, bigger in the bust and hip, longer in the leg than the five-foot-five Rebecca Chandler. It was the eyes that were the biggest surprise, though. Rebecca had expected brown, dark brown that would be almost black, Greek eyes. But Wonder Woman's eyes were blue, bright blue like the sky above the Parthenon.

"I must say," Rebecca began, using all her skills to modulate and control her tone, "I am surprised to see you here. Bearding me in my own den, as it were."

"You are the second person to make that reference in as many hours," Diana said. "But it is my understanding Daniel was cast into the lion's den by his enemies. I do not wish to be your enemy."

"It is my understanding." She talks of the Bible as though it were just a collection of stories that she hasn't bothered to learn properly yet.

"I'm afraid there is not much choice there, Diana," Rebecca said, again putting extra emphasis on the name. "Unless you have come here to tell me you renounce this paganism, this heresy you preach?"

"I preach no heresy," Diana said. She sat with her long legs crossed, leaning back in the chair, her hands draped loosely, casually on the arms. *What must that be like,* Rebecca wondered, *to be so sure, so utterly and completely self-aware, self-possessed that you know nothing can hurt you, no one can harm you in any way, and so you can sit, stand, lie, open, easy, not at all on guard, on the defensive?*

Rebecca became aware of her own posture, how she sat bolt upright in her chair, her knees together, her hands clasped on the top of her broad, black desk. *Does she read body language? Did they teach her that little trick on her hidden island, those women, those Amazons?*

Rebecca forced herself to relax, to sit back in her chair as Wonder Woman sat in hers. "You must know that's not true," Rebecca said. At least she was maintaining control over her voice, the voice that was her power, her greatest weapon, clear and strong and irresistible. "We are a Christian nation. Judeo-Christian, as some will insist. There is only one true God, and his Son, Jesus Christ."

"I know this story," Diana said. There was no antagonism in her tone. She spoke quietly, conversationally, as if—and Rebecca could not bring herself to truly believe this—she did not understand the full import of what she was saying. "And I do not deny the existence of your gods. But surely there is room enough in the Universe for many gods. I have walked with those who live in the marble halls of Olympus. I have battled those who spanned the dimensions from Apokolips and New Genesis. I have seen divinity in many forms, some good, some terribly evil. If you could only speak to your God, or to this man Jesus, to discuss this . . . they would tell you what I say is true." Wonder Woman paused.

Rebecca felt the heat rise in her throat and cheeks. "Are you . . . are you mocking me, Wonder Woman?" The title slipped past her lips before she could catch it.

"Mocking you? No. Why would I do that?" Again, to Rebecca's eyes Wonder Woman seemed completely genuine, unaware of what she was saying, of the meaning in her words.

She is a consummate actress, I'll give her that.

"One does not 'talk' with our Heavenly Father, or His Son. Not in the way you mean, at any rate. I pray, as all good Christians pray, and I believe my prayers are heard and answered."

Diana frowned. "I understand that is the way your faith operates, but I find it difficult to comprehend. How are you supposed to believe in these gods of yours if you have never met them, never even seen them?"

"*. . . these gods of yours . . .*" *The contempt in her tone! Is it just me, hearing it, or is she really dismissing God and Jesus, the Word, the Truth, so blatantly?*

"I don't have to meet them to know they are real." Rebecca allowed her lip to curl in a deprecating sneer. "Perhaps it is your so-called 'gods' who are the lesser, the unbelievable ones, since you have met them, have talked with them. I think I would have a great deal of difficulty believing in so mundane, so accessible a god."

Diana's dark eyebrows rose. "Why? Is it necessary that your gods be so much beyond you as to be unknowable?"

"Oh, I know my God, Diana. I know Him very well. And He is with me always, here, out there—" she gestured toward the broad expanse of window "—everywhere. He is in every blade of grass, every raindrop. He is in the hearts and minds and souls of those who love and worship Him. The Universe is His work, His canvas, and I am a part of it."

"I see you are sincere, and I admire your conviction," Diana said, and Rebecca was surprised by the other woman's lack of anger, at the absence of any hint of emotion in her tone or her face, "but how does this conflict with what I know to be true? There are countless legends of the Creation, and I know they cannot all be correct, so I choose to see them as a mosaic, each telling a small part of the greater story. Do you not see that your God is a part of this?"

Rebecca snapped to her feet, bristling despite herself. "I do not! God is not 'part' of anything! Everything, everything that lives, everything that exists is part of Him!"

Diana also rose, though Rebecca realized it was out of some sense of proper courtesy, rather than to take advantage of her height, her physical power. "I'm sorry," Diana said, "but that does not entirely make sense. There are many tales that go back to the beginning of the Universe, to the moment when Time and Space sprang forth from nothingness. All the gods, in one form or another, were born of that moment, of that timelessness. They are as much a part of the Universe as we. Vastly more powerful, many times wiser, but not separate, not outside. How could we worship them, how could we even comprehend them, if it were otherwise?"

"We comprehend as much as we need to comprehend," Rebecca said. She was aware of her ragged breathing, of the color burning like flame in her cheeks. *Where is Ramsey? Why did he sneak away? He has answers to all this. All the things he told me when he set me on this path, on the road to the destruction of Wonder Woman and her heresies.* "What we understand of Jehovah is only an infinitesimal fragment of His greater all. And He is the Alpha and the Omega, all there is." The last words she spat like bullets, hard edged and irrefutable.

Incredibly, Wonder Woman shook her head. "Perhaps you would understand better if I took you to Olympus. Is there a time when such a trip would be convenient to you?"

Rebecca felt her knees weaken. She lowered herself back into her chair, hoping the movement looked intentional and not necessary to keep herself from falling. "Take . . . me . . . to . . . Olympus?"

"Yes. I can arrange an audience. Not with Zeus, I suspect, but certainly Athena. She can explain all this better than I, though I am said to be blessed with her wisdom."

Rebecca swallowed in a dry throat. "This is just foolishness, now. I'm not in the mood for games, Wonder Woman." The name had slipped out again. Rebecca gritted her teeth, felt her jaw muscles harden to rock.

Diana looked genuinely perplexed. "This is no game. I can, when you are willing, transport you to Themyscira, and thence to Olympus. You can, at your discretion, meet my gods and goddesses. Surely that will show you I am sincere in all I say."

Rebecca managed a bitter bark of a laugh. "You must be joking. You think you can hypnotize me, brainwash me into thinking I'm going off to Olympus, and this will make me abandon my faith in the one, true God?"

Diana heaved an audible sigh. "Why do you set yourself forever in contention with me, Rebecca?" It was the first time Diana had used her name, and Rebecca felt it almost as a physical blow, a slap, as if Wonder

Woman were showing her in that single word that she knew the psychological game Rebecca had been attempting to play and had now demonstrated herself at the least Rebecca's equal in it. "I do not wish to turn you from your faith. Indeed, perhaps, since they are both gods and highly placed, I might be able to persuade Zeus to call upon your Jehovah and arrange for you to—"

"Get out!" The words exploded from Rebecca's chest like cannon fire.

"What?" Diana had actually taken a step back, the fury of Rebecca's outburst catching her unprepared.

"Get out of my office. Take your damned lies and get out. Go back to Gateway City or wherever you want to call your home and understand, understand, Wonder Woman, that whatever your scheme was in coming here today, you have failed. You have not corrupted me, not confused me, and I will not let you hypnotize me or brainwash me or use some damnable telepathic powers to make me see visions and think I've been transported to Olympus!"

"Rebecca—"

"No! I won't hear another word from you, Wonder Woman! Not another word until you are ready to come on my show, on national television, and tell the world that everything you say is nothing but a goddamned lie!" She paused, leaning heavily on the desk. "And now you've made me blaspheme. Get out." Tears ran hot on her blazing cheeks. "Get out before I have you thrown out." A hollow threat. She raised her face, her eyes looking at Wonder Woman, expecting to see her smiling, even laughing at Rebecca's distress.

Instead, the Amazon seemed deflated, reduced, sagging on her own skeleton as if some portion of life had been sucked from her flesh. "I am sorry," Diana said. "I did not come here intending to cause you this distress. I came to offer a hand of peace and make a reasonable proposal. If you will not accept either—" she turned, taking a few steps toward the elevator, "I shall leave, saddened."

"Not that way." Rebecca groped, blinded by her tears. Her fingernails scuttled like crab claws across the desktop, seeking a small array of buttons. She found them, pressed one. Behind her the curving, slanting windows shifted and slid, and the cool lake air whistled into the room. "Don't take the door, take the window. Fly away. I don't want you talking to my people."

Diana nodded, passing close to Rebecca as she crossed to the window. "I am sorry," Diana said again. "Sorry you are not prepared to see the Universe as it really is. You deny yourself so much."

"Get out," Rebecca hissed.

Diana stepped through the open window, as Rebecca had imagined earlier, stepped into the air and rose, gently, easily, flying up and away from the Crystal Tower.

Rebecca sagged, collapsed into her chair.

"Bitch," she said, lowering her head onto arms folded on the smooth, cool desk. "Bitch. I'll see you burn in hell before I let you poison one more mind. I'll see you burn in hell."

CHAPTER THREE

T HERE are times in a man's life, Donald Morris knew, when the Fates combine to play small games. *We call them "coincidence," but sometimes I think they are really something else. Something much more.*

Tonight was to be such a night, though as he sat lost in thought at the back of the big bus, Father Morris was not contemplating the Fates. He was thinking only of Wonder Woman, of what she meant, what she represented. He was wondering, for the hundredth time, if this pilgrimage to Gateway City would accomplish anything. Anything at all.

He had chosen to take the bus because he could not afford a plane or even a train. He had taken his small life savings, cashed them out, and bought himself a ticket—a one-way ticket, which he hoped was not somehow symbolic—to Gateway City. He carried with him only his worn old Bible and an equally worn old bag, now riding in the rack above his head.

A lifetime in a single bag, he thought. *So little to show. So little to show.*

Not so long ago he would have said he had much to show for his sixty-seven years on Earth. Not physical riches, not houses, cars, suits, exciting adventures in faraway places. No, his legacy was his good works, the people whose lives he had touched, perhaps saved.

So few saved. So few souls to carry in my bag, to say, "These are the ones, these are the children I never fathered, all mine, all touched and shaped and saved by me."

It was, he knew, dangerously close to hubris, to the sin of Pride. But he was past considering the consequences of sin, past considering sin as anything that required his thought at all. He was on a mission to find the reality of the world, the truth behind the truths he had cherished for so long and now could no longer tolerate.

He looked out of the window. The night was pitch black, save when a sudden bolt of lightning cut a jagged line down the heavy sky. Wind lashed sheets of rain against the sides of the bus, and thunder shook it. He felt—an amusing analogy—as though he were riding through some interminable car wash, dark and loud and very wet. The bus shook and groaned as it heaved along the highway. Father Morris tried not to think of what condition the old vehicle must be in, based on the low cost of his ticket. But, then, he had to buy the cheapest he could find. He did not know how long he would be in Gateway, or how much the days and nights spent there would deplete his tiny pool of cash.

I want to find Wonder Woman, he reminded himself, as if drawing some comfort from the thought. *I want to find her, talk to her. It could take a day, it could take a week. Even after I find her, if I find her, even if she'll be willing to talk to me, tell me what I need to know, there is no conceivable way my questions could be answered in a short time. It might take months to understand all she has to tell me, if she will tell me.*

Unconsciously he patted his jacket, the place where his wallet bulged against his chest—and he wished *bulged* were more accurate a word. It felt to him not a great deal thicker than it did when it was empty.

"This storm is getting very bad."

Father Morris turned at the words. In the seat next to him sat a tiny woman, birdlike, of indeterminate age. In the twelve and a half hours they had ridden side by side in the back of the old bus she had said nothing, not a single word to break the monotony and silence. She had not read a book, not looked at a magazine. She simply sat, arms folded across her chest, staring straight ahead, as if oblivious to everything except whatever might wait for her in Gateway.

"Yes, it is bad," Father Morris said. His voice caught in his throat. Twelve and a half hours without speaking had made his throat dry, his tongue thick. "They said it might be bad. They even said it might not be a good idea to be on the road tonight." *But I felt as though I had to go today. I had to start this today, or not at all.*

"No one said anything like that to me." The woman's voice was soft, like sand rustling in the bottom of an old bucket, Morris thought. There was no emotion he could detect. Only the words. "If anyone had said anything like that to me, I might not have come. I don't like storms. I don't like traveling in storms."

"I'm sure we'll be fine," Father Morris said, though even as he spoke he noticed others on the bus were stirring, waking, looking around. Hands were cupped between eyes and glass as people peered out into the darkness. *Are we there yet,* he could almost hear them thinking. He saw men and women glancing at their watches, trying to calculate how close they were to Gateway. *Half an hour or more yet,* he thought. *And, yes, that is a long way in a storm like this.*

As if to underline his thought, the lightning flashed and thunder crashed almost simultaneously. The bus shuddered down its whole length, and beneath him Father Morris felt the wheels spin, felt them for a moment fail to find proper purchase on the rain-washed road.

"I don't want to die tonight," the woman said. She turned for the first time to look directly into Father Morris's eyes, and he saw tears welling. "I came here to die, you know," she said. "I have cancer, and I came back to Gateway City to die where I was born. But not like this."

Father Morris reached out a cautious hand to pat her shoulder. "No one is going to die. Not yet. The driver is well trained, I'm sure. And the bus is old, but it seems serviceable."

"It's not the driver or the bus I'm worried about," the woman said. Father Morris began to think she was really quite young, perhaps no more than forty. "I've kept track of Gateway since I left. Thirty years ago. When I was a girl. I've kept track. I've read about the city in the papers. Seen things on TV. It used to be a beautiful city. Bright. I remember. But it's gone to hell. Greedy politicians and all the wrong kinds of people moving in. Whole neighborhoods turning over, turning bad." She turned to look ahead again, down the long aisle to the broad front windows and the wipers that whipped back and forth in what seemed to Father Morris a vain and fruitless battle with the rain.

"I have read some of that myself," he said. "But surely things have improved now. Now that Wonder Woman is there, I mean."

"Wonder Woman." The woman narrowed her eyes. "I read about that, too. I wonder what good she can do. She can fight monsters and space aliens and go off and lead the Justice League, but can she fight a crooked politician? Can she make sure the man who gets a million dollars to rebuild a road actually *spends* a million dollars to do it?"

"You sound as if you're talking about something specific," Father Morris said.

"I am. This road. This very road we're on. It washes out all the time. Every couple of years, with the combination of the earthquakes and the rains. It washes out. Huge chunks of it just fall off the hillside and slide down into the bay. And I've got to ask myself, when that happened the last time, when the road washed away the last time, did they get someone reputable to fix it? Or did they get the mayor's brother-in-law who never did anything like this big a job before, but who promised to kick back half the million dollars he was paid to the city council?"

Father Morris turned to look out into the rain again. "I'm . . . sure we'll be fine. This is a busy road. They wouldn't cut corners."

"Sure they would."

But in the next twenty minutes, as the lightning flashed and the thunder crashed, the bus stayed firm and sure on its path, and Father Morris sensed a calmness coming over the people who rode with him.

The storm was not getting any better, but it was not getting any worse. The driver seemed capable. The wipers might even have been winning a little bit in their war with the driving rain. People settled back into their seats again. One or two heads nodded, as sleep overcame worry.

And when disaster struck, therefore, no one was ready for it.

It came suddenly. Disaster took its name from the Latin for *evil star*, Father Morris knew, and like a shooting star, the lightning flashed down across the front of the bus. The driver swerved. The brakes squealed and the bus slewed sideways, fishtailing.

Father Morris felt the wheels beneath his seat trying desperately to grab the road. Almost succeeding. But then the road betrayed them.

It started as a low groan, a rumble, a flutter through the frame of the bus that longtime Gateway residents thought first to be the initial rolling shock of an earthquake. There was even the familiar liquid feeling as the ground shifted sideways, the solid earth moving in ways that contradicted all that common sense knew and comprehended of how rock and soil should work.

But it was not the ground this time, and it was not an earthquake. Undermined by water running down from the steep hills above the road, the cheap tarmac beneath the bus had shrugged its tar and concrete shoulders and surrendered to the terrible combination of weight and water. It buckled, folded, doubled in on itself. As the wheels of the bus twisted on the road, the road itself twisted beneath them, shaking itself free of the last slender bonds to the ground beneath and beginning to march across the precipice toward the unforgiving waters of the bay.

In an instant the bus filled with screams. As the bus tipped and turned, luggage leapt from the racks above the travelers' heads. Suitcases, valises, briefcases, Father Morris's battered old carpetbag hurled themselves into the aisle and seats, crashing down on people trying in sheer animal panic to pull themselves from their suddenly confining spaces.

The bus rolled. Father Morris clamped his teeth tight against his own scream as invisible hands plucked his seat partner from her place, throwing her like a broken doll into the back of the big man who had spent most of the trip snoring loudly across the aisle. Panicked by this attack from a new quarter the man lashed out, and the little woman bounced back to land in Father Morris's arms as he was himself up-rooted and thrown toward the roof of the bus.

There was a moment of horrible, yawing, wrenching vertigo as the tumbling motion turned floor to ceiling, and in midarc, Father Morris felt himself suddenly turned from flying up toward the ceiling to falling down toward it.

In midair, Father Morris felt his senses sharpen—he felt and saw every detail of what was happening around him in sudden, mind-searing slow motion. He heard the screech of metal on metal, the crash of breaking glass, the blare of horns as the bus—with all the cars and trucks around it—hurtled sideways to crash through oncoming traffic, unable to stop itself from being swept into the whirlwind of careening metal on the slick road.

He felt a dozen impacts rattle the bus as cars slammed into it. The roll made the ceiling now the side of the bus, and he looked in horror as a wide section suddenly buckled, embossed with fantastic force by the top of a car his hyperactive brain managed somehow to recognize as a late-model Buick. Cracks opened, and the rain and the night air poured in. Ceiling, car, and flying luggage smashed down on soft, vulnerable flesh. The snap and crack of bone was added to the banshee wail of tearing metal. Blood spurted red, arcing across the cabin of the bus, seeming poised, immune to gravity, glistening like a scatter of ruby beads.

Then time and motion seized the bus once more, and the tumbling began again. Over and over. Rolling and rolling, bus and Buick locked together in an obscene embrace, until the ground vanished beneath them and the bright, black waters of the bay, lit for a searing moment by lightning, flashed across Father Morris's vision as he looked down through the gaping wound across the top of the bus.

And then it stopped.

Suddenly. Wrenchingly. The cartwheeling ended. The bus jerked, shook, rattled, and was still. Morris crashed down onto the back of a dislodged seat, pain burning into him as the impact cracked ribs down his right side. He grabbed the seat back like a drowning man with a passing log and held on for dear life.

Silence moved in around him. A long, slow silence that hung for more than two dozen heartbeats before it shattered under the weight of too many pent-up screams. The cabin of the bus became a tunnel leading straight into the mouth of Hades, and all the demons of the underworld were screaming at once, bellowing and yelling as the fires licked and snapped at them.

Beyond the tangled bodies and twisted metal, Father Morris saw the fearful yellow flower of fire blooming against the darkness. The Buick had pushed all the way through to the bus's gas tank. Fuel was spraying onto the trapped passengers, and from some evil place an errant spark had broken free to touch and ignite the gasoline. In a very short time, Morris knew, the inside of this bus would look like the inside of a coal furnace. In the confined space the fire would burn hot and hard, and the struggling, screaming humans would, in next to no time, be transformed into the shapeless, blackened things news reports referred to as "burned beyond recognition."

Father Morris realized that he was not trapped. He was in pain—the least movement to test his freedom sent daggers up and down his side, and he tasted the wet saltiness of blood on his lip—but he could move, could shift himself around. And that meant he could help.

If there was time. People were struggling, pushing, clawing their way in frantic struggles to escape, and as they did Father Morris realized the bus was moving once again. Shifting. He blinked against the rain and spray of gasoline and saw the full horror of their situation; the Buick, fused as one with the bus, had come to rest at such an angle that it had prevented the larger vehicle from making that last half-turn that would roll it over the cliff and send it plummeting into the bay. But as the passengers struggled to free themselves they were redistributing the precariously balanced weight within the bus, and with a low moan the tortured metal was threatening to surrender its tenuous grip on the no-longer-solid earth.

"Don't move!" Father Morris's yell earned him a mouthful of gasoline. "Don't move," he shouted again. "You'll tip us over!"

For a fraction of a second, he thought he had gotten through to them as the passengers stopped their struggles. They looked around, eyes wide, faces ashen, slack. They saw just where they were, how delicate was the slender thread that held them.

But before calm could grip them, a scream ripped through the cabin. Someone had been touched by the spreading fire. Morris craned his neck and saw a young girl, no more than eight or nine, squirming and screaming as the bright orange flames licked at her feet. Already one of her rubber-soled sneakers was aflame. In an instant her scream was joined by others, and mad panic was unleashed.

The bus lurched. The Buick groaned, slipped, spitting sparks and new fire into the night as it buckled under the shifting weight of the bus. The ground gave way. The bus finished its half-roll and pitched out over the water.

And held there.

Father Morris opened his eyes—and snapped them shut instinctively in blind and blinding terror.

The water was below. The struggling, screaming passengers were all around. The impaling Buick was itself sliding, whining, and screeching out of the perch it had so violently torn for itself.

But the bus was not moving, not falling, not rolling. And as the Buick pulled away, Father Morris saw why.

There was an angel hanging in the air outside the bus. Pale against the darkness, one hand held out to support the giant vehicle, the other turning now to hold aside the Buick, extracting it as easily as a mother might extract a splinter from the finger of her child.

Lightning lashed the sky, and in its bright blue light Father Morris saw the golden gleam of the stylized W's that adorned the angel's bosom, the bright silver stars on her hips, the fairy glow of the lariat that hung from her waist.

"Wonder Woman!"

The words became a cry, a cheer through the bus. "Wonder Woman! Wonder Woman!"

She heard them and smiled. "Hold fast to what you can," she called above the howling of the wind and rain. "I will have you all on solid ground as quickly as I can."

Then there was the moment of vertigo again as Wonder Woman rose and the twenty-ton bus rose with her.

"It's a miracle! It's a miracle!"

Father Morris turned at that cry to find his former seat partner pulling herself from beneath a jumble of bodies and luggage to point to Wonder Woman, her tiny eyes wide as a child's on Christmas morning.

"No," Father Morris said, softly, under his breath. "I know a little about miracles, and this is not a miracle. This is something else altogether."

Later, Helena Sandsmark would say it seemed amazing to her that two people so diverse in their origins, their personalities, their needs of the moment, should have seen in her, Helena, a way of getting to Wonder Woman.

In that awful clarity of hindsight, of course, it would be obvious that Helena was the perfect conduit—a message to her would reach Diana. And a blow aimed at her would strike her famous friend.

The blow, when it came, was in the form of a knock on the door at seven-thirty Wednesday morning. More than a knock, a firm, hard pounding as though the unexpected visitor meant to smash the upper panel from the door, perhaps smash the door itself.

Still bleary-eyed from a combination of a late night and far too much coffee, Helena staggered to her front door, pulling her robe tight around her and trying not to trip as her slippers did their best to live up to their name.

"Yes?" The open door revealed two large men, one black, one white, both extraordinarily bland of feature, and a small woman with pinched eyes and a mouth that did not appear, to Helena, to lend itself easily to smiles.

"Professor Sandsmark?"

"Yes?" Helena tried to find the woman's face in her memory file, failed.

"I am Dorothy Kilgore, Professor," the woman said, seeming from her tone and pose to think this should have some meaning to Helena. "I am with the Office of Child Welfare."

Helena blinked. "Cassie . . ." The air moving through the doorway grew suddenly cold. "Has something happened to Cassie?"

The woman's pinched eyes closed even more, narrowing to most unpleasant, reptilian slits. "You don't know where your daughter is, Professor?"

"What? Of course I know where she is. She's spending the night with her friend Trisha. But when you said—"

"Why would you think something had happened to her, Professor?"

"What?" Helena's moment of shock and fear was fading. "Look, what is this? If you have something to say, Ms. . . . . Kilgore, was it? If you have something to say, I suggest you say it."

In response the woman produced a folded, very formal looking piece of paper. "This is a writ, Professor. It authorizes me to question your daughter, Cassandra Elizabeth Sandsmark, and, if I deem it necessary, to take her into protective custody."

"Protective? . . ."

Bracketed by her burly escorts, Dorothy Kilgore was already stepping over the threshold into Helena's small entrance hall. "I suggest you call your daughter, if you really know where she is, and instruct her to come here as quickly as possible."

•   •   •

The office was large, the ceiling high, the tall walls paneled in deep and lustrous mahogany. Portraits in ornate yet dignified frames glowered down, bookcases stood filled to bursting with thick, heavy tomes whose leather bindings added a scent reminiscent of men's clubs to the warm, still air. The overall effect, in fact, was of entering the innermost sanctum sanctorum of a prestigious, old-fashioned, and extremely select men's club, and Rebecca Chandler knew, as she strode across the burnt umber carpet, that this impression was not entirely out of place.

This was the office of the publisher of the *Gateway City Guardian*, an old and venerable newspaper that, in an age of instant communications, satellite hookups, and worldwide webs, had still managed to remain a force to be reckoned with in the Fourth Estate, and in the city. There were many in Gateway, from the mayor on down, who did not entirely believe something was true unless they read it in the *Guardian*.

William Winget rose as Rebecca entered his office. He was tall and heavyset—Rebecca thought immediately of the Spirit of Christmas Present in Dickens's tale of Scrooge—and came around his big Victorian desk to extend to her a hand that looked to Rebecca to be almost as big as her head. He was in his sixties, the latest of a long line of Wingets to sit in the publisher's chair.

"Miss Chandler," Winget smiled, showing big teeth the color of old ivory. "A great pleasure to meet you at last. My wife admires your work, especially your charities. We contribute to them often."

"And most generously." Rebecca allowed her small hand to vanish into the warm, dry folds of Winget's big fist. He shook her hand twice, gently, leaving her with the distinct impression that he could remove her arm from her shoulder with little more than a small jerk of his wrist. "That is why I asked to see you, in fact," Rebecca said, accepting an offered chair and watching as Winget took his place again behind the massive desk. "I thought I saw in you a friend, someone who would be willing and able to help me in this most vital crusade."

Winget frowned. "This would be the matter of Wonder Woman?

I have been following some of what you have had to say on this, and, I must confess, I do not entirely see your point. In a world full of super heroes, what difference does one super-powered woman make?"

"It is not her powers that concern me," Rebecca said. She consciously crossed her legs so that her demure skirt rode up just enough to show Winget a discrete length of smooth white thigh. She did not much enjoy using her sex as a weapon, but she knew from her research that Winget had a fondness for a pretty woman, and Rebecca Chandler was nothing if not that. "It is the stories she tells, the anti-Christian stories."

"'Anti-Christian'? I was not aware of this. Oh, I know she tells these fairy tales about being created by Zeus or some such nonsense, but surely no one believes them."

"Tell me, Mr. Winget," Rebecca said, keeping her voice calm and her face immobile, "do you believe that Superman is an alien being from a world called Krypton?"

"Why . . ." Winget paused. "Well, I don't suppose I ever gave it that much thought. Superman had been around for a while before the story of his origin came out. And he looks so human . . . but, yes, I suppose I believe it." He smiled. "I mean, why would Superman lie?"

"Exactly. We trust Superman. We tend to trust all these so-called super heroes. And so we—and our children—trust Wonder Woman. And when she says she was created out of clay, and brought to life by the gods of ancient Greece—well, the parallel to the story of Adam is unmistakable, isn't it? Wonder Woman sets herself up as someone who exists by right of divine intervention and then claims that divinity to be a set of gods all sensible and truly righteous people consider nothing more than fiction, myth."

Winget leaned back in his chair, the old, worn leather creaking beneath his weight. "Yes, I read all this in the *Guardian*." He smiled. "Like all well-informed people in Gateway City, I get my news from the most reliable source. But you see this as something more than a story, I take it. You see some kind of agenda being served."

"Do you believe in Satan, Mr. Winget?" Rebecca saw from the

brief flicker in his eyes, the way his expression changed for a moment, that the question had caught him unprepared, as she had hoped it would.

"I . . ." Winget paused. "This is a serious question? You really want an answer?"

"I really want an answer."

"Well then . . . I would have to say I am not entirely sure."

"Do you believe the story of Jesus, as told in the New Testament?"

"Of course."

"And you recall that Jesus is tempted by Satan?"

"Yes . . ."

"Then you believe that there is a force for evil in the world, there is a creature, a being, who works always to undo God's plan, to destroy the souls of men and women."

"I . . . I must confess I do not really think of it in quite those terms, but, yes, I suppose I do. I suppose if one is truly to believe the Bible, one really has no choice but to accept that Satan exists in some literal form."

Rebecca nodded. "I believe that literal form to be Wonder Woman. I believe she is here, on Earth, specifically with the intent of undermining the faith of our children, even our less cautious adults. By telling her stories, seeming by her deeds and powers to be proof that those stories are real, she compels unsuspecting people to consider, to actually accept the existence of those old gods, of Zeus and Athena and all the rest."

"Yes, I suppose she does." Winget frowned, and Rebecca liked what she read in his face. "I never really thought of it quite like that."

"No one does. That's the problem we face, since accepting Wonder Woman as a creation of familiar if mythological gods is far less difficult, for most people, than accepting that Superman came to Earth from a planet light-years away. And people have accepted that easily, almost gladly."

"There is a degree of comfort in knowing we are not alone in a large and often hostile Universe," Winget said.

"Yes. And there is a greater degree of comfort in knowing that there are gods who can be seen, touched, interacted with. That is what Wonder Woman preaches—accessible gods. Not gods that demand faith without hard proof, as so many will say God does. You see how insidious it is? How subtle?"

"Yes." Winget sat for a long while in silence. Rebecca was aware of the ticking of the grandfather clock that towered against one wall, aware of the shadows of clouds moving across the wall behind her host, framed by the square panels of the window opposite his desk. Time seemed slowed, as though it moved carefully, cautiously, as William Winget sorted through what she had told him, looking for the first time at something he had seen a hundred times but had never completely understood.

Rebecca was not worried. She had been working carefully herself for a year now, making contacts, talking to people of increasingly higher social and political status, showing them what she knew, making them understand. No one had turned her away yet. No one had disputed her conclusions. She did not expect Winget to be the first.

"Yes," he said again, finally. "This is serious. More serious than I would have ever considered, if you had not told me." He leaned forward, placing his big hands flat on the glass top of his desk. "There is a rot in this country. There has been for years. People have always had ways to explain it, excuse it. But I begin to see there is something much more than the mechanism of social decline at work here. There is too much of a conscious agenda, a plan in the destruction of our moral base, our family values. Amazing that I never saw any of this before today."

"Yes." Rebecca smiled, finding an ally, adding a soldier to her cause. "And you will use your power, your paper to make sure this is made clear to the largest number of people?"

Winget stood. "I will. Thank you for coming in today, Miss Chandler. Thank you for bringing this to my attention." He let out a long, slow sigh, as if he had been holding his breath as he pondered the implications of what Rebecca had said. "You may consider the *Guardian* ready to fight this on every level, at every opportunity."

Rebecca stood also, shaking his hand again. "Thank you, Mr. Winget. You will not regret this."

CHAPTER FOUR

 HE night seemed longer than
any Diana of Themyscira could easily summon to memory.

There was not just the bus to save, but more than two dozen other
vehicles, cars, trucks, vans, recreational vehicles, all caught by the sudden failure of the stretch of road on which they traveled, all sent spinning across cracking, splintering tarmac and concrete to the cliff above
the bay. Most she had been able to catch while they were still on the
road, as she first caught the bus—the largest, and therefore represent-
ing the most people in immediate danger—but some had slipped away
while she saved others, and no less than eight cars had to be dredged
from the churning waters.

Nineteen died in that horror. But more than a hundred were saved.

As she emerged from the hospital, wiping back a strand of black
hair that had escaped from its confinement behind the tiara of her
princely office, Diana looked up into the morning sky, into the clear
blue and the summer sun, marveling once again at how quickly storms
could come in this part of the world, and how quickly they departed.

There were a dozen or more television camera vans parked—more
accurately scattered—along the sidewalk in front of the hospital.
As Diana walked down the steps toward them a swarm of reporters

surged up to meet her, thrusting microphones and cameras at her like weapons.

"Wonder Woman! Wonder Woman!" There was a frantic quality in this chant that had not been present even in the voices of the people she had rescued the night before. Diana shook her head, wondering what forces drove these people, that there could be in them such agitation, such near panic, when the worst thing that could befall them was that she might choose to step off into the air and fly away without granting them an interview.

With calm practice learned from previous experience, Diana held up her hands, signaling for calm from the onrush. "One at a time, good people, please," she said, and her smile was as warm and genuine as the summer morning. "I will be happy to answer such questions as I can."

They gained some modicum of reason, and one by one the familiar questions came: how did she hear about the disaster, how many people were saved, how many lost, what did she think of the political situation that allowed the roads to fall into such disrepair?

Each one she answered to the best of her knowledge, side-stepping political and personal questions—"Wonder Woman, what about you and Superman? Is it true you're romantically involved?"—until there came a question that stopped her dead, her voice catching, words failing.

"Wonder Woman, what do you say to the charge that you engineered this disaster in order to make this 'heroic rescue' and redeem yourself?"

Diana blinked. " 'Redeem'? I was not aware I was in need of redemption."

The questioner moved closer, and the other reporters, sensing something new, some additional, unexpected layer to their story, parted to let him pass. Diana studied his face, recognizing him as one of the star reporters of the *Gateway Guardian,* a man named Simon Kirby.

"Surely you can't deny that you have been considerably diminished," Kirby said, "by the charges leveled against you by Rebecca Chandler. Her points are known and accepted by many as valid, and you have done nothing to respond to them. Do you now deny that you rigged that road to collapse in order to deflect attention from those charges?"

"I most certainly do!" Diana felt herself stiffen, her muscles tensing as though in anticipation of a physical assault. "I have no reason to endanger the lives of the people of this city in order to defend myself against Rebecca Chandler's attack. I have spoken with Miss Chandler and—"

But the rest of her words were lost. At the simple phrase "I have spoken with Miss Chandler" the reporters lost all composure and exploded in questions of when, where, how, what was said. They surged up the steps, thrusting their microphones, shouldering each other aside, jostling, pressing in, until Diana launched herself straight up from the front of the hospital, hurling herself away from the madness.

Hera and Athena give me strength! Her breath came now in rapid, shallow gulps, and she paused in the air, high above the face of Gateway City, forcing herself into a slower, steady rate of breathing, exercising her warrior's training. *I have faced demons and devils, angry gods and monsters beyond the imaginings of Men, but I will never be prepared for the sheer ferocity of a reporter who thinks he has stumbled on a story!*

She let the gentle breezes carry her across the city, exercising no more control than was necessary to simply keep herself aloft. She lowered her head, closing her eyes, and let the calm serenity of her Amazon philosophies seep slowly back into her limbs, her mind. Her pounding heart slowed, her bosom rising and falling less rapidly.

Rebecca Chandler again! It would seem I am not permitted to escape this woman's attentions for an instant. Nor am I allowed again to underestimate her. If even one person could conceive such an insanity as to suggest that I would willingly sabotage a highway, place hundreds of people in jeopardy, even cost the lives of more than a dozen, simply to make myself look good. . . .

She shook her head, drifting through the bright blue sky. *I have never heard such a thing said of any other whom the press calls a "super hero." Yet now I, who have come here only to spread the word of peace and kindness, to teach and to defend, I am to be made the target of such accusations!*

She turned, bending herself against the wind, moving away from the towers and streets. She needed a calm center, she realized. And a kind of wisdom Helena Sandsmark could not, by virtue of her youth, possess.

But there was someone else she might talk to. Another who possessed a deep understanding of the ways of faith, and whose faith itself, though different in many ways, was kindred to the faith of Rebecca Chandler.

The office was small and crammed with filing cabinets, these likewise overly crowded with manila folders stuffed with sheets of mismatched paper, forms, charts, foolscap covered with hastily scribbled lines of nearly illegible text.

Whole lives are changed by the words on these pages, Helena Sandsmark thought as she tipped her head to read—or try to read—some of the things written there. *Children are taken from their parents, families exploded, all on the basis of what is written here.*

She had never had an occasion to doubt that the Family Services department of the Gateway City government performed a valuable task, protecting children and young adults, even saving young lives on many occasions. And it had never before occurred to her that there was anything wrong with the system, that there might be something even vaguely Inquisitorial about it all—charges leveled and acted upon, with the accused having precious little to say in the matter.

I suppose they need to act that way, sometimes. If a child's life is in danger, there's not much time to spend on checking the facts, finding the corroborative details. You get in there, you get the child, and you worry about the fine points later, when the child is safe.

But her daughter was in no danger! Helena turned from her inspection of the files, looked at the cluttered top of the old metal desk that squatted in the center of the room. Unlike the files it was tidy, meticulous. There was nothing—not even photographs—to suggest that a human being used this place as a workstation. There were no papers on the desk, no pens, no Post-it notes. Even the blotter was brand new, showing no sign of use at all. Helena compared it in her mind with her own blotter, on her own desk at the museum. There were a hundred and one memories on that stained surface. Notes to herself, written in faded ballpoint or felt tip pen, some still having meaning, some whose message was as lost as the most obscure hieroglyphs. But all pieces of her life at the Gateway City Museum of Antiquities, all reminders of her steady climb from a graduate student working part time in the Assyrian Antiquities department, on through her days as an assistant curator, a full curator, a department head, and now, after long, hard work, finally head of the whole Classical Antiquities division. It was all there on the ragged-edged blotter, in code, the main reason she was never able to bring herself to replace it with a new, more serviceable one.

But here, in that small office, with the filing cabinets crowding close—*Why filing cabinets, anyway? They could put everything on a computer that would take up a fifth of the top of the desk*—Helena looked at a desk that could not be more devoid of any hints of the personality of its owner if it had been deliberately planned that way.

And maybe it was. These people spend their lives poking into the lives of others—again, she had not thought of it that way before now—*maybe they develop a kind of instinct, a kind of self-preservation thing, that keeps them from putting out anything in the office that speaks of who they are, of what their lives are all about. They don't want anyone to know of them what they seek to know of others.*

"Professor Sandsmark?"

Helena turned. The man entering was small, smooth faced, unimpressive. He wore a neat brown suit, a white shirt, a brown tie. His shoes were brown and neatly polished, if ten years out of style. His hand, when he extended it to shake Helena's, was smooth, dry, manicured. On his right wrist he wore an ordinary Timex watch, such as Helena knew was for sale in drugstores all over Gateway. *The blandness of the desk continues to its owner.*

"Yes, I am Helena Sandsmark."

"Martin Lieber. Won't you please be seated?" He stepped around the desk and took his own place in the small chair that faced the room. He set a slim manila envelope on the unblemished blotter and laced his fingers atop it. "I must say," he said after a moment, "that this case comes to me as something of a surprise. I have read some of your books on the ancient world. They are quite brilliant."

"Thank you." Helena kept her voice flat, unmodulated. Her stomach was roiling, her whole body near to vibrating with emotions—anger first among them—but she was not about to let that show now, here.

"So you can see," Lieber said, "how I would be—and am—quite surprised to be informed that you have turned out to be such a poor mother that you have allowed your daughter Cassandra to be placed in a situation of almost constant jeopardy."

Helena fought to restrain herself, catching her instinctive first reactions, tamping them down. Forcing her voice to remain calm, she said, "You understand that that is a completely preposterous charge, do you not?"

"Is it?" Lieber unlaced his fingers, opened the manila folder. There were only half a dozen sheets of paper in it, Helena noted, and three of them were some manner of forms. "It's true that you not only hired Diana Prince—Wonder Woman—to work at the museum, but also rent the apartment on the top floor of your house out to her? It's true that you allow your daughter, Cassandra, to interact with Ms. Prince whenever she chooses? It's true that you have, on occasion, even asked Ms. Prince to function as a baby-sitter when you were—shall we say—otherwise disposed?"

Helena felt the color rise in her cheeks. She had been most discreet in her relationship with Jason Blood, the world-renowned demonologist who entered her life shortly after she first met Wonder Woman. But she could not deny that there had been occasions when she had asked Diana to look after Cassandra while she, Helena, spent time with Jason—sometimes even a whole night. "Diana has looked after Cassie once or twice, yes." Helena felt familiar emotions bubble inside her.

Emotions she had thought long since gone. She heard her mother's tones when Helena told her she was pregnant, heard her telling her to "get rid" of the baby, to not bring such shame onto the name of Sandsmark. She heard the doctors, the nurses, the counselors telling her there would be no shame in putting the child up for adoption, Helena being barely more than a child herself—eighteen when Cassie was born—and ill-prepared for the rigors attendant to full-time motherhood. She heard her father—the only one who had been on her side—worrying that she might be forced to sacrifice her career, her mind, to the task of raising a baby. She might have had to leave college, find a job, support herself. Her father loved Helena more than life itself, she knew, but she knew also that he was no match for her mother. And if Janice Sandsmark saw in this unfortunate event a blemish on the family name, Gunnar Sandsmark was not about to debate with her.

"Our records indicate," Lieber said, "that Prince—" Helena was very aware of the sudden deletion of "Ms." "—has 'taken care' of Cassandra on at least four separate occasions. And on one of them she even allowed her to use some Amazon artifact that enabled her to fly."

Helena swallowed. She had been annoyed, herself, when she learned Diana had permitted Cassie to try on the fabled Sandals of Hermes, but she was not about to admit to that here, now. "Diana comes from a culture very different from ours, Mr. Lieber," she said, putting on her best professorial voice. "The Amazons are trained from childhood to be warriors, to take care of themselves in any situation. Diana saw in this nothing more or less than a proper part of Cassie's training as a young woman." She paused for a moment, wondering if the next thing she intended to say might sound too much like an apology. She elected to press on. "She has also been teaching Cassandra some of the more easily learned Amazon ways of self-defense—something I think you will admit is of great use to a young girl in a city like Gateway."

Lieber sat straight in his chair. "I would advise you not to take that tone with me, Professor," he said, and his narrowed eyes gave his face a coldness Helena had not seen there before. "You may think your high position at the museum and your high position in your professional community has earned you some kind of special status, some form of invulnerability from the considerations of we mere mortals—" the sarcasm in his voice compelled Helena to once again bridle her emotions—"but here, in this office, you are just another parent who has been accused of endangering our most precious national resource, our children. And—" Lieber leaned back, and a small, thin smile of satisfaction played about his lips—"I should perhaps warn you right now that this investigation began because someone of vastly higher position and importance contacted this office and suggested we make a study of you and your daughter."

Helena's eyebrows rose high beneath her straight, brown bangs. "And who might that be? I believe the Constitution of this country still guarantees the accused the right to confront the accuser."

"Oh, indeed," Lieber said, continuing to smile. "But don't fool yourself into thinking there is any avenue of escape there, Professor Sandsmark. The one who brought your case to our attention was none other than Rebecca Chandler herself!"

Esther Schorr had weathered many things in her life, many crushing blows that might have annihilated a lesser soul. As a girl she had survived the Final Solution Adolf Hitler and his Nazis attempted to work upon her people. As a young woman she endured the rigors of making a life in a new land, without the language, without the skills necessary to make even a beginning.

She found joy in a husband who loved her, but saw him taken from her when he was only thirty-eight, the victim of a senseless, violent crime that would, eventually, serve as the inspiration for her son Michael to seek a position with the Gateway City Police Department. In that, though there were ever-greater dangers as Michael moved along in his career, Esther found great pride and satisfaction in the sense of a job well done, a son well raised.

But Michael had one more test for her. As she moved about her small apartment, dusting, cleaning, doing the little things she did each day to keep her body and her mind occupied, Esther thought back to the day some three months ago when Michael had come home, sat her down, and told her he thought he was in love.

Esther remembered her joy, the way her heart swelled in her narrow chest. Michael, at thirty, had begun to seem to Esther a perpetual bachelor, one who would date, who sought the company of pretty women, but who seemed determined never to settle down, never to give Esther the grandchildren she so longed for.

"My job is too dangerous, Ma," he would say when she pressed him. "How can I ask any woman to tie herself to a guy who might be dead the very next morning?"

So when he came home, sat Esther down, pulled up the ottoman in front of her, sat himself, took her hands in his, and looked into her eyes, saying, "Ma, I think I'm in love. . . ."

But Esther remembered the hesitation in his voice, and remembered how, even at that moment, she knew there was something much more to this than his unwillingness to ask a woman to share his dangerous life.

"She's not Jewish?" Esther had asked. Michael understood how she was about such things. She had seen her people hunted, almost exterminated. To perpetuate the culture and the faith was more than a fond wish to Esther Schorr—it was a mission.

"Oh boy, is she not Jewish!" Michael laughed then, Esther recalled, and it was not at all the reaction she had expected.

Now Esther paused in front of the collection of family pictures on top of the big sideboard in the living room. There was Max, her husband, looking so handsome, so tall and regal, in his college graduation picture, in their wedding picture. There he was holding Michael in his arms, the day his son was born. And here were half a dozen pictures of Michael, different ages, different dress, looking small and dark and not at all like his father.

He takes after me, Esther thought. *Better he should have taken after Max, to be tall, to be slender like a young god.* She smiled. She remembered what Michael said when she had blurted out her reaction to his news.

"Oh, Michael," she said, knowing it would make him mad, "a *shiksa?*"

And he had laughed again, surprising her again. "A *shiksa* goddess, Ma! Ma, it's Wonder Woman."

Esther opened the top drawer of the sideboard, pulling out the big scrapbook Michael did not know she kept. It was brand new, but already full of clippings, articles, stories, all about Wonder Woman.

Wonder Woman! That Michael should even meet such a person! Esther opened the scrapbook and paged slowly through it. Such an amazing story, contained in those pages. She had had to go to the public library over on Thurmon Street, go through their back issues and photocopy some of the earlier pieces, but she had assembled the whole history of the Amazon Princess called Wonder Woman. *And how many mothers can do that? How many mothers can go to the library and find whole magazines about the girl their son is dating?*

Well, not actually dating, Esther reminded herself. She was not really sure exactly where their relationship stood. She knew Michael made no secret of his feelings toward Diana—*a nice name, a good name*—but she thought Diana was perhaps a little naive in these things.

She grew up on an island with no one but women there! She was fully grown before she first even met a man! Esther shook her head. She had read in some of the articles that people had actually asked Wonder Woman what the women of Themyscira did to ease their sexual needs—*The things some people ask, these days! Like it's anybody's business!*—and she understood that Diana had come to what she called "Patriarch's World" thoroughly unversed in the ways between men and women, and there was nothing to suggest that this had changed in the years she had been here.

She closed the scrapbook and returned it to the drawer. As she slid it closed the buzzer sounded from the hall, and Esther hurried to see who was at the downstairs door.

"Hello?" she said into the small microphone by the speaker.

"Good morning, Mrs. Schorr," replied a voice familiar even through the tinny buzz of the speaker. "It's Diana. May I come up for a moment?"

Father Donald Morris pushed himself up out of dreams. They fell away, and like so many of his dreams, vanished almost at once, at least in detail. There remained only the sense of something not right, something most unpleasant at the edges of his perceptions.

He opened his eyes, looked around, and understood the reason for the unpleasantness of his dreams. He was in a high bed, in a small ward shared by two other patients. The smells and sounds of a metropolitan hospital were all around him, familiar and disturbing, and he knew at once that these had worked their way into his unconscious.

For a moment he could not quite remember the sequence of events that had brought him to this place, this bed. Then images of the night before—*Only the night before? How long have I been out?*—came back to him, and he remembered the fear, the horror, and the rescue the small woman called miraculous.

"*Miraculous.*" He frowned at the word. *How easily we toss that around, calling anything "miraculous."* He remembered a year or so ago when an airplane crashed into a rugged Andes mountainside. More than a hundred people died, but the first reports indicated that a whole family of four, father, mother, and two children, had survived. It had been called a miracle. Relatives interviewed on the radio and television, in the first hours, used that word over and over. A miracle, a miracle. But then it came out that only the father and infant son had survived. Mother and daughter were dead. *And so,* Donald Morris thought then as now, *did that make it only half a miracle?*

And he remembered, too, Frank Hume, his best friend before he went into the seminary, joking with him about his calling, making good-natured sport of the beliefs he held so dear. "So Jesus walked on the water and fed all those people and came back from the dead, and you want to call that a miracle?" Frank would say, nudging Donald with a friendly elbow. "But Jesus was the Son of God, Don! That was just his everyday *shtick*. Now, if *I* did it, then it would be a miracle!"

But the news reports were calling Wonder Woman's rescue of the victims of that highway collapse a "miracle." Donald Morris had already seen some of the stories on the TV as he sat in the emergency room insisting that others with greater injuries be attended to before the doctors and nurses got around to him.

He wondered how the more detailed stories in the morning newspapers read, and reached to the side of the bed for the signal button to buzz for a nurse and ask for the papers—and breakfast! He found, to his surprise, that he was absolutely famished.

Papers and breakfast were brought, and with the activity came wakefulness in his two roommates. They had questions, of course. It had gone all around the hospital by now, Morris was sure, that he and the others in other rooms were the ones who had been saved by Wonder Woman. Sudden celebrities, in a strange, small way. *We did nothing more than be in the wrong place at the wrong time, and be fortunate enough to have a super hero in the area to save us,* he thought, rueful as always, *but there are some among us who will, I'm sure, make a fortune on the talk-show circuit, with their embellished tales of their personal interaction with Wonder Woman.*

Father Donald Morris shook his head, eating his scrambled eggs and reading the papers. *People are so gullible, so eager to believe the most outlandish stories.* And, despite himself, his mind-set, his overwhelming sense of gloom and futility made him add a thought that would have been utterly alien to him only a year ago. *In the way those foolish Palestinians believed all those outlandish stories of a man called Jesus? Believed them? Cherished them? Compiled them?*

He sighed. *Is it always like this? When a man who has dedicated his whole life to something, to a job, a woman, a faith—when that man finds a flaw in the object of his dedication, is it always a pendulum effect? Does the adoration always turn to disgust, the love to hatred?*

He sipped his coffee, horrible, bland hospital coffee. *I gave my whole life over to the service of God and Jesus, the Father, the Son, and the Holy Ghost, and I never doubted in all the years that what I was doing was exactly right, exactly true. I saw all the super heroes of the world, all the super villains, some of them boldly declaring themselves to be gods, New Gods, and I was able to take it all in and think "Yes, well, there is ego for you, and in the end they will pay a price for it." And I never doubted that it was all true, what I believed. Not in all the years of seeing children die. Seeing them crushed and broken by the uncaring clockwork of the Universe.*

Father Morris considered the phrase. *Yes, that's how I've come to see it, isn't it? "Uncaring clockwork." All mechanical, all random mathematics, like the scientists say. God? Who is God? What is God? A kindly old man with a long white beard? Charlton Heston in his greatest role? And if God is everything we want Him to be, how can there be suffering, how can there be children dying of cancer, leprosy, tuberculosis—in this modern world! Tuberculosis! And AIDS. Bubonic plague. All the ills of Man, still out there, still torturing and tormenting even the youngest and weakest. And why? To test us? To test our faith?*

Morris nibbled at his toast, tasting nothing but bile. He wanted to leap from the bed—though the pain the least movement generated in his side suggested "leaping" would not be among his activities for a while—and run to the rooftop to scream at an unhearing Universe, an uncaring God.

And what good would that do? Remember Matthew, Chapter 6, when Jesus scolds the hypocrites, as he calls them, for their blatant display of their supposed faith, having trumpets announce them as they made their way to the Temple. Pray in private, He tells them. Go to your closets and commune with God alone, keeping your faith so personal and private it is as though your left hand does not know what your right hand is doing. Because God knows all. God does not need public displays. Public displays are for the glory of man, not God.

And so, Donald Morris knew, if he went to the rooftop and screamed his outrage, it would be for his own satisfaction, not for any good it might do in catching the attention of God. God, if He existed, already knew the least thought of Donald Morris. Already knew the mission that brought Donald Morris to Gateway City.

He returned his mind to the matter of reading the papers. They all carried the same story, varied only by the individual styles of the writers, the editorial styles of the papers themselves. The staid, old-fashioned *Gateway Gazette* carried no pictures on its front page, and only small headlines. There he found WONDER WOMAN IN HEROIC RESCUE. In sharp contrast to the *Gateway Star Ledger*'s LIKE LIGHTNING! WONDER WOMAN TO THE RESCUE IN HIGHWAY HOLOCAUST.

He read each article, in search of any clue to how he might find Wonder Woman, might contact her. When he picked up the *Gateway Guardian* he stopped for a moment, blinking, as if to dispel the clearly erroneous headlines his tired eyes were forming out of the tall, black letters on the front page.

WONDER WOMAN FAKES "RESCUE" AFTER HIGHWAY SABOTAGE, said the main headline. SELF-STYLED "SUPER HERO" ENDANGERS HUNDREDS FOR SELF-GLORIFICATION.

"What?"

The others in the room looked up as Morris blurted out the question. "What is it, Father?" his closest roommate asked.

"This headline." Morris held the paper for the others to see. "What are they talking about?"

"Oh, that!" Mr. Appleby, occupying the bed in the opposite corner, his broken leg angled up before him in a concoction of wires and pulleys. "I saw that on KGCT last night, too. They seem to think Wonder Woman sabotaged the highway to make herself look good."

Morris doubted his hearing as well as his vision. "Why on earth would she do that?"

"Because of Rebecca Chandler." That from Mr. Johnston, only slightly scraped and bruised after amazingly—*though not miraculously*—walking away from a small plane crash. "She makes sense, and 'Wonder Woman' is obviously worried that more and more people might begin to realize she makes sense."

The sarcastic emphasis around Wonder Woman's name was not lost on Morris. "You believe that Chandler woman? Why?"

"Why?" Johnston seemed shocked at the question. "I thought you were a Catholic priest, Morris. Thought that would put you on Chandler's side automatically."

"Not quite," Morris said. *The Catholic Church is not quite so rigid and unyielding as some people think. But the last thing I need right now is to get involved in a theological debate with people who take their religious lead from televangelists!* "I came to Gateway City hoping to meet Wonder Woman and talk to her, but I'm afraid my brief encounter with her last night may be as close as I get. I confess my plan did not include any really clear means of making contact."

"Why don't you get in touch with the museum?" Appleby fluffed up his pillow as best he could, seeking some kind of comfort in the unnatural position forced on him by the healing process. "The Gateway City Museum of Antiquities. You know she works there, as Diana Prince."

"No," Morris said, "I didn't know that." *A super hero with a day job?* Of course, it made a kind of sense, he thought. "I think," he said, lifting his breakfast tray to the side to slide his feet off the edge of the high bed, "that I had better find myself a phone."

INTERLUDE
IN WASHINGTON

I N the Oval Office, in the executive wing to the side of the White House, the President of the United States was troubled.

On three television screens, mounted in a long sideboard by the door to the left of his desk, he saw variations on the same image: people marching around the White House, placards and voices raised, here and there fists raised, while nervous policemen looked on and wondered just what they should be doing.

The placards all featured some variation on the same slogan: DOWN WITH WONDER WOMAN.

"At least it's not you they want to pull down this week, Mr. President." The Speaker of the House sat on the edge of his chair, perched like some small rodent waiting for food to fall from a table, the President thought. The American people would be most surprised, he considered, to see the two of them, the Speaker and the President, together, alone and without the rhetoric. Especially given the identity of the third man in the room.

"I wish I could say it was a pleasant change," the President said. "But I don't know how to deal with this kind of thing." He tapped the papers piled on his desk—*The Daily Planet, The New York Times, The Boston Globe, The San Francisco Examiner, The Gateway Guardian,*

The Chicago Tribune. Excepting the *Guardian*, none of them had yet to come out with an editorial statement, a policy concerning the Wonder Woman question. Even the three networks were being cagey, as their coverage of the marchers showed.

The President swiveled his chair to face the third man in the room. "What do you think? You know her better than we ever will."

"Yes, sir, I do." There was a subtle shading in the deep, smooth voice. The President could not say for sure what it was, but it spoke of something deeper, something hidden. He was not about to ask what it was.

"Do you think any of this has merit, then?" the Speaker asked.

"No, sir, I don't." With a gentle billowing of his scarlet cape the third man crossed to stand closer to the President's desk and the three television screens. "Diana and I have fought side by side on more than one occasion. Even fought creatures who professed themselves to be gods. She has never seemed interested in destroying the faith of the American people in their own gods. She has never seemed interested in destroying anything. She's more concerned with nurturing, building."

The President took note of the hint of a Midwest twang in the man's voice and was once again astonished, amazed that this greatest of all heroes should be so very much an American boy, so very much the personification of the American dream.

He's even an immigrant, the President thought. *An immigrant who came to this country—this planet—and became greater than he ever could have if he'd stayed at home. The ultimate Horatio Alger story.*

"Do you intend to do anything about this?" the Speaker asked.

"No, sir. Not yet." He turned from the televisions. "Mr. President, Mr. Speaker, there are matters that concern me in Metropolis just now. I really should be getting back there. I'll keep an eye on all this, of course, as I'm sure others will in my . . . community. If by some chance, this all turns out to be true, we'll be ready to do whatever is necessary to stop Wonder Woman."

"And if it's not true?" the President asked.

"Then, Mr. President, I'm afraid there's not very much anyone will be able to do that Diana can't do on her own."

And with a quick step to the doors to the Rose Garden and a brief, unconscious flourish of the cape, he was gone, hurling himself skyward so fast he seemed simply to vanish.

"I wonder . . ." The Speaker of the House left the words hanging in the air for a moment.

"Yes?" The President thought he could make a good guess at what his visitor wanted to say, but he preferred to hear the words before he spoke them himself.

"I wonder," the Speaker said again, "if this was true about Wonder Woman, would we have any way of knowing it *wasn't* true about all the rest of them?"

"What do you mean?"

"I mean, all these super heroes. All these people with powers and abilities far beyond ours. Suppose they were all part of some scheme, some great plan to bring down this nation of ours. If that were true, if they were all in on it together, and Wonder Woman was just the first one to get found out . . ." He paused for a long time, shaking his head. "Mr. President, if they were really to turn against us, do you suppose there is anything, anything at all that we could do to stop them?"

The President turned to look at the French doors. "Do anything to stop them?" He shook his head in turn and, rising, crossed to look up into the bright blue sky above the Washington Monument. "We were just having a conversation with Superman, a man who died and came back to life," he said after a long silence of his own. "What can *anyone* do against a force like that?"

CHAPTER FIVE

CASSANDRA Sandsmark had a secret. A big secret. The kind of secret that threatened to bubble up and explode out of her almost every time she opened her mouth to speak. Cassie was very proud of herself, that she managed to keep this secret for the weeks it had been in existence. She knew, too, that she must continue to keep it a secret. Must not let the least hint of it slip out, since it was exactly the kind of thing these busybodies were talking about, the kind of danger they were insisting Helena had been carelessly subjecting Cassie to.

Because Cassandra Sandsmark was, occasionally, a super hero herself.

It began innocently enough, with Diana allowing Cassie to try on—and try—the Sandals of Hermes, the mystical sandals that allowed the wearer to fly, free, fast, and high as any bird. The first time she tried them, Cassie almost killed herself, flying too high, too fast, before she learned how easy it was to control them. But since then, without Diana's knowledge, Cassie had borrowed the sandals several times, along with the polished armband known as the Gauntlet of Atlas, which multiplied the wearer's strength tenfold. With those, and a black wig and goggles as a disguise, Cassie had gone out to make her own little war against the things that were wrong in Gateway City, and when asked, when confronted in her disguise had called herself Wonder Girl.

Now, as she sat in the small, spare waiting room of the Family Services department, slumped in her chair, sullen and disgusted in the way only a teenager can truly achieve, Cassie thought it was so absurd that these people would try to take her away from her mother, believe her mom was careless and uncaring, when Cassie had proven—at least to herself—that she didn't need constant supervision. She could not only take care of herself, but could, when called upon, take care of others, too. She had donned the gauntlet and the sandals and gone out to be a super hero, just like Diana.

And the greatest irony was, of course, that if she were to reveal that to these people, she would probably never see Helena again. They would throw her mother in the deepest, darkest cell they could find and lose the key.

Jerks.

But that still left Cassie with a significant problem: She couldn't afford to be cut off from Diana at a time when everything seemed to be going wrong for her best friend. A lot of the kids at school were starting to parrot the words of Rebecca Chandler, and too many of their parents were taking those words and embellishing them, expanding them, making Chandler's thoughts their own.

Cassie had fought for Wonder Woman when she could, with words of her own, but she was having great difficulty convincing the ones who had turned on Diana that what they thought was wrong. Just plain stupid.

So what if Diana believes in some old gods no one else believes in anymore? Who cares? Isn't America supposed to be about religious freedom? Isn't that what they drill into us in school, tolerance and understanding? Acceptance of others?

She wondered if this sudden attack on Helena's suitability as a mother could have anything to do with the attack on Diana. Pretty egotistical, Cassie supposed, to think so, but then her life had expanded a lot since Diana came into it. A few months ago, she was just another fourteen-year-old girl whose biggest worry in the world was how she was going to meet boys while attending an all-girls private school. But on the first day Diana came into her life, Cassie found herself not only confronting danger on an order she had never known or could have even guessed at before, but even being able, in a small but significant way, to help Wonder Woman defeat that danger.

After that it seemed as though Cassie's life was touched by excitement—and danger—on a regular basis, as if Diana herself was some kind of magnet that drew the bad things that came to Gateway directly to her.

And maybe she is. Maybe that's how super heroes are supposed to work. They're bigger and stronger and tougher than the rest of us, so something about them is like a magnet, and when some stupid super villain turns up he'll go after the super hero instead of regular people who might get hurt.

Not that "regular people" didn't get hurt anyway, when Wonder Woman—or any other super hero—fought these high-powered bad guys. But, Cassandra reminded herself, there were a lot fewer people getting hurt compared to the ones who could have been hurt if the heroes hadn't been there. Like that road collapse, yesterday. Nineteen people killed. But they might *all* have been killed if Diana hadn't gone to the rescue.

Sounds drew Cassie from her darkening thoughts. She hopped off her chair, crossed the three steps to the door, and held an ear close to the painted wood to listen. People were talking in low tones in the next room. A couple of men and a woman, she thought. She did not recognize any of the voices. She turned from the door.

"Holy spit!" Cassandra nearly leapt out of her skin.

"Don't be afraid." The big man stood in the center of the room, tall, dark, handsome in a way Cassandra thought was more than a little cruel. He wore dark clothes that hung on his broad frame in a way that accentuated the power of his body.

"Who're you?" There was no door into the room other than the one Cassie had been listening at. No window—and in any case she could not imagine this man climbing through windows—no means of entry at all. "How did you get in here?"

"That does not matter," the man smiled, and his teeth were brilliant white against the darkness of his beard. "You want to help Wonder Woman, don't you?"

Cassie raised a skeptical eyebrow. "Well, yeah. I mean, she's my friend."

"That is good." The stranger laid a large hand on Cassie's shoulder. She felt the weight of it, and the heat of it, even through her denim jacket. "It is fortunate indeed for Diana that she has such friends as you."

"You know Diana?" Cassie was beginning to worry less about how this man got into the room than about discovering his purpose for being here. If he was there to help Diana, that made him a friend, and Cassie was willing to overlook his mysterious entrance. *Could be he's some kind of super hero himself.* She studied the dark face, the dark eyes bright and clear.

"I know Diana very well," the stranger smiled. "I have just come from talking with her, in fact. Talking at length about this situation, this strange menace she faces."

"What menace? Rebecca Chandler? She's no menace to Diana. Diana could pop her head off with one hand."

"She could indeed," the stranger smiled. "But, of course, she may not do such a thing. So, instead, she and I have conceived a different approach. An approach that requires your special help."

"Kewl!" Cassie felt her heart swell, her breath quicken. She knew she could trust him, whoever he was. Any friend of Diana's was a friend of hers. "What do I have to do?"

"Something very simple," the stranger said, "but something that may be difficult for you to do."

"There's nothing I wouldn't do to help Diana. She knows that."

"Yes. Yes, she does. But what you have to do now, Cassandra, is betray her."

"Some people say that the Christian God and the God of the Jews are the same," Esther Schorr said, pouring a cup of tea for her guest and settling back into her most comfortable chair. "I've never been quite able to see that. Christians and Jews believe in different things. Like the Messiah."

"This would be the man Jesus of Nazareth?" Diana sipped her tea, and Esther studied her, so calm, so cool. She wore a simple blouse and skirt, not her dramatic costume, and sitting on the couch across from Esther she seemed almost—though not quite entirely—reduced to human proportions. She was still tall, powerful—*And, let's face it, this is no average figure we're talking here!*—but as she sat with teacup in hand, legs demurely crossed, hair pulled back into a soft ponytail, she looked very much like a girl any mother would be pleased to have her boy bring home.

If only she didn't believe in such . . . unusual gods.

"Jesus is called the Messiah," Esther said, "but we don't think He is. God promised us a messiah, to lead us out of bondage. Would He send us one we wouldn't recognize?"

"But you have known what it was like to be persecuted for your faith," Diana said, bringing the conversation back to her key point. "This is something I do not fully comprehend. On Themyscira, of course, we all worshiped the gods of Olympus, and so there was no chance of a schism, no reason for one group to consider itself superior or holier than another. Yet, since I have come here to Patriarch's World, I have been aware of all the differences, and all the trouble they cause. But it was not until now that I understood how deeply rooted those differences are. How much hatred they can cause."

"There are a million reasons people hate the Jews," Esther said, seeming to Diana to be picking her words carefully. "But not one of them is real. Do you know, there used to be talk of a Jewish-Communist conspiracy. In Russia, the Jews were persecuted as maybe nowhere else outside Nazi Germany, and yet people would look at the bad things in the world and say it was a Jewish-Communist conspiracy."

Diana shook her raven-tressed head. "Do you understand why Rebecca Chandler would suddenly seek to attack me like this? Why she would see me as such a threat? Do *you* see me as a threat?"

Esther leaned back in her chair and considered the question. "You want an honest answer. That's not so easy to give. In a way you are a threat. My son is very fond of you, you know that."

"Yes, Michael and I are great friends."

"Well, maybe more than friends, from his way of looking at it. But even if that weren't quite so, understand that we, the Jews, believe a child should be raised in his mother's faith. So if, for example, you and Michael got married and had a baby, that baby would not be raised in the Jewish faith. He would be raised to worship your gods. In that, a little, you are a threat."

Diana set aside her teacup, focusing her attention on the question at hand, sidestepping, in her own mind, the concept of a deeper relationship with Michael Schorr. "But I would expect such a child to be taught the faith of both his parents, and allowed to chose for himself."

"Maybe. It's not that easy. And someone like Rebecca Chandler, well, she doesn't think there should be even that much choice. She thinks she has found the one true answer, and she wants everyone else to follow her thinking." Esther paused for a moment. "You know," she continued, "I think Rebecca Chandler is sincere. With all the attention she's been getting lately, I've listened to her a couple times, and I think she means what she says. Some of those others, they're just serving themselves, lining their own pockets. But I think Rebecca Chandler really believes what she preaches. And, of course, this means she believes you are evil and out to destroy her faith."

"Yes," Diana nodded, "I was impressed by the strength of her convictions when I met her. But why are so many others following her? Why do people I have never met, never touched in any way, wish to do me harm? There are more and more stories in the newspapers, on the television. And now, this nonsense about my sabotaging the highway, risking all those lives. . . ."

"Do you know what some people think about why Hitler started out to kill all the Jews in Germany? All the Jews in the world, if he'd won?"

"I am not clear on the details," Diana said.

"Well, some people say Hitler, he really didn't have anything against the Jews. Some people even say he was horrified, himself, when he found out how far things had gone with his 'Final Solution.' I doubt it, but maybe, *maybe* it's true. In any case, he came to power at a time when Germany was in a really bad way. Pitifully poor. People hungry, out of work. And he got this idea that what the German people needed was a scapegoat. Somebody they could blame for their troubles. Like the way people in this country like to blame television or movies for all the problems we have. So he picked the Jews. People already didn't like the Jews, didn't trust the Jews. Maybe if there had been a lot of Chinese people or black people in Germany, he would have picked them. He wanted someone visible, easy to spot. And the Jews, because some of them dressed differently, because they went to different places to worship their God, because they lived in isolated neighborhoods, in ghettos—well, they were visible. So Hitler told the German people—and the Jews were Germans, too, remember—he told the German people that the Jews were the evil ones, that all the problems Germany had were caused by the Jews."

"And people believed that?"

Esther sighed, fighting back the emotions that threatened to choke the words in her throat. "I was there, darling. People in trouble will believe whatever they have to in order to survive. The Germans needed to believe we were the cause of their troubles, and they didn't want to know how their leaders were taking care of the problem. As long as it . . . as we went away." She shook her head, sitting silently with her memories for long moments before looking back up at Diana and forcing a smile. "It doesn't even have to be something as big as Hitler's Germany. When I was younger there was a man in this country who came along one day and said all the juvenile delinquency that was such a problem was caused by comic books. Comic books! Like I could imagine something less harmful than a silly comic book! But he said this, and because he was a psychiatrist, and because he had a nice Viennese accent, people listened. People were looking for a scapegoat."

"And America is troubled now, so people are looking for another scapegoat."

"Sure. And what could be better than someone like you? You have such amazing powers, so right away people are jealous a little, maybe. You are more beautiful than any woman on earth, so women are envious, men are resentful. And you talk about gods that no one believes in, and tell people that these are real gods, and that you've met them." Esther tipped her head, studying Diana to see the effect of her words. "Would you be surprised if I told you even I don't believe that story?"

"You don't?" Diana said, genuinely surprised. "Why not? Why would you think I would lie about such a thing?"

"I don't know. But I believe in my God, and I know in my heart that He is the one, true God, who created the Universe, who created all the people and the animals, the birds and the trees and the flowers, and who, in all that, still has time to look down and make sure that little Esther Schorr is okay, that she has bread in the breadbox and milk in the icebox. I believe in Him, Diana, and I think He maybe believes in me. So, sure, I don't like that you come and say 'Here are these other gods, and I know they are real because I have met them.'"

"You know that when Mike and I first met he came to Themyscira with me?" Diana wondered how much Michael Schorr had told his mother of the beginnings of their relationship. "You know that he stood by me, helped me to defend my homeland against an invasion."

"Yes, I know this. I was very proud of him, even more proud of him, if such a thing is possible, when he told me."

"And he told you that the leader of the invasion was a being known as Darkseid. A god from a world called Apokolips?"

Esther frowned. "No. No, that he did not mention."

Diana nodded. "There are many gods in the Universe, Mrs. Schorr. Virtually every inhabited planet has gods and goddesses, and they were all created, it seems, by an energy wave that was hurled out into the Universe by the destruction of an old world, the One World on which all the gods lived at the beginning of time."

"All the gods?" Esther swallowed. Her mouth was dry, her chest heavy. "Diana, you know I can't believe such a thing. You know I can't believe that my God is just one god out of hundreds or thousands or millions."

"No," Diana said, lowering her eyes, feeling a weight press down upon her broad, strong shoulders. "No, I see now that you cannot. And, perhaps, no one raised in this country, in this culture, truly can." She looked up, meeting Esther's troubled gaze. "I was raised to accept the concept of a plurality of gods," Diana said. "I was raised to believe in gods who were physical, who walked among us, talked with us. I have been to Olympus, seen them in their homes, seen them about their daily lives. I comprehend my gods, Esther, but I see now that the very core of so many faiths in this land is the incomprehensibility of their god."

Diana stood, tall and straight, staggeringly beautiful, Esther thought, in the sunlight spilling through the tall windows at the end of the room.

"I have much to consider," Diana said. "Thank you for the tea. And for the wisdom."

William Winget spread the proof of the first page of the afternoon *Guardian* on the top of his big desk.

The headline was bigger and gaudier than he liked for the paper—the *Guardian* was not so staid as the *Gazette*, but neither was it the *Star Ledger*—but it delivered the message he wished spread across the city.

PUBLISHER DEMANDS ANSWERS. WINGET CALLS FOR INVESTIGATION OF WONDER WOMAN.

Beneath, filling the rest of the page, a picture of the Amazon Princess looked most unpleasant and sinister. *If I were truly a public figure*, Winget thought, *I would never go out where I could be photographed. Or if I did, I would never move my face, never blink.*

High-speed cameras, auto-focus, auto-advance. All these added together to capture the slightest movement of a celebrity's face. In the
huge picture morgue downstairs, Winget knew, were hundreds, thousands of pictures of celebrities ranging from the Queen of England to
Sylvester Stallone, and only a small percentage of them were anything
close to what might be called flattering. An editor—or a publisher, in
this case—could conceive a headline and, in minutes, find a picture of
someone caught in midblink, or midsneeze, or midyawn, or any of
countless variations of expression that, taken out of context, created a
perfect illustration of the point being made.

So, here, a shot of Wonder Woman. An unfortunate—for her, not
for William Winget—combination of shadow and half-formed expression warping her otherwise beautiful features, making her look for all
the world like someone who could, yes, be here to destroy the things
that mattered in this country, the core of our faith in God Almighty, the
morality of our children.

"Perfect," Winget said.

His city editor smiled, nodding. "I was pleased to find that shot. It
wasn't easy. She is so damned gorgeous."

"Camouflage," Winget said, and found, to his surprise, he believed
what he said. He would have admitted, if anyone asked, that it was
Rebecca Chandler's physical attractiveness—no Wonder Woman, but a
nice, neat little package—that had pulled him into this fight. He was
not so old, after all, that he did not still enjoy the beauty of a woman,
and enjoyed more than an appreciative glance.

"Maybe." Jack Kubica turned his head to look again at the picture.
"Anyway, it does the job."

"It does the job," Winget repeated. He smiled. "Fax a copy to Miss
Chandler at once. I want her in on this from the start. I want her to
know how much I am helping."

"Of course she will do what we ask of her," Stephen Ramsey smiled.
"She is a troubled child desperate for someone to trust. She cannot

turn to her own mother, the source of her troubles, so she will surely leap into the arms of the first trustworthy adult who shows her the least bit of love and compassion. Certainly an adult like you, my dear Rebecca, fits that bill to perfection."

"The poor child." Rebecca Chandler sat behind her wide desk, the high back of her chair casting a long shadow across the room. Ramsey, standing at the edge of that shadow, seemed to her almost to blend into it, his black suit fading into the dark oblong in a manner that seemed, when she thought about it, sinister and more than vaguely supernatural.

She decided not to think about it. Stephen Ramsey had been far too much use to her, backing her financially, building up her empire—as he was not at all hesitant to remind her—and most of all, fueling her campaign against Wonder Woman.

"Yes," Ramsey said solemnly. "Poor child indeed, yet most fortunate for us." He chuckled, and Rebecca felt the sound rumbling in the pit of her stomach. For a moment her thighs seemed to liquefy, and she was glad to be sitting.

"Really, Stephen, to take any pleasure in the torment of an abused child—"

"Yes, yes, of course." Ramsey's smile broadened. "Still, we are not responsible for her troubles, are we?"

"No, but—"

"All I meant was that considering your current crusade, Cassandra Sandsmark's misfortune could not have come at a better time. Imagine the impact upon the world when they hear the child's tale. And of Wonder Woman's part in her travails." Ramsey crossed the room to look out across the lake. "This is going very well, now, Rebecca." He turned to look at her, and, not for the first time, Rebecca saw in his eyes a fire that had nothing to do with the sunlight streaming through the tall windows. "We can proceed to the next phase immediately."

"We're that far along? I don't want to risk rushing—"

"We can proceed to the next phase immediately."

In spite of the many objections she could raise to such a move,

Rebecca held her tongue. Something in his voice. Commanding, compelling. Of course, he would know best.

"Yes," she said with a dry mouth. "As you say."

In the official report, the witnesses to the melee were not able to say with any certainty that Mike Schorr had thrown the first punch. Logic would suggest that he had. One moment, Gary Miller had been standing, taunting the smaller man, and the next he was halfway across the room, sliding on the wet floor toward the showers.

Mike Schorr was not a man quick to anger. The witnesses testified to that, at least. In his years with the Gateway City police, as he rose from patrolman to SWAT specialist, he had learned to control his temper. There were too many situations in the daily life of a cop that could explode out of control at the least word, the smallest action motivated by rage instead of calm common sense.

So Michael Schorr, who would be among the first to admit to a short fuse in his younger days, learned to control his emotions, to temper his thinking, his actions. To be sure, to be careful.

But today he was angry. Today the back of his neck burned and his teeth ground behind lips drawn thin. His face—oddly boyish, despite a nose smashed flat in his Golden Gloves days—already dark of skin, was darker still, his brows drawn down over eyes that shone like steel.

"Miller, you are so full of crap your eyes are brown," he said. Miller was a full head taller than the bantam-sized Mike Schorr, but he drew back a little before the rage everyone in the room sensed was only just being held in check.

"Look, Schorr," Miller said, "everybody in the department knows you're sweet on Wonder Woman, so I don't think you got a whole lot worth saying here, right?"

Mike stood his ground, clenching and unclenching his hard fists in a ritual he had used countless times to moderate and modulate his anger. He found himself instinctively measuring distances, from himself to Miller, from himself to the lockers, to benches, to rough, white walls.

There were two dozen men in the room, policemen all, mostly SWAT, like Mike and Miller. Mike factored in their positions as they moved about, some by their lockers, some seated, some emerging from the showers at the far end of the long room, towels around their wet forms, feet slapping on the cold concrete floor.

"I've got as much right and more," Mike said. "I've seen Wonder Woman up close, in action. I've been to her homeland. I know what she says is true."

"Sure," Miller said, poking a thick finger into Mike's chest. There was a disadvantage of more than size here, Mike realized, should this argument come to blows. He wore only a T-shirt and boxers, while Miller was still in the molded, reinforced Kevlar body armor the Gateway City SWAT teams had been wearing for nearly three years. Mike had used the armor many times himself, and he knew its weaknesses, but he also knew a blow from one of Miller's gauntleted fists would do a lot of damage. Still, Mike Schorr was not about to back down now.

"Oh sure, Schorr," Miller sneered, "you come back after being missing for half a week and say you and Wonder Woman went back to Paradise Island and had some business, but you don't want to talk about the business. You're all tight-lipped about that."

"Diana asked me to keep to myself what I saw on Themyscira," Mike said. "Not a whole lot of people from the outside have visited there." *And, anyway, it was enough to ask people to believe I'd even been to Themyscira. If I started talking about battles with angry gods and stuff like that, they'd toss me in the booby hatch. As it is, the captain has been keeping an eye on me ever since, waiting for me to show I'm really nuts.*

"Handy," Gary Miller said. "Seems like Wonder Woman has maybe a whole lot too many secrets she doesn't want the rest of the world to know."

"Well, if we knew," Barney Kingsford chuckled from his place by his locker, "they wouldn't be secrets, would they?" He winked at Mike, his smile bright in his black face.

"Keep out of this, Kingsford, unless you have something worth adding," Miller snapped without turning to look at Mike's friend. "All I said was that Rebecca Chandler has a good point—we're all too quick to trust Wonder Woman—and Schorr here has to try to jump down my throat to protect his girlfriend." Miller leaned his big, flat face closer to Mike's and smiled a most unpleasant smile. "And, y'know, maybe if I was getting a piece of that action, I'd be defending her, too."

At which point Miller suddenly went careering across the concrete floor, the armor on his back screeching, his head bound for a sharp, painful impact with the tiled rim of the door to the showers. Men in towels leapt aside like clumsy ballerinas, two not quite fast enough to avoid the sudden missile that whizzed past their feet. They tumbled, and as Miller cracked into the wall he found himself under a pair of naked bodies.

"Geddoffame," he snarled, surging to his feet. He staggered from the blow to his head but fought off the vertigo and hurled his armored form down the length of the long room.

Mike Schorr realized in that moment that there was an advantage to being nearly naked. He moved with speed and grace he could never have achieved in the armor. The SWAT teams worked out regularly, getting limber, getting used to the way the armor moved, but it was still bulky and cumbersome. It had saved more than one life, stopping bullets, blocking shrapnel, even knives, but getting into hand-to-hand combat with a man in his underwear, he proceeded to demonstrate to Miller, is not very different from wrestling a greased pig.

Mike moved quickly, easily. He aimed careful, flat-handed karate blows at the points he knew the armor to be weakest, the joints, the seams, especially knees and elbows. Miller wound up spending too much of the fight—if it could be called a fight—trying to stay on his feet, or getting back to them.

He managed to land a couple of strong hits, and Mike went reeling, stars dancing before his eyes, but he recovered fast—his Golden Gloves training—and pummeled Miller again and again.

"Awright, cudditout!!"

The voice ripped across both men. Mike danced back, Miller lurched. In the door to the squad room Captain Alonzo Vasquez stood like a conquistador, dark eyes afire, fists planted on his hips.

"What the hell is this?" Vasquez advanced menacingly into the locker room. "Miller? Schorr? What the hell are you doing?"

Both men flapped their gums, speechless, faces red. They were members of the top, the best, the Gateway City's crack SWAT team, the bravest of the brave, the brightest of the bright, and they were caught brawling like drunken hooligans.

"My office," Vasquez snapped. "Now." He turned on the others in the room as Miller and Schorr marched out, heads hanging. "And the rest of you—I want full reports on this." He narrowed his black eyes. "Pay special attention to explaining why none of you were doing anything to stop it!"

There were more steps mounting to the broad portico of the Gateway City Museum of Antiquities than Father Donald Morris had expected.

Holding his coat tight against the pain in his side, Morris paused halfway up the steps and wondered if he would be able to make it the rest of the way. Passersby paid little attention as he hunched forward, folded over his pain, and he could not say that he truly blamed them. He had not had another coat stashed in his old carpetbag, and the one he wore, though cleaned by the hospital laundry, looked very much like what it was, a garment that had seen too many years of use even before it survived a rolling, tearing ride in a bus bound for oblivion.

Feeling a little better, Father Morris again started up the steps, planting his feet carefully on the worn stone, focusing on each step in turn, and keeping his eyes averted from the rise before him. *Don't look at the top. It will come soon enough, if you just keep going. But if you look, it will just seem an impossible distance away. Don't look at the top.*

Abruptly—thankfully sooner than anticipated—the last step flattened out into the broad landing before the tall glass doors of the museum. He paused for a moment to catch his breath, then pushed through the central revolving door.

At once he was struck by the museum's size, the hugeness of the halls, the way sounds bounced and reverberated. Ten thousand alien aromas mingled and drifted on the conditioned air, everything from the scent of coffee brewing in the cafeteria downstairs to the barely detectable odor of age, of time sunk deep into the fabric of things brought here over many years, from great distances.

Stationed in the center of the entrance foyer, looking strangely new and out of place against a high, smooth marble wall, was an information kiosk, bedecked with fliers and pamphlets, posters announcing shows in various parts of the museum—including, Morris noted, at least one that, by the dates, had ended two weeks before.

He crossed to stand in the short line before the kiosk, listening to the sounds of the museum. Looking past the foyer to the first hall, he saw the array of glass and wood boxes, display cases, containing fragments of history, from bits of stuff that were completely unidentifiable at this distance—and likely to be so close up, he supposed—to outlandish suits of armor, festival clothes, ritual garments. Sunlight slanted into the museum through a high clerestory along the top of the broad north face of the museum. The light was orange and gold, painting the drifting dust motes, making them dance like tiny fairies across Morris's vision.

He stepped up to the kiosk, his turn at last, and asked for directions to Helena Sandsmark's office. Given them, he crossed the great hall to a small side passage, making his way down a flight of stairs leading into the lower levels of the museum.

This will be the frustrating part, he told himself, preparing for a long wait. He had called ahead, of course, to make a proper appointment with Professor Sandsmark, only to be told that some personal distress was keeping her out of the museum. She would, however, be stopping in at random times, whenever she could find a moment, and, the secretary suggested, if Reverend Morris—he smiled at the term—would like to come in and wait, he might catch her. Usually, he was informed, Helena Sandsmark managed to find some time to come in in the later afternoon.

So he was there, in what he supposed could be called the middle of the early afternoon, making his way painfully down the steep steps to the level that housed Professor Sandsmark's office.

Of course it was a long shot. He knew that, on many levels. There was no guarantee that Professor Sandsmark would come in that afternoon. "Personal distress" was the precise phrase the secretary had used, and Donald Morris had not felt it his place to question further. If Helena Sandsmark was diligent enough in her work that she would find time to stop in at the museum when she could, then fine. If she found such time today, this afternoon, even better.

Otherwise, he would come back tomorrow, and the next day, and the next, even though he knew, deep down, that making contact with Helena Sandsmark was not, after all, a direct conduit to Wonder Woman. Professor Sandsmark would have to decide, herself, that Donald Morris's mission was of sufficient importance that she should report it to her Amazon friend, and Wonder Woman would then have to decide that, having heard that report, she wanted to act upon it.

And how capricious is she? How much attention is she prepared to pay to the small lives around her? The demands on her must be great. I am only a priest, and God knows, I understand what demands people can make. Every man sees his own needs as the most important in the world. I am likely to be, what, one of thousands who petition Wonder Woman at any given time?

He recalled seeing the news reports of the first appearance of Superman—even before he had donned his familiar costume—when he had saved a crashing spaceplane that had been scheduled to land at Metropolis as part of the centennial celebration. When Superman—not yet called "Superman," Morris recalled—landed, with the crippled spacecraft, he was immediately besieged by the press. And not just the press. The cameras showed an ocean of flesh, people crowding in on the dark-haired young man, pressing in, reaching for him, clawing at him. *Had he not been Superman, he would surely have been crushed to death!*

And all demanding, all seeing in him and in his amazing act some kind of miracle that, in their eyes, needed to be immediately exploited to their own advantage.

Perhaps that's why, the next time Superman appeared, he came in that costume of his, that uniform. It was his way of saying, "Yes, I am here to help, but only now, only when I am 'on duty.'"

And for Wonder Woman? Superman was not known to have a "secret identity"—unlike other super heroes, he wore no mask—and neither was Wonder Woman. But Superman was elusive, while Wonder Woman had chosen, for reasons of her own, to live among the people she served as one of them. Unlike Superman—it was hard to imagine him with a day job—Wonder Woman had a place she went on a regular basis, a paycheck she collected to take care of the day-to-day things, and even a name, Diana Prince.

Of course, Morris had looked in the phone book for that name, but, wisely, Diana Prince was not listed—or, at least, had not had a phone long enough to be listed.

So, acting upon the information garnered from his hospital roommates, Morris came to the museum, looking for this one sure connection to Princess Diana of Themyscira. If he was more fortunate than he had any right to expect, perhaps he would find, through her, a connection to something that would answer the most perplexing questions of his life.

"You may believe in Jesus—" his words to the Mother Superior kept running through his head—*"but Wonder Woman has had lunch with Zeus."*

CHAPTER SIX

REBECCA Chandler herself was
astonished at the speed with which things were happening.

True, after her own meteoric rise—from little more than nothing to
this pinnacle in slightly less than two years—she realized there should
be nothing, or at least very little, left that was capable of surprising
her. Nothing, except whatever Stephen Ramsey, the ever-elusive and
ever-mysterious Stephen Ramsey, had a hand in.

*And I still know almost nothing about him. No, be honest. I know
absolutely nothing about him. My organization is vast, it has many, many
eyes and ears—all paid for, of course, and sponsored by him, nurtured
by him, as I have been—and yet not one of them, not the highest, not
the lowest, has been able to find out a single thing about Mr. Stephen
Ramsey. I know now only what I knew two years ago—he is rich, impossibly rich, he is persuasive, and he is irresistible.*

Rebecca had not felt herself physically attracted to Ramsey, despite
his good looks and undeniable power. There had been times, she would
admit, when his sheer physical presence seemed almost on the verge
of overwhelming her, but there was always, always, something just
at the edge of her perceptions, something that seemed to place him
beyond such things. Beyond the concerns of mere mortal men and
women.

It's quite insane, and yet somehow, if you were to tell me he was from Mars, from Krypton, from somewhere far beyond this world, this Universe, I would not be completely disinclined to agree. He is alien. He is strange—wondrously strange, I suppose, but strange, nevertheless. And he has never made any improper moves toward me, either.

For a moment Rebecca puzzled over that. *Am I unattractive to him? Unappealing as a woman?* It was the worst kind of vanity to even think about such things, she knew, since she was not, as she protested to herself, interested in anything Stephen Ramsey had to offer beyond his financial support for her enterprises, yet Rebecca Chandler was, after all, a woman, and enough of a woman that there was a small part of her, call it her ego, that could not help but wonder, in a small way, what it was that made Ramsey as immune to her charms as she was to his.

She remembered how they met. Two years, yet it seemed like two centuries. She had been working in a Christian Science Reading Room, filing mostly, sorting the books. She lived in a tiny room, a single room with a shared bath in a boarding house on the South Side of Chicago. Her life had been drab, colorless, and she would have been the first to admit she was, herself, very much like her life.

I was a bland and boring little nobody. I had nothing to distinguish me from a million other people in Chicago, all with small lives, small thoughts and minds. I wanted to be more, I wanted so much to be more. There were times when I thought I would sell my soul for a way out of that life.

Rebecca froze. She had been going about one of her normal daily functions—reading selected mail, making notations as to which letters would receive which of a hundred carefully crafted form responses. It was something she had done so many times in the past two years that she could do it automatically, scanning only the first line or two of each paragraph, sometimes nothing more than the first and last paragraphs. It was the sort of thing she could do while her mind wandered free.

Now she stopped. The words on the page grew faint and distant.

She had never thought of it before in quite that way. Never put just that string of words together in her mind. *I would sell my soul for a way out.*

Rebecca felt the color drain from her cheeks, her fingers growing cold, the letter she held slipping from her hands.

No. No, it couldn't be. It couldn't be that.

Like many Christians, Rebecca believed there was a creature, a being, an entity—*there is no really suitable word*—that embodied the forces arrayed against God, against the Word and the Truth. Call that being Satan, if that were convenient, though Rebecca was sufficiently versed in the Bible and its history to know that a satan, in its proper form, was an angel sent by God to block the path of some mortal, someone whom God had chosen to take another route. As he had blocked Balaam's ass, and the beast, more in touch perhaps with the fundamental forces of the world than Balaam himself, refused to proceed when it saw the satan.

And Stephen Ramsey certainly changed my course. But did I sell my soul to do it? I don't think so. I don't recall ever saying anything, doing anything that could be viewed as entering into such a diabolical— literally—arrangement.

No, she decided, Stephen Ramsey, whatever else he may have been, was not Satan, not Lucifer, not anything supernatural at all. He had about him something of the manner and the way of a conjurer, he moved without sound, seeming to pass without disturbing the air around him, but that was something Rebecca attributed to the sheer force of his presence, his maleness.

And he has given me all of this, all this power to spread the word of God, in exchange for nothing more than my promise that I will use some of it to reveal to the world the truth about Wonder Woman. She paused. Her brow creased. *And have you ever asked him why this is so important to him? Have you ever even wondered aloud, in his presence, why the destruction of the Amazon Princess is even necessary within the frame of his needs, his view of the world?*

Rebecca understood why she needed to see Wonder Woman

brought down. Those observers who said she was completely sincere in her beliefs were correct. She was no charlatan hiding behind the Bible as an easy source of wealth and power. She had amassed a fortune for herself, and lived well by it, but she made sure the vast majority of it—more than 99 percent, she was assured by her accountants—went to the glory of God, not the betterment of Rebecca Chandler.

And she wanted Wonder Woman destroyed because the Amazon represented, by her very existence, something ancient and evil. *Early Christians took the form of their demons from the gods she worships. There was a reason for that. They understood the evil inherent in those beings.*

Rebecca was surprised again, for a moment. She did not think, in all the times she had given thought to such things, that she had ever before given the old gods, the Greco-Roman gods, the credit inherent in referring to them as "beings." To do that would be to give them a kind of life, to acknowledge them as something that existed, that was real.

This was something Rebecca had never considered, never allowed into her thoughts. Even as a girl, watching reruns of *Star Trek*, she had been deeply offended—though she had not been sure why, then—by the episode that proposed the Greek gods to have been space travelers, that suggested Apollo might be alive, out there, somewhere in the Universe.

They were never real, she thought, feeling strength returning to her in a sense of renewed purpose. *They might have been some half-guessed shadows, hints of the greater Truth that Humankind was still struggling to comprehend*—after all, they did prefigure some significant portions of Judeo-Christian lore—*but they were never the real beings Diana claims they are, creatures you could meet, talk to, even mate with.*

Rebecca shuddered. What a thought! Such an inherent blasphemy! As if a real god, a true god, would ever lower himself to engage in sex with a mortal woman. It was all pagan storytelling, bringing the gods down to human dimensions, in a vain attempt to make them and their actions comprehensible.

Rebecca checked off a few more letters, marked one specifically—a woman in need of a lifesaving operation—to receive a check from the Soldiers of Salvation. She shuffled the different-sized pages into as neat a pile as possible, setting them on the corner of her desk.

Glancing at her watch, she reached past the pile to tap one of the hidden contacts in the ebon surface. The wall before her parted, the big TV screen lighting. She selected ABC, settled back in her chair as the mellifluous tones of Peter Jennings drifted from the speaker. There had been a protest march in Washington. A group of black Episcopalians had taken up her crusade and marched on the White House bearing standards and posters demanding that the President take a special interest in Wonder Woman, demanding that Congress look into the matter of this so-called Amazon Princess and her outlandish, heathen stories. The demonstration had been peaceful enough, but the videotaped images of the protesters clearly showed the rage etched on their faces. Their outrage was palpable, and Rebecca could only wonder at the power, the raw emotion her words had led to. Would eventually lead to.

Jennings ended the story with a wry look into the camera. He had little time, Rebecca could tell, for something he considered so patently foolish.

She made a mental note to contact the head of ABC. Pressure would be brought to bear. If the network was to cover this story, they would have to cover it in the proper fashion. Knowing NBC would not have led with the same story as their chief competitor, Rebecca switched to that channel, finding Tom Brokaw beginning coverage of the demonstration.

Now get it right, she thought, and listened for the least bit of inflection in Brokaw's voice, the least suggestion that he, like Jennings, was not fully in Rebecca Chandler's camp.

Were she in a better mood, a better situation, Helena Sandsmark might almost have been able to find humor in what was happening. A kind of insane, frustrating, totally irrational Monty Python humor, but humor nevertheless

I am beset by bureaucrats, she thought. *And because they are bureaucrats they have no interest in forwarding the public good, in dealing with the problems presented to them in a straightforward, logical manner. They are interested only in perpetuating their bureaucracy.*

In her position at the Gateway City Museum of Antiquities, Helena had often had to deal with bureaucrats—in search of funding, or special travel and shipping permits for the artifacts that flowed almost daily in and out of the various departments under her supervision. She had gone to war on more than one occasion with virtually every level of government, civic, state, even federal. She had fought with Republicans and Democrats alike and had come to the repeated, almost humorous conclusion that the main difference between the two parties was the spelling.

But now Helena could find nothing to make jokes about, even the dry, thin jokes that were her trademark.

They have taken my daughter from me. They have taken Cassie, and I have spent the better part of a day just finding out where it is they have taken her.

When this is all over, she decided, when this is all behind and the people who have initiated this absurdity are revealed for the idiots they are, she could make some kind of legal response, maybe some kind of class action suit. *I'll sue the bastards for a hundred million dollars and settle for ten,* she thought, and a grim smile settled onto her lips. *After all, the museum could use the money.*

The Department of Child Welfare was a cluttered box deep within the rabbit warren of Public Services. It had taken Helena some twenty hours of phone calls, office visits, more phone calls, more visits, being shunted physically and electronically from one place to the next, from one bureaucrat to another, but she felt she was at last closing on her target. She had in her pocket a name and an office number. The name was Thomas Odynsky, and the office was here, on this floor, behind one of these doors.

Helena's hard heels clicked loudly on the stone floor as she marched down the narrow corridor. The place was oppressively hot—for some reason the furnace was going full blast, although the day outside was warm—and the air was heavy with PineSol and other indeterminate smells.

Helena came to her destination. She paused at the door to take a deep breath, held it, let it out slowly. She reached for the knob, and, in that moment, thought better of it, abandoning her original plan to storm in and hit whomever she found beyond the wood and frosted glass barrier with everything she had, fueled by every ounce of rage bubbling inside her. Feeling as close to under control as possible under the circumstances, Helena raised her right hand and tapped lightly but firmly on the glass with two fingernails.

"Come."

Helena stepped into the office. It was small, crowded, windowless. It was an oven, and the man behind the desk sat in shirtsleeves, his bald head glistening, the few strands of remaining hair that arced sadly across his pate plastered down with sweat.

"Are you Odynsky?" Helena decided to forgo polite titles.

"Yes. You must be Professor Sandsmark." His voice was deep, bigger than his small frame. "Won't you take a seat?"

"Not until I see my daughter. Where is Cassandra?"

"She's not here," Odynsky said. Helena saw him draw himself in, saw him shrink slightly, as if in preparation to protect himself from physical assault.

She sighed. "All right, I've been all day running around this rat's maze you people have built for yourselves. I can go a little further. Where is she?"

"I'm not at liberty to tell you that, Professor."

Helena blinked. "I beg your pardon?"

"I said, I am not at liberty to tell you where Cassandra has been taken."

"Like hell you're not." Helena felt her heart begin to pound faster than she would have thought possible. She wondered if Odynsky's small, self-protective movement had been learned from past experience; how many parents, presented with this bureaucratic moron, actually hurled themselves across his desk and tried to throttle him? *Which I am* not *going to do. Yet.* "You people may have exercised your arcane rules to the point of being able to take Cassie from me without anything like due process, but you are not going to be allowed to prevent me from seeing her. I demand to see her. I demand that you prove to me, right now, that she is all right, that no harm has come to her."

Odynsky essayed something Helena found altogether too much like a sneer. "I find such concern particularly ironic, coming from you, Professor. Especially after everything Cassandra has told us."

"What Cassie has told you? What are you talking about?"

"Your daughter has been most cooperative, Professor Sandsmark." The sneer was quite clear now, quite undisguised. "Oh, not at first, I grant you. At first she refused to talk at all, to tell us anything about you, about Wonder Woman, about anything we needed for our files. But then she had a sudden change of heart. It was quite amazing to see. Just like someone had thrown a switch. I suspect—" Odynsky narrowed his eyes "—it happened at the point at which she realized this was her first real chance to get away from you, to escape the pattern of abuse to which she has been subject."

"'Pattern of abuse'?" Helena felt the walls of the room drawing away, as though she were shrinking, sinking in the middle of some invisible quicksand, all logic and reason suddenly and forcibly being sucked from the Universe. "What? . . ."

"Shall we start with your boyfriends, Professor? Cassandra presented us with quite a list. 'Uncles' she called them. All the 'uncles' you've been bringing home over the years. Sometimes as many as three a week. Different men, at all hours, coming and going, not only in your room, but Cassandra's."

"But that's—"

"And since Wonder Woman arrived, moving into the apartment on the top floor of your house, well, it's just become worse and worse, hasn't it? You and this Amazon . . . well, we know what Amazons were all about, don't we?" Odynsky's cheeks were beginning to flush, Helena noticed, the color bright in the otherwise incredibly drab room. "I would have thought your concern for your professional position would have compelled you to be more careful, Professor. To be at least discreet about your relationship with Wonder Woman. But I suppose you thought no one would ever catch you. You had Cassandra so fearful, I'm sure you thought you could get away with anything."

Helena sat down heavily, her legs drained suddenly of the strength to hold her up. "Cassie told you this? *Cassie?*"

"She did." Odynsky shoved a manila folder across the desktop with much the same motion and contempt, Helena thought, that a man might show pushing a bowl of excrement away from himself. "You can read the report, if you wish. By law I am forced to allow you to do that much, at least." Odynsky rose, rounding the desk and heading for the door. "Now, if you will excuse me, Professor, I need some fresh air. The stench in this office is suddenly quite unbearable."

Of all the powers granted to her at the moment of her creation, the one Princess Diana most appreciated was that given to her by the god Hermes, the power of flight.

There was nothing she could summon to memory, no experience she had ever known, that could compare to the sheer, visceral thrill of simply stepping off the earth, stepping out of the clinging bonds of gravity as one might shed a coat, and rising into the air, rising faster and faster until the wind was whipping past and whistling in her ears.

Diana had flown more times than she could count, since the first time, still an infant, when she rose from her mother's arms and bobbed about the nursery built in the palace with great care and special attention for her. She remembered bouncing off the ceiling then, like a wandering balloon. She flailed her arms and legs as if swimming in the air, and, in fact, that was precisely what she had been doing. She had been far too young, then, to understand that her flight, her speed and direction, could be controlled by her thought, her will.

And now, of course, it was all unconscious. For Diana to take to the air required no more effort or deliberate direction than it took another woman to lift and place each leg in the process of walking across a room.

And if Diana was grace personified on the ground, if her least movement was a harmony of fluid ease and economy, then in the air she was a symphony. Her body was at home on the crest of the wind, light, supple, yet at the same time strong. She controlled the current, riding the wind, and beneath her it was as docile and compliant as a well-trained stallion.

The sky was as much her home as the ground, and when she was troubled, when the problems of her life pressed in too close, it was always to the sky that Diana went to find solace, some small release. There, above the clouds, where the air was sharp and clean as a warrior's blade, where the sounds of the city dwindled down to nothing, she found peace, a blissful tranquillity that was unequaled in her life by anything beyond her quiet moments of contemplation in the Temple of Athena.

The Temple of Athena. She remembered clearly the first time her mother, Hippolyta, took her there. Diana had been no more than three years old, as mortals measured time, and yet the details were as clear in her mind as if the moment had been yesterday. No small part of this, Diana knew, was due to the simple fact that the temple had stood, perfect and unchanging, for all the years Themyscira had been in existence, and was the last time she had visited its cool, shadowed halls exactly as it had been on that first day.

I have been granted by Athena a portion of her own wisdom, Diana thought, as she rose above the smog and noise of Gateway City, *but either it has now deserted me, or the problem that confronts me is beyond even Athena's wisdom to comprehend.*

Diana had never been reticent in confessing that her primary emotion, since she had left Paradise Island, was one of confusion. Having lived the first twenty-two years of her life in the ordered serenity of Themyscira, where all things were understood and each person had a place and a duty to perform, Diana's journey to the world outside, the place her mother called "Patriarch's World," was one of constant revelation. Sometimes too much so.

In a few short years she had seen for the first time disease, poverty, crime, perversion, and the kinds of senseless wars Humanity unleashed all too frequently upon itself. Diana was an Amazon, and an Amazon was nothing if not a warrior. She understood the need for war, but she had yet to see a war fought by mortals that had in it any of the glory, the grandeur, the simple, pure necessity that she had always understood to be the central reason for unleashing martial fury upon one's neighbors.

She had seen wars fought—and so many in the short time she had been here!—over everything, it seemed, but honor and righteousness. Man had taken up arms against man over wealth, over faith, over internecine squabbles that seemed to her so petty, so far below proper intellectual and emotional consideration that she would never in ten thousand years be able to imagine herself raising a hand or a sword in their cause.

And, the nature of her mission and her powers having thrust her into the role of "super hero"—she was still far from comfortable with the term—she had seen senseless cruelty and greed, eruptions of rage and fury all for the smallest, most trivial and insignificant reasons. She had seen men and women who found themselves suddenly possessed of great power—and used that power, not for the betterment of all around, as Diana had been taught all her life, but for their own aggrandizement. These individuals the press and television had dubbed "super villains," another foolish term, Diana thought, and they were seen as aberrations, somehow separate and apart from the norm, the natural configuration of the heart and mind of man.

Yet are they really? With all the cruelty and senseless violence I have seen in the few short years since I left Themyscira, can I really believe that these "super villains" are so very different from the average man or woman? Granted great powers, how many people would turn to altruism?

The sad fact, as Diana well knew, was that the "villains" outnumbered the "heroes" manyfold.

And she wondered, as she glided out over the Pacific, leaving behind the west coast of the United States, and with it the noise and jangle of Gateway, she wondered if this new and puzzling menace that had risen to vex her was in some way a manifestation of that very thing, the baseness of the human spirit. The Christian church—the very institution against which Diana was said to stand in opposition—taught that all men were born in sin, that all men carried a burden of evil they must purge before they could go on to their final reward. The sentiment was not uncommon, Diana knew.

If Man is inherently evil, she thought, is it not natural to expect that the race will produce more evil men, more Hitlers, more Attilas, more Caligulas, than it will Schweitzers or Mother Teresas? And is it not natural to assume that this basic core, this rotten center, constantly battled, constantly denied, would nonetheless drive people to seek villains, enemies, targets on which they can vent their own dissatisfactions— scapegoats, as Esther said, for their own frustrations?

Diana rose almost to the edge of breathable atmosphere. Unlike Superman she could not for long withstand the rigors of naked space, and so she did not push up beyond the slender blanket of air, only high enough that what she drew into her lungs was thin and colder than the coldest ice, chilling her, yet at the same time sharpening her thoughts.

Is this, in the end, why I am here? I have sought a central purpose all the time I have traveled in man's world. In my years in Boston, in my time with the Justice League of America, in my few months in Gateway, I have searched for something that will give me a center, a distinct purpose to my mission here. My mother sent me out as a peacemaker, an ambassador, but that is only the smallest part of what an Amazon is *meant to do. I am trained to fight—to fight, and, when necessity de-mands, to kill, to defend all that I hold to be true and worthy. Is that why I am here, now? Is that what this new vexation is all about?*

She had been tested before, by both Man and gods. It was not alto-gether unlikely, she knew, that this was all part of some new test, and that, when she emerged on the other side of the gauntlet—as she knew she would—she would have been made stronger by her passage.

So be it. She released her hold on the tenuous fibers of the air and al-lowed herself to fall, dropping straight and true toward the broad blue Pacific almost fifty miles below. *If I am to be tested, let me face the test and master it. Let me show the people, the gods, and most of all myself that there is a reason the world has come to call me Wonder Woman!*

Cassie had never seen such luxury in her life. *Decadent,* she thought, not entirely sure of the meaning of the word, but almost certain it prop-erly applied itself to the room, this massive, sumptuous, utterly unbe-lievable hotel room.

If I'd known it was gonna get me this kind of treatment, I'd have ratted out Mom and Diana right away! She kicked up her feet, lying back on the impossibly huge and yielding bed, laughing to herself. She was, perhaps, too young to appreciate the finer points of irony, but Cassie sensed there were layers to this situation. She had only pre-tended to turn on her mother and her closest friend—what was Diana if not her best friend?—and not only was she allowed to infiltrate the heart of the enemy, but she was being rewarded with luxury and deca-dence while she did it.

She was quite pleased with herself, too. At first, she thought she might not be able to get away with the really outrageous lies she was telling. She began with a single fib, a small thing, more of an exaggera-tion than an outright lie, but seeing the reaction it elicited in the Child Welfare people, she built quickly, laying one fabrication atop another, until her imagination utterly outstripped itself and she began plundering memories of *Beverly Hills 90210* and *Melrose Place* to flesh out her prevarications.

She thought the suggestion that Diana and her mother were—what was that silly phrase?—"more than friends" was particularly brilliant. The Child Welfare people were all so tightly wound, she had quickly noticed, all so utterly unhip and painfully repressed that the suggestion of a lesbian relationship was just enough to push them over the edge. After all, no matter how liberal and understanding the rest of the world might be—and Cassie had friends at school who were already displaying lesbian tendencies, which she herself had no problems with whatsoever—these people were paid to think evil thoughts, to see darkness at the center of everything.

And I guess they mostly do a good job. There're lots of kids who are abused, kids who need to be rescued. But sometimes, like this time, they go too far. She remembered a girl who went to her school, briefly, who one day announced to her circle of friends that she was so thoroughly and completely pissed off with her parents and their stupid rules and regulations that she had decided to take herself down to the Child Welfare department and say that they, her parents, had been abusing her.

"Had they?" the other girls had asked in horror.

Of course not, admitted the plotter, but that was not the point. She wanted to teach them a lesson, and this, she had decided, was the perfect way to do it.

Of course, the other girls reported this when they learned that she had actually gone through with her plan, but still there had been sufficient hesitation, enough of a gap between the discovery and the report that damage had been done, and even though the lie had been revealed, the parents would go through the rest of their lives with people looking at them just a little askance, with the eternal questions of *What if it's true? Or why would she say those terrible things if they weren't true?*

So it had been easy enough for Cassie to spin the kind of web of lies her mysterious visitor—she still had no idea who he was— wanted. And it had worked so well that now Cassie was ensconced in the luxurious suite, eating chocolates and drinking shakes, ordering hamburgers and pizzas by the long ton, and knowing that every penny of it was being billed to the Soldiers of Salvation and Rebecca Chandler.

I wonder if I can eat enough pizza to really make a hole in her fortune, Cassie laughed to herself, reaching for the phone to call room service.

And this afternoon, she thought, *I think I'll tell them the story that was in that way wonky movie that was on HBO last month. They're so willing to believe anything. I bet I could even get away with telling them I'd been abducted by space aliens.* She laughed out loud. *Maybe I'll tell them mom is a space alien!*

Looking out the tall corner windows of his office high in the elaborate face of City Hall, Mayor Benjamin Garrison peered through the thick cloud of cigar smoke that seemed always to circle his head, surveying the portion of Gateway City arrayed before him and considering his next move.

"This is a tricky one, Your Honor," Sheldon Minsky said. He had been Garrison's chief aide and counselor for more years than either of them really cared to remember, and in that time he had shepherded Garrison's career through many places high and low. Small and gnomish, with perpetually bad skin and weak eyes behind thick glasses, Minsky had said of himself that he had a "great face for radio," and he realized very early in his life that any political aspirations he might possess would have to find satisfaction in his manipulation of the careers of others. And in the tall, patrician, utterly unimpeachable Benjamin Garrison, Minsky found the perfect instrument.

Garrison took the stubby cigar from his lips, studied the chewed end. "Define 'tricky,'" he said. It was an old trick of his, when he did not understand something clearly, to demand that the speaker "define" what he or she was saying, as if the fault lay in the delivery of the information, not the listener.

"There are about twenty different polls on the subject," Minsky said. "All seven local radio stations, all four network affiliates, the Browning Corporation, a couple of colleges, even one bank asking its customers what they think. And the city is split about right down the middle, if you ignore the uncommitted. Thirty-five percent think Wonder Woman is just swell, thirty-seven percent think she should be burned at the stake."

Garrison turned from the window. "So the nays outnumber the ayes by a small margin?"

Minsky shrugged. "There's a three percent margin of error, either way." He shuffled the sheaf of papers in his hands, feeling small and unimportant, as he always did next to Benjamin Garrison. *Without me he's nothing*, Minsky reminded himself. *Without me he's still a lawyer with a couple of high-placed clients and no ambition beyond a big house and a very young wife.* Minsky's first task, when he adopted Garrison as his protégé, had been to persuade him to reconcile with his wife of twenty years and put his Playboy Bunny girlfriend on the most distant of back burners.

"Three percent." Garrison frowned, and Minsky saw the first signs of trouble.

He's thinking. He's trying to make decisions for himself. Never a good sign.

"Three percent isn't enough to make a difference, Your Honor. Three percent one way and suddenly the majority is on Wonder Woman's side. And, remember, there's the uncommitted."

"The uncommitted rarely vote," Garrison smiled. He sat behind his desk, crushing out his cigar butt in the big ashtray, and took a new, dark Havana from the tall humidor. These were the one vice Minsky permitted him, and much effort was made to disguise the path by which they were smuggled in from Canada, where the stogies, illegal in America, were available. Garrison puffed the cigar furiously, filling the air around him with thick blue-gray smoke. "See if you can narrow this down, Shel. Find me a really good grip on this. If the people want to side with Wonder Woman, I want to seem like I was the first to do so. Otherwise, I want to throw the first torch on the fire."

"Of course." Minsky smiled inside, hearing Garrison speak as though he were no more than a ventriloquist's puppet. The long years of shaping and training paid off almost every day now. *Sometimes I think I could safely leave him on autopilot. Sometimes.* "I'll get our own people on it. They can scrape up more solid data, usually."

"Let me know what you have as soon as you have it." Garrison leaned back, the cigar thrusting from his lips like some oddly displaced cannon. "I want to be on the forefront of this one. However it goes."

CHAPTER SEVEN

THE first effigy appeared on a
Friday, after a quiet Thursday with no news, no new disturbances. The
Guardian had been continuing its demands for an investigation of
Wonder Woman, and on local news shows, the anchors and reporters
alike, unknowingly mimicking the mayor, sought without success for
the real direction of public sentiment.

Then, early on that chilly Friday, a plume of smoke rising from the
edge of Gateway Park brought a single fire truck and a half-dozen
smoke-eaters wailing through the dawn, each and every one hoping
there was nothing to deal with but a cigarette tossed carelessly into
dry leaves—and not too dry, if all was well.

Instead, as the truck pulled up alongside the old stone wall that
edged that side of the park, what they saw was a crudely shaped figure
dangling from an even cruder gibbet. Only the juxtaposition of the two
forms, in fact, identified the dangling thing as anything recognizable
as a human body. Certainly there was nothing that even remotely suggested that the subject was supposed to be the most beautiful woman
on Earth. Nothing, but a scrap of cardboard nailed to the sign and
bearing the rough legend "Wonder Woman" in Magic Marker. The
placard was so poorly executed that the last three letters in "Woman"
were crowded together to fit them on the card.

"Bozos R Us, huh?" laughed fireman Harry Briggs as he hosed down the effigy, not even sufficiently alight to emit more than the curl of smoke that had summoned the firemen.

"Maybe not," said fireman Dennis Quarry. He snatched down the cardboard sign and stared at the crude lettering.

Another fireman turned from the truck, listening. "What? Whaddaya mean, Denny?"

Quarry shrugged. "Me an' my ol' lady been talkin' about this Wonder Woman thing. Charlene thinks Rebecca Chandler is right."

"You're kidding!" Harry Briggs had served with Quarry only a few months, but he believed he knew him better than this. "Wonder Woman saved my butt once, when I got caught in the Claymore fire."

"Sure," said Quarry, tossing away the sign so it spun across the open grass like a poorly engineered Frisbee. "But didja ever stop to think that maybe Wonder Woman set that fire, just so she could be the big hero and rescue you?"

Briggs opened his mouth to speak, but for a moment there was nothing he could say. After a long silence he found the words. "No," he said, feeling uncomfortable even saying it, "I never thought of that. Not till now."

"Man, this sucks! This really, *really* sucks!"

In her small apartment, upstairs in Helena Sandsmark's house, Diana of Themyscira, Amazon Princess, heir to the throne of Paradise Island, looked over the shoulder of Michael Schorr as he squatted before her television set. "Yes," Diana said, "I would be forced to agree. This does, indeed, 'suck.'"

Laid out in flickering horizontal lines, a riot boiled across the small TV screen. Seen from a hovering newscopter, perhaps 150 people yelled and swarmed, shaking baseball bats, pitchforks, shovels, anything they could find in their garages and basements that even remotely resembled a weapon. A police barricade held a thin black line before the rioters, keeping them back from the steps of City Hall. Scattered across the seething crowd, signs—professionally lettered signs, Mike noted—demanded the arrest of Wonder Woman. One, not professionally lettered, demanded something far less civilized. A newscaster rattled on pointlessly, describing what the picture clearly showed, but adding a little spin here, a little emphasis there, spinning the story into something more than it was.

"They all talk like they're covering the freakin' *Hindenburg*." Mike turned off the TV sound. "I can't listen to this." He straightened, pounding a fist into his open palm. "I should be down there. I should be helping to control those idiots." *Mostly I should be making that one rat bastard eat his stupid sign. With a side of broken glass.*

"There is nothing you can do, Mike." Diana laid a comforting hand on her friend's shoulder. She was a head taller than Mike Schorr, and he had to angle his head when he turned to look into her eyes.

"I know. Three weeks suspension without pay for brawling in the locker room like some idiot rookie." He thumped fist into palm again. "But I've got to do something. I've—"

"Diana . . ."

The voice was barely more than a whisper, a croak. Both turned at the small sound, shocked to see Helena Sandsmark framed in the door to the stairs out of Diana's apartment.

"Helena!" Diana was at her side before Mike could move. She caught her friend, Helena looking for all the world as if she was about to collapse. Diana helped—almost carried—Helena to the only chair in the room, a battered old thing Helena had passed along, with a table and the small bookcase on which the TV stood, just so Diana's apartment would not be totally devoid of furniture.

"Helena," Mike said, as he dropped to one knee beside the chair. "What the hell happened to you? You look like you've been dragged backwards through a rose bush!"

"I feel like it." Helena coughed. "Can I have a glass of water? Thanks."

Diana filled a glass from the sink in the small kitchenette, handing it to Helena. "You were attacked?"

"No. Not per se." Helena gestured to the TV. "I was in that. I had to go right through the middle to get to my car."

Mike swore. "They'll all be made to pay, Helena. One way or another."

Helena shook her head, and Diana realized for the first time that her friend had lost her glasses. Helena squinted to see. "That doesn't matter, Mike. What matters is Cassie." Suddenly her eyes filled with tears. "Oh, Mike! Diana! You won't believe it! I've been hearing the same thing over and over for two days, and I still can't believe it myself!"

Father Donald Morris walked slowly up the steep hill. Gateway City was known throughout the country for being built all on hills, but he was firmly of the opinion that Helena Sandsmark had chosen for her home a house on the very top of the very highest hill. And, of course, it would be one of the streets up which the buses did not run.

He felt bad—more than just the fact that he was tired, tired of waiting, of walking—as he trudged up the hill. Morris was here because he had committed a small crime.

Well, perhaps "crime" is too strong a word. It had not taken him long to learn the routine of Helena Sandsmark's secretary, and the previous day, Thursday, as he whiled away another afternoon waiting for Helena to maybe stop by her office, Morris had seized on an opportunity. When the secretary had gone to get herself a cup of coffee—Morris had politely declined her offer to get him one, too—he had stepped quickly around her desk, flipped open her Rolodex, and found Helena Sandsmark's address and phone number. The latter, he noticed, had been marked with an asterisk, which he took as an indication that it was, as he knew, unlisted.

Now, with Helena's address in hand, he trudged up the hill toward the house. *And please let her be home,* he thought, in something he recognized as very nearly a prayer. He had not prayed in weeks, and not sincerely in months, perhaps years. *Hard to pray when you're not sure there's anyone there to listen.*

He reached the house. It was one of a row of nearly identical units, distinguished and individualized only by the color of their trim—all were white, to give a kind of unity to the block, but the gingerbread crowding around doors and under eaves was of all the colors of the rainbow.

And finally, at the summit of his climb, Father Morris was confronted with another height to scale. The living levels of the houses were set on the second floor, above the single-car garages on which each house perched, frogs on boxy lily pads, and to get to that second floor Morris would have to climb a long flight of steps.

He climbed, panting all the way, leaning heavily on the railing by the time he reached the top. His heart was pounding, his brow damp, and for the first time Donald Morris realized he might have a time limit on his quest. *I'm worn out,* he thought. *My soul, my body. Everything is worn out.*

He crossed the porch, narrow and deep beside a wide bay window, and thumbed the doorbell. For a long moment there was no sign of life in the house, no movement or sound. He rang the bell again. *Please be home.*

At last he heard the sound of feet on stairs—*more stairs?*—and a shadow fell on the curtain covering the inside of the glass center of the door. The door opened.

"Yes?" asked the most beautiful woman Donald Morris had ever seen.

Nobody told me I'd have to make a fool out of myself doing this!

Cassandra Sandsmark stood before a trio of full-length mirrors in one of the bedrooms of suite 2512—the *presidential* suite!—of the Gateway Plaza Hotel, rotating on the balls of her feet, looking with mounting revulsion at the infinity of images radiating out from her into the glass.

Rebecca Chandler had sent her a dress to wear. Apparently, Cassie decided with the combined disgust and pity only a teenager can summon for her elders, the clothes she normally wore—usually some combination of sweatshirts, denim jackets, and spandex jogging shorts above oversized sneakers—didn't fit the image Rebecca Chandler felt her newest convert should present to the world. And so she had sent Cassie a dress. This dress.

Well, "dress" sorta describes it. It was all pink and white ruffles and fluffs, something that evoked in Cassie's mind not so much thoughts of fashion as of pastries; she looked, she thought, rolling her eyes in disbelief at the image, like some kind of bizarro wedding cake.

And this without considering the fact that the confection of lace and taffeta showed off all the things Cassie believed were wrong with her figure. Helena had assured her daughter that she would, eventually, grow out of her gawkiness, but for the present Cassie was still composed predominantly of elbows and knees, and in the ridiculous dress it was precisely those features that were emphasized. Her arms stuck out like knotted pipe cleaners, her legs protruding from the flouncy hem of the dress like something manufactured by an artisan who had once seen human limbs, a long time ago, and remembered them poorly. Added to this were the tiny high-heeled pumps—a demure high heel, but Cassie had never learned the art of walking in those things—and the effect was, in Cassie's eyes, completely grotesque. She could not walk without wobbling, and every step set the layers of the dress off on miniature tsunamis of bilious pink and white.

Shoot me. Shoot me now.

Still, there was a job to be done, Cassie reminded herself, and this outfit, gross as it was, could, in a pinch, be considered part of her disguise, a part of the elaborate construction she was building around herself, the pattern of careful deceits and partial truths.

If I've gotta look like a dork to help Diana, I guess I gotta. But if my picture gets on TV or in the paper looking like this. . . . When this was all over, when she returned to school, Cassie knew she had small hope that her actions to help Wonder Woman would in any way serve to balance, in the eyes of her classmates, how utterly and completely ridiculous she looked in this dress.

There was a knock at the dressing room door. Cassie turned—a bit too fast; she almost toppled in the strange and uncomfortable shoes. "Yeah?"

"It's Mrs. King, dear," said a voice from beyond the door. "Are you ready? Miss Chandler is here to meet you."

Oh, really? Cassie took a deep, deep breath. This was going to be the hardest part of all. Making up horrible lies about her mother and Diana, well, Cassie had always had a highly active imagination, and storytelling came easy to her. What did not, what had never been easy for her to do, was containing her emotions. When people annoyed her, she told them so—and Rebecca Chandler brought a whole new level to the meaning of "annoy."

I can't let her get to me. I can't blow it now. If I go ballistic and tell this bitch what I really think of her, this whole thing'll be for nothing and there won't be anything I can do to help Diana.

"I'll be right there, Mrs. King." Cassie scrunched her feet deeper into the pumps, clenching her toes in the hope that she could somehow hang on to the insides of the shoes and prevent herself from falling off them and breaking both ankles. Cautiously she attempted the few steps to the door, managed them successfully, and, with mounting confidence, opened the door and stepped into the bedroom.

"Oh, Cassandra, you look beautiful!" Mrs. King's eyes were wide, and, so far as Cassie could tell, her statement was genuine. *She really thinks I look good in this thing!* The peculiarities of the older generation never ceased to astound Cassandra. Then again, considering the dowdy business suit—complete with the ubiquitous Soldiers of Salvation band on her right arm—and the silvery hair tied up in a bun at the back of her head, maybe this prom dress from hell look really was her thing.

"Where's Miss Chandler?"

"She only just arrived and is waiting in the living room." Mrs. King reached out to pat Cassie's hair. The unruly mass of yellow waves had resisted all attempts to corral it into anything more demure than the tumbling-over mop Cassie normally wore. Mrs. King shook her head. "You'd look so pretty in a ponytail," she said, "or maybe even pigtails with nice ribbons."

Excuse me while I puke, Cassandra thought, but kept her good-girl smile plastered on her face. "Mom always made me wear my hair real short on the back and sides like this." She raised the lower lids of her eyes, simulating the approach of tears. "I do my best with what I have, Mrs. King."

Mrs. King put her arms around Cassie and pressed the girl's head against her shoulder. "There, there. All that's behind you now. Miss Chandler is going to take personal care of you from now on, Cassandra. Why, you'll never have to shed another tear, child. You're really just the luckiest little girl in the world."

Cassie sniffed loudly and straightened, shaping her face into what she hoped would look like a brave little smile. "I know I am, Mrs. King. I can't wait to tell Miss Chandler how happy I am that she's come to save me." As an afterthought, Cassie added what she considered to be an inspired line. "All my prayers have been answered."

"Yes, they have," Mrs. King beamed. "Now, come along. Let's not keep the dear lady waiting."

They crossed the bedroom arm in arm, and Cassie felt her heart beginning to pound so hard she wondered if Rebecca Chandler would be able to hear it. Only a few days ago she had been sitting in front of the television set in her mother's house, eating a peanut butter sandwich and hurling derisive comments at Rebecca Chandler's video avatar. Now she was going to meet the woman, face to face, under circumstances that were not entirely Cassie's to control.

Don't blow it, she repeated to herself, making it almost a mantra. *Don't blow it. You won't be able to help Diana if Chandler guesses for even one second that you don't mean what you say. Don't blow it. Don't blow it.*

She stepped through the doors into the living room and stopped as Mrs. King stopped. "Miss Chandler," Mrs. King said, "this is Cassandra."

Rebecca Chandler turned, and in the moment before she extended her hand, Cassie thought she saw something flicker in the woman's eyes, something Cassie could not quite identify. *Am I just being paranoid?*

"Cassandra," Rebecca smiled and shook Cassie's hand. Rebecca's hand was small, dry, her grip firm. "I want to thank you so much for your help. You have been closer to Wonder Woman than almost anyone else. Your decision to speak against her will carry a great deal of weight."

"Thanks," Cassie said, releasing Rebecca's hand. Already she found herself in a scenario not at all like the one she thought it would be. Rebecca surprised her. She was no taller than Cassie, and there was nothing overbearing in her posture or attitude. She wore a simple, fashionable suit, modestly cut, showing a discrete amount of knee and just the right hints of what her figure might be like. Her skin was smooth, her voice likewise. Despite herself, Cassie realized that in any other circumstance, this was a woman she would almost certainly like.

"I've ordered lunch in a private dining room downstairs, Cassandra," Rebecca said. "Are you hungry?"

"Way this girl puts away her food, I don't think she could ever get hungry," Mrs. King chuckled, and Cassie blushed.

"I could go for lunch, sure," she said. "But it doesn't have to be anything fancy like a private dining room. Pizza or something would be cool."

Rebecca smiled gently. "As a public figure, I have put myself into the very center of people's lives, and it is sometimes hard for them to understand that I do not really know them. They believe I speak personally to them when I preach from the Crystal Tower. I'm afraid if I did not seek privacy, I would never find any personal peace."

Cassie looked around the sumptuous suite, something close to awe on her features. "Well, I guess if you need privacy, this is the way to do it, huh?"

The presidential suite was, Rebecca knew, a horrible expense, a terrible waste of the money collected by her Soldiers to do the Lord's work, but Rebecca understood the necessity of overwhelming

Cassandra Sandsmark, of keeping her constantly in a whirl, off her toes, so she would not have the chance to think through to the ultimate consequences of her actions. She had, of course, stayed at places like this herself, on occasion, as the guest of wealthy followers who insisted on nothing but the best—or their idea of the best—for Rebecca Chandler. They meant well but seemed unable to understand, no matter how much they claimed to follow and to accept her message, that such opulence was mere window dressing. From nothing she had come, to nothing she would return, and in the arms of the Heavenly Father she would find all the comfort and reward she would ever need.

Stephen Ramsey understood her message—understood, she was certain, most everything. It was he who had suggested overwhelming the child with all this opulence and attention. She had to give Ramsey credit for that, as well as for knowing of Cassie's situation. What must be the extent of his contacts that he knew the trouble Cassie was in? It had to be more than luck. It was as though the good Lord knew of her need and had sent Cassandra, through Ramsey, to her.

"So, shall we go? And while we eat, if it is not too difficult for you, we can discuss what we're going to do, how you're going to help me reveal to the world the truth about Wonder Woman."

"Yes," Cassie said, and her smile was not at all for the reasons Rebecca might have thought. "I'll help you tell the world all about Diana."

Vanessa Kapatelis had been following the news stories with a mixture of fascination and disgust. She felt, she was sure, almost exactly as a passenger in an automobile must feel, passing some horrible accident on the highway. The blood and the pain, the torn and mangled bodies were terrible to behold, and yet they held the eyes, seized the senses until the natural forward motion of the vehicle carried one past the accident. Yet even then, Vanessa knew, there was a tendency to turn the head, to crane the neck, look back, seek a last glimpse of the carnage.

That was how Vanessa felt as she read in the latest *Newsweek* the articles about Wonder Woman. There were many, it being the cover feature—a slightly unflattering cover, Vanessa thought—and they presented a variety of different views. Even George Will, writing in his column at the back of the magazine, had his opinions, though they were less about Wonder Woman than about the people who once accepted her without question and who now seemed just as willing to accept her detractors. Not surprisingly, Vanessa noted, the commentator found in all this the opportunity for a baseball metaphor.

It was all of deeper significance to Vanessa than to almost anyone else. She and her mother, Julia, were among the first people with whom Princess Diana of Themyscira had made contact when she arrived on these shores. The gods of Olympus—sometimes it still seemed astonishing to Vanessa that she had actually met these beings—realized Diana would need a native guide, someone who understood the culture and the foibles of her soon-to-be homeland, and so directed her to Julia Kapatelis, archeologist and professor of Greek culture at Harvard.

It's hard to believe Diana's gone, Vanessa thought. *Even now, after all these months, I still expect her to step through the door, or come flying in the window.* Although the rift between them had long since healed, Vanessa found herself still feeling bad, at certain moments, that she had allowed herself to be so hostile to Diana when she had first arrived. It was a natural enough response, of course. Julia, who had perhaps been older than she should have been to have a teenage daughter, had adopted Wonder Woman almost instantly; they shared at an intrinsic level more than she and Vanessa ever could, not the least of which being the ability to converse in ancient Greek. Vanessa preferred, still, not to consider that her reaction to Diana's arrival had more than a little to do with the Amazon's astonishing beauty—the beauty of Aphrodite, some said, and it was not hard to believe—which served, without meaning to, to underline Vanessa's own lack in that area.

A lack, she would be pleased to point out, if she addressed the issue, she had largely overcome in the years since Wonder Woman arrived.

Then, Vanessa had been barely more than a child. Now, as she considered which college she should enter after completion of her senior year in high school, Vanessa was much closer to being a woman.

"What are you reading, honey?" Julia's throat was dry before her morning coffee, her voice barely more than a croak.

"*Newsweek* and the morning paper," Vanessa said, looking up from the kitchen table as her mother entered.

Julia pulled a baggy robe tight around her middle and crossed to the sink to peer out the window. "Looks like a beautiful day." She poured water into the kettle and set it on the stove. "What's the latest bad news?"

"There are still marchers in Washington," Vanessa said. "And the President still won't say anything one way or another."

"Of course not." Julia took a loaf of bread from the refrigerator, popping two slices into the toaster. "I wish she was here. I wish she hadn't had to leave." They had seen Diana only once in the time since she left Boston, and that had not been the happiest of circumstances. Julia felt a great sense of unfinished business between them, and she knew Vanessa felt likewise.

Vanessa nodded. "But you said at the time that you understood."

"I understood. I *understand*. That doesn't mean I have to like it." Julia spooned instant coffee into a big mug. She added the cream and sugar while waiting for the water to boil. "After everything that had happened in her life, discovering so many things had gone wrong on so many levels, I understood completely why Diana felt the need to break away. She needed to find another place, somewhere she could start fresh."

"But you didn't have to suggest Gateway City, did you? I mean, you could have suggested somewhere closer. Somewhere we could drive to in, like, less than a week."

"That's why they have airplanes, honey," Julia said.

"Do you think we could go, then? Go to Gateway? See Diana."

"I've been thinking about it. We're a bit short on funds just now.

Replacing the roof last summer pretty much emptied the piggy bank. And I don't know what we could do, really, except provide two more people for Diana to have to worry about if things got really bad."

Vanessa's eyes widened. "What do you mean?"

"I was watching *Nightline* last night. They did a whole ninety minutes on this business. There is a strong groundswell rising against Diana. Oh, I know it doesn't make much sense, but it's there. There are a lot of people, it seems, who just don't trust super heroes in general."

"That's ridiculous. I mean, they're here to help."

"Mm. That's easy enough to say. But I suppose there are some people who might be inclined to resent that. Resent being 'taken care of,' as it were."

"Maybe. But that's kinda stupid, isn't it? I mean, Diana never tried to do anything that people didn't want her to do. She just helps people who need help."

"Yes. Still, it's not too hard to understand this Rebecca Chandler's point. Not to agree with it by any means, but certainly to understand it. I still remember how I felt when Diana started introducing me to the gods! Do you remember when Hermes was here?"

"Yes." Vanessa giggled despite herself. "I called him 'Mr. Hermes.' "

"And he corrected you. 'Lord Hermes,' he said. Still, that was all very strange. I'd studied those beings all my life, and I suppose I'd known there was more than a kernel of truth to the stories, but to actually *meet* one of them. . . ."

"It's funny that people can't accept Diana without thinking that she's some kind of threat to their religion. But, then, I guess people have never been too quick to be tolerant, have they?"

"No. We have a bad habit of inventing enemies, we humans." Julia sighed, crossing to lift the whistling kettle from the burner. She poured hot water into her mug, stirred, sipped. "That's better," she smiled.

"Still," Vanessa said, "I wish you'd thought of somewhere other than Gateway City to suggest to Diana."

"I suggested Gateway because Helena Sandsmark was there, and I knew she could provide Diana with the kind of support she was going to need."

"I thought Helena was a bit of a stiff when I met her," Vanessa said. She did not add that she was at first furious to discover Cassandra's "Wonder Girl" identity. Vanessa felt suddenly as though she had been cheated of something. It was only a small consolation to learn that the Sandals of Hermes and the Gauntlet of Atlas had not even been in Diana's possession until the very end of her stay in Boston.

"Helena is absolutely brilliant in her field," Julia said, failing to notice the small cloud that had crossed her daughter's face. "Top of her field, in fact."

"Except for you?" Vanessa found a small smile in the midst of her pressing gloom.

"Well, her disciplines are a bit different from mine." Julia returned her daughter's smile. "She's very different from me, but I was sure she would respond to Diana in the right way. Besides, knowing that there was a position open for a visiting lecturer at the Gateway City Museum of Antiquities—well, I thought that would be a perfect way for Diana to establish herself in the community and earn some money. I wouldn't want to see her back at Taco Whiz."

"That was kind of hard to take."

"And," Julia added, "Helena's daughter was about the same age you were when Diana first arrived here. I thought maybe the dynamic would be similar enough that Diana would feel comfortable, allow her to feel at home that much faster in a strange city."

"It doesn't look like things have worked out quite that way." Vanessa tapped the front page of the *Globe*. "Take a look at what young Ms. Sandsmark has been saying."

"What?" Julia crossed to pick up the paper, briefly skimming the article. "Oh, my!"

She stepped to the phone by the back door, dialing Helena Sandsmark's number from memory.

"Hello?" The voice at the other end sounded thin, drawn, even in that single word.

"Helena? My gosh, is that you? This is Julia."

"Julia! Oh, it's so good to hear from you!"

"How are you, Helena? I've been seeing all this nonsense about Diana, but now I see in this morning's paper—what's going on, Helena? Why is Cassie saying all these awful things?" Julia held the paper in her free hand. She looked again at the article. "I mean, this business about you and Diana. That's total fabrication."

"It's all fabrication," Helena said. "I don't understand it at all, Julia. Everything was fine between Cassie and me until all of a sudden the Child Welfare people came and took her away, and the next thing I know, she was telling all these stories. It's not like her."

"How's Diana taking it?"

"I'm not sure. She seems confused by everything, these days. And then last night, this priest arrived. That was very strange, too."

"A priest? He came to see Diana?"

"Yes. A Father Donald Morris. He asked to talk to Diana in private, and they were alone for hours. They left together a little while ago."

"They left? Diana left you alone at a time like this? That doesn't seem like her."

"I told her to go. I wanted her to go. There's nothing she can do for me." A long pause, as the telephone signal spun its invisible thread from Gateway to Boston, rising beyond the atmosphere to touch a stationary communications satellite along the way. In the silence of the conversation Julia heard the whistle of the carrier signal, bouncing through space, and thought of the Music of the Spheres. *Not what the ancient philosophers had in mind, I'm sure.*

"Do you want me to come out there, Helena?" Julia began to do the calculations in her head, how much money she could scrape together— the ticket would not be cheap on such short notice—who could look after Vanessa and the house. She was sure Nessie would protest that she was quite able to be left on her own, but Julia was not ready for that step just yet.

"No," Helena said. "I'm fine, really. I need to deal with this business, and I need not to have to worry about Diana as well, for a while."

"What about this priest? Do you have any idea what he wanted? I mean, Helena, for Diana to go off with a priest when things are going on like this—"

"I don't think he was a threat of any kind, Julia. He seemed . . . I don't know. I had the impression he was looking for something, answers of some kind. That he thought maybe Diana could give them to him."

"What kind of answers?"

"I'm not sure."

"Do you know where they went?"

"Oh, yes," Helena said, and the simple matter-of-fact manner in which she said it told Julia her erstwhile student had accepted Diana just as Julia and Vanessa had, several years before. "She's taken him to Paradise Island. She's going to take him to Olympus."

CHAPTER EIGHT

"**N**ORMALLY I would fly under my own power, Father Morris," Diana said, "but it would be a long way to carry an unprotected human."

"Especially an old one," Morris smiled, wondering what it would be like to be lifted like a baby in Wonder Woman's strong arms and swept away over the tops of the clouds. It would be, he supposed, one more amazement in what had proven to be an amazing encounter.

"Stand back a moment," Diana said. They were on the street outside Helena's house. Diana had changed into what looked to Morris like a modified Grecian gown, light and silken, short enough to show her long, firm muscled legs, short sleeved and cinched tight about her waist by a golden cord that shimmered and seemed almost to glow in the twilight. She slipped a hand inside the gown's bodice and produced what seemed at first to be a powder compact, save that it was completely transparent and, when Morris squinted to improve his failing vision, somehow soft about the edges. It seemed to ripple, slowly and subtly, as if alive.

"This was a gift," Diana said. "I have not had the opportunity to use it much, since I can fly under my own power, but I was promised it had other uses than mere flight." She touched a finger to the center of the strange disk, slightly larger than the palm on which it rested. It reacted to the touch, a silvery light radiating out from the point of contact, and suddenly the thing leapt from Diana's hand, stretching and attenuating, altering its shape and size until, to Morris's utter astonishment, something very much like an airplane stood on the street before him, delta wings catching the last rays of the sun as though the whole thing were made of nearly invisible glass.

"My goodness," he offered, finding absolutely no better words in his vocabulary.

"It is amazing, isn't it? All I have to do is think of the form I need, and it takes it immediately when I touch it."

"And it can fly? I don't see any engines or jets."

"It flies." Diana extended a hand, guiding Morris to the back of the left wing. "Step up, Father. It is more than strong enough to support your weight."

He did, reaching out a hand to steady himself as he stepped and half expecting his foot to pass cleanly through the elusive surface. It held beneath his sole and felt for all the world like tempered steel beneath his fingertips.

"Go ahead," Wonder Woman said, stepping onto the wing behind him. "It will open to let you in."

Morris was, by that point, operating entirely on trust. He stepped toward the side of the plane, to where he supposed a door would be if the thing had a door, and, as Diana promised, the phantom skin of the fuselage folded back, *flowed* back, smooth and liquid in the streetlights. He stepped in, seeing the rough outline of a seat looking for all the world as though it were formed from the air itself. Cautiously he lowered himself into it and found not hard metal but a softly yielding cushion, which shaped itself at once to the contours of his body.

Wonder Woman stepped in and sat behind him. Looking over his shoulder he saw no joystick, no control surfaces of any kind. "How do you . . ." he started to say, but the plane was already airborne.

"It flies by manipulating the electromagnetic forces of the Earth itself," Diana said in response to Morris's unspoken question.

"How far is it to Paradise Island? It's in the Bermuda Triangle, as I understand?"

"Sometimes," Diana smiled. "Themyscira is not, strictly speaking, a part of this world. It touches all places at all times."

"Then . . . I don't understand. Why do we have to fly there? Why not just, well, be there, now?"

"It is not so easy to enter Themyscira as it is to leave. The gods placed all forms of protection around the island. To go to Themyscira requires that one follow a specific path."

"How far away is it, then?"

"Roughly, as you might measure distance, three thousand miles."

"And how long will it take to get there?"

"A little over three minutes."

I may be suspended, but there are still things I have to do.

Mike Schorr drove down the steep hill of Plantagenet Street, one foot on the gas, the other on the brake. Around him Gateway City was drawing itself into shadows and darkness as twilight faded into night. This was the beginning of the bad time, Mike knew. It did not matter that there were things going on in the city, aberrant things spinning in crazy circles around Diana. That was just a layer added to a particularly overripe onion. As a cop he had seen too much of the underside of Gateway. He knew that no excuse was needed when the darkness came, no excuse needed for things to crawl out of their holes, blinking in the dark, waking to begin anew their twisted, inverted day.

And with effigies being burned in the park and people marching with placards, well, that would just give those things a focus, something new to play with.

Often he wished he did not think in just that way. He had tried, in his years on the force, to cling to the optimism that brought him into uniform in the first place; he had been so sure when he joined the academy, fresh out of the Marines, that one man in one place could work wonders for the city—if he was the right man, and it was the right place. And while he did not entirely believe he was that man—his ego was not that large—he nevertheless believed he could make a significant contribution, if only he had the chance.

After a decade, he still thought he had a contribution to make. What had changed was how he viewed the ones who stood in opposition. He came onto the force with all the proper training; he was clear in his mind, square in the notion that there were no truly bad people, only people who had come to bad ways through accidents of circumstance. He understood that the abused child would oftentimes grow into an abusive adult. He knew that the kid who grew up with an alcoholic father or mother stood a much greater likelihood—illogical as it seemed—of becoming an alcoholic or substance abuser of some kind himself. He knew, too, that those who had suffered the worst from violence would be the most violent, that those who had suffered the most from substance abuse would be the quickest to get others hooked. The cycle was clear, and Mike was sure he could break it, if he could step in at the right time, in the right place.

That was before he began working the streets of Gateway City. Before he entered into the soul-numbing routine of being a cop there, of facing, every day, day in and day out, the grime, the crime, the festering sludge that bubbled always just beneath the surface of this one-time jewel city.

Soul-numbing? Yeah, it's soul-numbing. But you have to let yourself go numb, let the center of yourself go to sleep, even die a little, because if you don't, the city will win, will wear you down, grind you down, and in the end it will beat you. And in the end, the bad guys will have won.

Mike turned right off Plantagenet onto the easier grade of South 110th. The old buildings marched past him, tall and ornate, and if he squinted he could blot out, a little, the graffiti, the broken windows, the screens, the iron grates, the garbage, and maybe get a sense, a fleeting sense of what the city was like in her prime, years before his own birth.

He drove carefully. This was no armored squad car he rode in, no

SWAT tank ready to plow through anything and everything that got in his way. It was his own car, his pride and joy, a '68 Dodge Charger, restored from the ground up, with his own hands, on his own time. A labor of love if ever there was one, and Mike did not like driving it through neighborhoods like this, at times like this.

He heard the rioters before he saw them.

Two blocks short of Bleecher, where 110th began a series of undulations, becoming not so much a street as an asphalt snake, slithering down uneven rows formed by some of the oldest buildings in the city. This was Parkertown, less than a neighborhood, still something more than a ghetto. An ill-defined clump of old sandstone and shingle buildings, burned-out shells some of them, others leaning against their neighbors like drunken trolls pausing in the midst of a night's debauchery. Broken windows stared down like blind eyes; doors with smashed hinges bent in and out like the snaggled teeth of ancient crones.

Mike heard shouting, glass breaking, and the all-too-familiar sounds of metal on metal, metal on stone and brick. He pulled over to the curb and stopped the car. This was a lousy place to park, but there was nothing better in a ten-block radius. He slipped his spare nightstick from its brackets under the dashboard, sliding it under his jacket. Getting out of the Charger and locking it, he activated the alarm with the amulet on his key chain.

Not that I can expect that to do much good. In Parkertown an alarm was not a warning, but a call; the scavengers who lived there would swarm toward the sound, looking for anything they could grab, anything they could carry away.

Mike smelled smoke as he made his way to the corner of 110th and Bleecher. He shifted the nightstick to the ready position in his hands, aware that it was a small and puny weapon against what he might have to face, and edged toward the corner. Peering around it he saw what he expected to see, maybe fifty people, mostly young men, late teens through early twenties, running, yelling, brandishing anything they could grab that passed for a weapon. A few had handguns, firing them into the air, and Mike began, automatically, to mentally plot their positions in the crowd and count the number of times he heard them discharged.

He did not wonder where his fellow officers were in the face of the riot. Most likely no one had called 911 yet. If anyone ever did. In places like Parkertown, the "wretched refuse" took care of their own problems, and the police were as often as not willing to let them. After a while, the problems burned themselves out completely. "The self-cleaning oven," some on the force called it.

Experience had taught Mike that there was, unfortunately, some truth to that particularly cynical line of thought. He was also inclined to stay clear of this mob scene. He held his position at the corner, watching, measuring distances, getting the full layout. If there were people who needed protecting, he would act, but he was not about to risk a busted skull or a bullet just to try to keep the peace. There was very little here, after all, that could be broken any more than it already was. Only if he saw lives threatened would he act.

He watched, trying to determine the center of the trouble, locate the cause. At first it took him awhile to lock on, it was so obvious and yet so absurd. When he finally spotted it, he was not sure he could make himself believe what he saw.

Halfway down the block stood a small storefront, a Family Services clinic such as tended to dot the poorer neighborhoods, bringing information and counsel to men and women who had little use for either, trying to help an impoverished populace understand that the roots of their poverty lay in a lack of education and an ever-rising birth rate. No one could escape the cycle of poverty while tied to it by hungry babies, each of whom would grow to produce another generation of poverty, on and on, a möbius loop that grew larger every year.

The storefront's windows stood behind sliding steel gratings, but these had not protected them from being broken. The light of crude torches glinted and gleamed on shards of broken glass all around the edge of the windows, and in one, dangling in shreds from a single piece of tape, were the remains of a Wonder Woman poster.

And he saw something else, something far, far worse than a torn picture of the woman he loved.

There were people inside the store. At first he thought he was simply seeing a trick of the light, shadows cast by the tattered shreds of the poster, but no, there were at least three people—two men and a woman, he thought—inside. The mob didn't seem to care much, as they continued to stab through the grating with their primitive torches.

Were they inside with the grating down when the mob came, or did they somehow manage to lower it after the attack started? And why don't they get out the back way?

The most obvious answer, of course, was that it was highly likely the old building, crowded in tight against similarly aged structures on three sides, did not have a back way. *Which means those people are trapped—especially if a fire gets started, and with all those torches, that's more a matter of when than if.*

Mike shifted his position, edging down the street, hugging close to the wall as he approached the shifting, seething perimeter of the mob. All attention was focused on the storefront, so no one had spotted him yet, but he was still cautious. He wasn't in uniform, but the distinctive lopsided Y-shape of his nightstick would almost certainly get him tagged as an off-duty cop. The GCPD had been careful to ensure their equipment did not fall into civilian hands, so something as simple as a nightstick would mark him immediately.

He was trying to formulate something resembling a plan as he approached, but nothing was coming to mind. It was not as if he could simply order the crowd to disperse—"Move along, citizens! Show's over!"—and expect them to obey. If they were decent and law-abiding, they would not have been threatening the lives of those innocent people in the storefront.

As far down the street as he could get without actually entering the mob, Mike stopped, considering his options. *Wish to hell I had a way to get in touch with Diana. She'd sort through this mess in about two seconds.*

But Diana was not coming, and neither were the police or anyone else. Mike knew it was as close to futile as anything he had ever done, but he knew, too, that he had no real choice but to take some kind of action himself; if he stood back any longer, those people in the storefront would almost certainly die. The margin in their favor, the odds of their surviving, was too small for him to bank on.

So he stepped into the edge of the crowd. Carefully, at first. His instinct was to go in swinging, attack from behind and take down as many of the mob as he could before anyone noticed anything was happening. He could, he was sure, carve a swath quite a way into the press of bodies, but the only thing that would accomplish was to put him near the center of the mass at the moment they realized they were under attack. By a cop. *A single, stupid, unarmed cop!*

So he stifled his instinct and simply shouldered through, pushing and jostling as he worked his way across the heart of the throng, toward the front, the shattered window, and the endangered civilians. People pushed back as he passed, angry to be shoved aside but otherwise paying him no real attention—the nightstick was back under his jacket, for the moment out of sight—and he made good progress. These people were too focused on their target to give more than token resistance to him. Mike had seen mobs before, admittedly from the outside of the crush in his capacity as a cop, and they were always a scary thing, seething with a life of their own, but there was something almost primal about this group. As though their minds were not their own, that there was nothing else in the world more important than their goal.

He reached the front of the crowd and paused, measuring the distances from side to side and from where he was standing to the storefront. The torch wielders were still at it, jabbing their flaming sticks through the cage of the grate. Mike saw that some of the torches were made of cloth—soaked in gasoline, he supposed—wrapped around table legs and broken baseball bats. It was a wonder that none of the burning rags had detached itself yet and fallen to the floor inside the store.

At this distance he was able to confirm the number of occupants, three, and could also see that they were terrified, far beyond any hope of comprehending what was happening to them, or why.

Okay, hero, Mike thought, *you're here, you're now. What are you gonna do?*

He pushed through, out to the front of the crowd. A small open space had formed around the broken windows, in which the men with the torches—four of them—danced and thrust, waving their flaming weapons with no regard for the safety of anyone, inside or outside the clinic.

Mike swung his nightstick hard and low, cracking it across the backs of the knees of the closest man. The man yelped in surprise and pain, folding and dropping his torch. Mike snatched it up and turned, spinning the nightstick in his free hand.

"Okay, police officer!" he shouted as a ripple of surprise ran through the crowd. "Everybody settle down and take ten steps back." In his mind's eye he saw clearly the absurdity of the situation, one man with a billy club and a torch facing an army of fifty or more. He knew his declaration of authority would carry absolutely no weight, but he could only hope there was enough—any!—sanity left in the mob that the sudden appearance of a policeman would serve, if nothing else, to remind them that they were breaking the law, that there were consequences to their actions that they might want to consider. *Of course, all they've gotta do is just kill me and there won't be anyone to identify them if they do torch the place.*

The other three men with torches pulled back from the windows, circling, forcing Mike into their center.

"Everyone okay in there?" Mike shouted over his shoulder without taking his eyes off the mob.

"We're okay," replied a tremulous voice. "How many of you are there, Officer?"

Just little old me, Mike thought, but said, "About twenty, spread around the rooftops with high-powered rifles and scatter-guns." He waved the torch in the general direction of the crowd. "So move out, people. Nobody wants any bloodshed here."

The mob stirred, nervous, not sure whether to believe him. From this close angle, Mike suddenly saw a flash of bright color in the otherwise dull mass. Then another, and another. Armbands. Pale blue, with white letters on them, interwoven around a golden cross in a logo Mike recognized, the standard of Rebecca Chandler's Soldiers of Salvation. There were half a dozen people wearing the armbands, and Mike noted height, weight, race, and gender. Only one was a woman, a particularly mean-faced woman he thought, but all were in their middle twenties. They shifted with the rest of the crowd, angry, boiling. Mike would have expected them to be trying to stop the madness, but he realized with a sudden sick feeling in the pit of his stomach that they were, instead, encouraging it. They were in the forefront of the assault on the store, and one of them, a tall, thin man with hair the color of the fire on Mike's torch, stepped forward with fists balled and teeth clenched.

"You don't want to be part of this, Officer," he said. "There are no men on the rooftops. Most of those rooftops would collapse if a sparrow landed on them. You're here alone. You walked into this accidentally and decided to do something about it."

"You just test that theory, junior," Mike said. "See how good you look with half your head blown off." He raised his nightstick as if in signal. "All I have to do is drop my hand. Want to test it?"

The redhead's eyes flickered, but his resolve did not weaken. "It's a bluff. It's a good bluff, but still a bluff. Step out of the way, Officer. We're gonna burn down this place and its pagan icons."

"Pagan? . . . What the hell are you talking about?"

"That!" The man pointed to Mike's left, to where Mike knew the shredded Wonder Woman poster hung still by its single scrap of tape.

"The poster?" It was so absurd Mike could barely get his brain to form the words, let alone speak them aloud. "You're trying to torch this place, you're threatening to kill three people—because of a Wonder Woman *poster*? Are you out of your friggin' minds?"

"He's one of them!" The mean-faced woman with the SoS armband shouted, her voice high and shrill. "He's one of the pagans!"

Mike poked the torch toward the crowd. "Don't get stupid, people," he warned. "This is nothing for anyone to get hurt about. It's just a poster. It's not a goddamn religious tract!"

"Blasphemer!" the woman shrieked, and the crowd surged forward a step. Mike took an involuntary equal step backward and toppled.

The man Mike had dropped, the man whose torch he held, was on hands and knees directly behind him. As Mike took his step back, his calves bumped against the fallen man, and he went over. The crowd pounced as if it were a single beast with many hands and kicking feet.

All Mike Schorr remembered after that was blood-red darkness and pain.

"I want to thank you all for coming," Rebecca Chandler said, beaming down from the stage, spreading her arms to encompass the gathering in a silent benediction. "I wish especially to thank the representatives of the Fourth Estate I see here. What we have to say this evening is of vital importance, and that it be disseminated quickly is equally important."

Sitting in the row of quasi-dignitaries arrayed behind Rebecca, Cassie kept her hands folded in her lap—as much to control the upward surge of the ridiculous starched skirt as to look prim and proper as Rebecca had instructed—and did what she could to keep anything approximating her real feelings from finding their way to her face.

She looked past Rebecca at the assembly, arranged on neat rows of folding chairs in one of the big ballrooms of the hotel. Down each side of the room men and women, neatly, plainly dressed, stood like Secret Service guards at a presidential function. Cassie saw the slender microphones that lay against the cheek of each, and on each right arm the blue, gold, and white band of the Soldiers. Faux crystal chandeliers hung from the ceiling of the long room; draperies along the walls served to muffle echoes and disguise service doors. The overall colors of the room were soft bronzes and subtle tans, and Cassie knew that her dress, all in pink and white, stood out in that subdued color scheme as much as her usual scruffy outfits had in the dignified halls of her mother's museum. The main difference, for Cassie, was that the latter was her choice, her own carefully calculated act of teenage rebellion, while this frilly monstrosity was Rebecca Chandler's idea, her attempt to control the world's perceptions of Cassie and thus the degree of credibility they would give her words.

She was more than a little nervous about that. She knew some of the faces she saw in the audience; famous journalists and TV people, some of whom, Mrs. King said, had made a special trip to Gateway City just to hear what she had to say. *What if they recognize where I stole some of my stories? I mean, these are TV people. They've got to know what's going on on TV. What if one of them busts me, says, "Wasn't that story on Melrose?" What'll I do then? Mom always says "life imitates art," but I bet they won't buy that as an answer.*

Cassie was beginning to realize that the game she was involved in was greater than she had originally thought. She was glad she had lifted her stories almost whole from other sources, so that at least she did not have to keep track of any total lies, but still there was the danger that she would quote too closely, and someone would call her on it.

She wondered where her mysterious confidant was. She had not seen or heard a word from the dark, bearded man since he had popped into the room where she had waited, all alone, ready to do battle for Wonder Woman until he persuaded her otherwise.

I sure am glad I think this is a good plan; otherwise I might start to get paranoid. There would be ample reason, after all, she thought. Suppose, just for the sake of argument, the bearded man was, in fact, some aide or ally of Rebecca Chandler's? What if this was all some scheme of hers, to get Cassie to say horrible things about Wonder Woman, and, in so doing, knock over the first of a whole string of dominoes that, Cassie now realized with a shudder, would be impossible for her to stop tumbling even after she revealed that everything she had said was a lie.

Man, this's trickier than I thought. I have to go along with this now, or I won't be doing squat for Diana. But just as quickly, Cassie realized that was ridiculous. She might be just a kid, but she thought she was a fairly good judge of character, and the bearded man had been nothing but sincere in his desire to help Diana. How could she think otherwise? Besides, Cassie thought she had scored some significant points with Rebecca, and she did not want to lose that now.

Lunch, Cassie thought, had been especially successful. "I'm so glad you came forward with your story, Cassandra," Rebecca had said, nibbling around the edges of a large Caesar salad. "For someone as close to Wonder Woman as you have been to come out with the truth like this—" She paused, a bite of lettuce halfway to her lips, her eyes suddenly pinning Cassie to her chair.

"What?" Cassie had blurted, very much like someone caught in a lie.

"It is all true, of course," Rebecca had said, lowering her fork but not her gaze. Cassie remembered being surprised by the power in that look, the fire in those otherwise cool gray eyes. "I mean, if any of this is made up, well, I will understand, Cassandra, that you are, of course, glad to be free of your mother and eager to be as helpful to my cause as you can. But it is vitally important that everything you say is absolutely true."

Cassie had used the chewing of a mouthful of garlic bread as an excuse to postpone the moment of her answer. "It's true," she had said at last, summoning all the skill on which she had been so complimented by Miss Hren, her drama teacher at school. "Every word of it is true." She had let her voice quiver on the last words.

Rebecca had reached a hand across the table to cover Cassie's, pressing it gently. "There, there. It's all right. No need to upset yourself, Cassandra. All the reasons for upset are behind you now."

Cassie had smiled, a timid little thing she felt most proud of. "Thank you, Miss Chandler."

"Rebecca."

"Rebecca. Thanks."

". . . Cassandra to say a few words on her own behalf!"

The sound of her name snapped Cassie back to the moment. Blinking, she rose, crossing to where Rebecca stood with her hand extended toward her. Cassie took the hand, standing for a moment in silence as, unexpectedly, a large portion of the audience broke into applause. Cassie noted the blue Soldiers' bands scattered among those applauding and wondered if those special agents of Rebecca Chandler had been the ones who had started it.

"Thank you, thank you." Rebecca released Cassie's hand and gestured for silence. The room settled down again, and Cassie stepped up to the microphone. She stared at it for a long moment, as people shifted and coughed in the audience.

"Go ahead, dear," Rebecca said, smiling.

"I'm not sure what to say," Cassie said.

"Just tell the good people what you've told me," Rebecca said. "Take your time. No need to rush."

Cassie turned back to the mike. "Well," she said, ordering her thoughts, summoning again the television script clichés, "I guess it all started when Wonder Woman came to work at my mom's museum. . . ."

Stephen Ramsey sat alone in Rebecca Chandler's office, high in the side of the Crystal Tower.

He had turned the tall chair to face the windows, and he looked out across the lake toward a horizon in darkness as the light of the city faded away across the waters. Had she walked in on him at just that moment, Rebecca might not have recognized her friend and ally of the past two years. It was not so much that Ramsey looked different; his form was essentially unchanged, his face still the one Rebecca first encountered in the small office at the back of the Christian Science Reading Room.

It was the expression on his face that Rebecca would have found completely alien. She had, by this time, seen Ramsey's face display what she would have thought were all the ranges of emotion of which a human being was capable, from rage to joy, and these always moderated, always carefully controlled. For Stephen Ramsey, Rebecca had long since determined, was a man who liked to be in control of all things at all times, his own body and emotions not least among them.

So the grin that split his face would have seemed most strange to Rebecca, as would the gleam in his eyes and the sheer ferocity of his jubilation. He would have seemed to her to be almost vibrating, and, indeed, his balled fists drummed on the arms of the chair, rising and falling no more than was caused by the clenching and releasing of the muscles of his forearms, but even in this Rebecca would have been surprised. The release of emotion was almost childish.

But Rebecca was not there. She was half a continent away, in Gateway City, and did not know that Stephen Ramsey was sitting in her chair, in her office, high in the silvery wall of the monument she had erected to her faith.

"Master, I have news."

Ramsey turned at the voice. "Say it."

"The plan proceeds on schedule. There are no less than one thousand of your agents now set in key positions throughout this organization. Elsewhere, nearly ten thousand more have been stationed across the country, inciting the populace. Thus far they have been instrumental in the generation of a great deal of violence."

Ramsey's eyes narrowed. "Violence is of only secondary significance. They are continuing to maintain the thrust of the plan? The focus remains undiminished?"

"Yes. Sentiment is rising fast against Princess Diana. Your agents in other countries report smaller successes there, as the word begins to spread."

"Good." Ramsey smiled again. "Excellent. Have the European—"

"Oh! I didn't know you were in here, sir. I . . ." Alyce Ruste froze in the doorway, the sheaf of fax papers slipping from her hand as her eyes went wide, her jaw slack.

Mr. Ramsey was not alone. Her eyes told her that, but her brain reeled. The visitor stood before the desk, a darkness in the center of the bright room. He was tall and lean, but Alyce's eyes found it difficult to define the exact boundaries of his form. He—if, indeed, it was a "he";

the form did not suggest gender—seemed to be standing on the edge of reality, slipping in and out of what was real and what was not, now in Rebecca Chandler's office, now somewhere else, leaving only a shape in the air, a portal that opened into darkness and fire. It was an effect no mortal eye was capable of encompassing, and Alyce's mind, expecting to receive and process only information about the three-dimensional world, discarded it completely.

Alyce did not see Ramsey move from his place at the desk, perhaps twelve yards away, but he was suddenly before her, interposing himself between Alyce Ruste and the unguessable, unnamable thing that stood in front of the desk. His strong hand closed around her shoulder and turned her, guiding her out of the office into the waiting room beyond.

"Thank you so much, Miss Ruste," he said, and his voice was smooth and soothing in her ear. "You should head on home now. No reason for you to be here so late."

"Oh . . ." Alyce tried to find words, tried to force her thinking processes into something more familiar. "I . . ."

"Yes," Ramsey smiled. "Run along now." His dark eyes twinkled, but when she turned to look into them, for a moment Alyce Ruste felt the world slip away beneath her, felt all her mind and soul suddenly teetering on the edge of an infinite abyss, the abyss she saw beyond the black centers of Stephen Ramsey's eyes.

"Run along now," she said, her voice, like the words, not entirely her own.

"Yes. Run along. I'm sure you must have something to do this evening."

"Something to do . . ."

"Something to do." He applied a gentle pressure to the center of her back and sent her on her way, down the length of the waiting room to the door.

He stepped back into Rebecca's office. His visitor was still before the desk, hovering, not quite touching the floor he seemed to stand on.

"You did not check the outer office to see that we would not be disturbed," Ramsey said. It was not a question.

The visitor seemed to shrink, to draw back in time and space. "No, master. I thought at this hour—"

"You did not think," Ramsey said.

He made no movement, but his visitor was suddenly gone, shards of darkness scattering across the room, shrinking and folding in upon themselves. In a moment nothing remained, save Ramsey's memory of a scream that would last ten thousand years.

The first question was not at all one Rebecca had expected. A woman in the front row rose to her feet at the instant Cassie showed a sign of completing her speech.

"Nancy Serlin, WGHG," she said, and Rebecca noted the press badge on her chest and the shotgun mikes that turned to focus on her. "Miss Chandler, I was wondering if you have any comment on the riot in Parkertown this evening?"

Rebecca blinked, as Cassie turned to look at her. The first questions should surely have been directed to Cassandra, Rebecca thought. What is this?

"Riot? I'm afraid I don't know anything about a riot, Ms. Serlin."

"Really? According to reports, it was started by your people."

Rebecca stiffened. At once it seemed the whole room was on its feet, shouting questions, any sense of proper decorum abandoned. Rebecca verbally fought her way through the onslaught, answering such questions as she could and, in the midst of it, weeding out the beginnings of an answer of her own: someone, some individual or group wearing Soldiers of Salvation armbands, had incited a riot in front of a Family Counseling office in one of the poorest districts of Gateway. When the police finally took the time to investigate, sending a half-dozen squad cars armed with riot gear, the mob had resisted their attempts to disperse them, and one of the Soldiers had been involved in a fistfight with two officers. An officer, apparently one who had been on the scene before the others arrived, had been hospitalized and was in critical condition. In all, some twenty people had been arrested, three of them wearing Soldiers of Salvation bands.

"Of course I neither condone nor encourage such behavior," Rebecca said, trying not to shout but finding she had to raise her voice simply to be heard over the crowd. "The Soldiers of Salvation is ever and always dedicated to peace, to the standards of brotherly love as dictated by Our Savior."

Her words had little effect. She stepped back from the edge of the stage, reaching out to pull Cassie to her side. "You must have questions for Miss Sandsmark," Rebecca said, feeling her face grow hot, tears of frustration burning her eyes. *The fools! Don't they see this has nothing to do with the real issue? Don't they understand that a few of my people—if they really were my people—acting on their own and far beyond their authorization, should not become the focus of a conflicting issue. It is Wonder Woman who is the problem here, not a few hooligans who might have slipped through my security screening process.*

No one, it seemed, was interested in anything more Cassandra might have had to say. In desperation, and feeling a sense of profound failure as she did so, Rebecca summoned her public relations people and, as they closed phalanx between the reporters and herself, Rebecca drew Cassie to the side of the stage and out through one of the concealed doors.

As the doors closed behind them, Rebecca leaned heavily on the jamb. She shook with emotion, and her grip on Cassie's hand was growing painful.

"I'm sorry, Miss Chandler." The speaker was George Peltier, one of the district liaison officers who had set up the press conference. "I don't know what—"

"I want the whole thing in detail in my room in ten minutes," Rebecca barked, focusing her emotion into anger. "I want to know who is the head of the Parkertown unit, I want to know who was arrested, and I want anyone who was involved and is still at liberty brought to me. I want answers."

"Yes'm." Peltier was thirty years older than Rebecca, at least, but as Cassie watched, he cringed back like a schoolboy before an irate teacher.

"Come along, Cassandra," Rebecca said, pulling Cassie after her. "We've got to get away from this noise and do some serious thinking. A stupid little incident like this is exactly the sort of thing the press loves to blow out of proportion."

For an instant, Cassie was torn. Rebecca was right, of course. The press, the papers and the TV, would be only too thrilled to blow this up way bigger than it really was, and if that happened there would be lots of vultures ready to pounce, to tear Rebecca down from her Crystal Tower.

But that hasn't happened yet. No, it hadn't, and until it did, Cassie knew her best, most helpful position was at Rebecca's side, monitoring her, ready to report back to Diana with all the secret machinations Rebecca Chandler might be engineering.

So Cassie followed, down the service hall to the elevator, up to the twenty-fifth floor again, where Rebecca Chandler had a suite, a mirror image of Cassie's own. They rode the elevator in silence, Rebecca staring at the floor, her lips moving. Cassie realized she was praying and, more, understood once again that this was not a show for Cassie's sake. Rebecca's beliefs, her faith, were sincere. It was only in her reading of Wonder Woman that she was mistaken. Cassie wondered if there could be a way of reaching Rebecca, some way of getting her to understand that there was nothing in what Diana said and did that was intended as an assault on Christianity, or anything else Rebecca believed in.

Prolly not. Diana went and tried to talk to Rebecca, and Diana is the most reasonable human being in the world. If she couldn't get through to Rebecca, no one can. Too bad. Looks like the only way you're gonna learn is if you take the big fall, Rebecca.

Cassie was more than a little surprised to realize this thought made her sad.

CHAPTER NINE

T HEY passed suddenly out of darkness into light—pure, clear light like the brightest summer day, the brightest noon above clouds white and tall as snowy mountains.

Father Donald Morris looked down through the nearly invisible skin of the strange ship and saw an island rising up on a clear blue sea. *That's not the Atlantic.* . . . "Where ?. . ."

"Themyscira," Diana said. "The island of my birth."

He squinted at the land rushing up to meet them. It looked not at all as he had imagined. The terrain was rough—torn, he thought, broken as though by some great conflict, and such buildings as he could see rose in the midst of fragments, ruins.

"What happened here? It looks like the aftermath of war!"

"It is." Diana looked down as well, seeing how much progress had been made, but how much there was still to do. "My homeland was invaded, a short time ago, by a being known as Darkseid. He calls himself a god, Father Morris, and he was seeking, through Themyscira and through me, access to the gods we Amazons worship. They are, he believes, an offshoot of the event that created him and his fellow gods, and he wants their power."

"You . . . fought him? You fought a . . . god?"

"I have fought many gods in my time, Father Morris. Ares. Hercules." At the mention of the second name Morris thought he heard a small catch in Wonder Woman's voice, but when he turned to look at her there was nothing in her face to confirm that. "The Universe is full of gods, and if Darkseid and his fellows are to be believed, it was a single event, the destruction of a single, ancient world, long before the Earth was born, that created all of them."

"'All'?" Morris wondered as the plane descended if he was now about to hear the things he had come for, the things he feared, the knowledge he dreaded.

"All the gods who walk among mortals in physical form, at least," Diana said, perhaps sensing his concern. "Your god is said to be older than the Universe, Father Morris, and so I suppose he would predate the destruction of the Old World."

"Can you tell me more of that?" Morris asked, needing and yet dreading to know.

"I wish I could," Diana said. "What I know I know from Darkseid, who is not to be trusted, and another god, a being known as Metron, who has agendas all his own. But what they say, and what I am inclined to believe, is that in the furies that birthed the Universe, in the middle of the unknown and unknowable energies of that beginning, a world came into being, and on that world dwelled creatures, entities whom we can only think of now as gods. Great was their power, and greater still their egos. They made war on each other, always, until at last they could no longer control the forces they unleashed, and the One World was destroyed, split in half by their last war."

"Astonishing!"

"But true. At least, I have seen with my own eyes the twin worlds that cataclysm created. In mortal tongues they are called New Genesis and Apokolips, and they are as opposite as their names might suggest, one bright and full of cheer and hope, one bleak and full of desolation and despair."

"And the gods, the Olympian gods came from those worlds?"

"No. The destruction of the One World sent energy spilling in all directions into the Universe. Some of that energy, in the millennia it took for New Genesis and Apokolips to congeal and bring forth new life of their own, struck other worlds, scattered through the cosmos. It planted seeds, so that mortals who evolved there were invested with the power of the old gods and rose themselves to godhood. Here on Earth it struck in many places and spawned the gods of Olympus, the Norse gods, the Aztec and other gods. All much more than mortal, all touched by something we might call divine."

Morris shook his head in disbelief. "It is all so utterly different from anything I was raised to believe. And yet, if there is room in this for the Christian God, if there is a place for Him before all this, still as the progenitor of Creation, perhaps there is still an answer to my questions."

"Perhaps." Diana pointed through the phantom nose of the ship. "Now, look, Father Donald. We are landing."

The ground came up smooth and silent, and there was no jolt as the invisible aircraft touched the soil of Themyscira. They slowed without any sense of deceleration, and the plane came to a rest. Diana leapt from her seat to the ground at once. Morris saw three women standing to the side of the broad, flat marble terrace on which they had come to a stop.

"Is one of those Hippolyta, Queen of the Amazons?" Morris asked. He had come to Themyscira prepared to be amazed but convinced he would need to rationalize whatever he encountered. He realized now that no amount of intellectualizing could ever fully prepare him to step into legend.

"My mother is not here," Diana said, raising a hand to greet the approaching trio. "She recently sent herself into self-imposed banishment. This land is now ruled by the former captain of my mother's army, Phillipus." Diana turned to look at Morris, seeming to read his thoughts. "Do not fear that Phillipus is in any way less qualified to deal with this matter than Hippolyta might be. She possesses all the wisdom one can accrue in three thousand years."

Morris swallowed. *Three thousand years. Almost as far back as civilization itself. She has seen the empires of Greece and Rome rise and fall, been alive when Egypt was in her glory. And*—he hesitated, letting the thought form—*she could easily have walked the hills of Palestine at the same time Jesus walked there. She could have met him, spoken to him. And if that is possible, if I accept that these women have indeed lived for millennia without aging or dying, then why would I doubt the existence of their gods?*

He felt again a sense of vertigo, as though he were moving through a dream. *If I were to be bounced awake now,* he thought, *and find myself still on that bus, still riding through that storm toward an unknown future in Gateway City, I would not be at all surprised.*

He felt Diana's strong hand under his arm, lifting him to stand on the wing. "Greetings, Phillipus," Diana said, extending both hands toward the tall, beautiful warrior so clearly of African extraction. Morris was surprised, not having expected a mixing of races. *Perhaps this, more than the absence of men, is why this place is sometimes called Paradise Island.*

"Welcome home, Princess," Phillipus said, stepping forward to link her hands with Diana's, each clasping the other's forearms. "We have taken the necessary steps in response to your signal." She released her grip and offered her hand to help Morris step from the wing of the plane.

Morris studied Phillipus. She was easily the second most beautiful woman he had ever seen—the first being his pilot, of course—but there was about her face and posture a sadness, a heaviness that, he thought, had more than the burden of her office to account for it.

He wondered what had transpired here. He had heard, he was sure, a certain subtle shift in tone whenever Diana spoke her mother's name, and he knew there had recently been a terrible falling out between mother and daughter. Diana had been tight-lipped on the subject, and Morris did not feel it was his place to probe, even as he asked her a thousand other questions, but he had gleaned enough to know Hippolyta had betrayed her daughter in some unspecified way. A well-intended betrayal, he thought, but still something Diana had not yet found the necessary personal peace and resolution to allow herself to forgive.

"Father Morris, you are welcome here," Phillipus said. "Princess Diana has explained your mission, and we understand it and have prepared for you. Would you care to rest before you embark? We have set aside a quiet place, and there is food and drink if you desire it."

"That would be grand," Morris said gratefully. "It has been . . . a busy day." He smiled, and Phillipus smiled back, her teeth bright and even in her dark face.

Friendly face, he thought. *Friendly eyes, voice. Yet if what Diana has told me is true—and why wouldn't it be—this woman is the leader of the Amazon armies, a warrior more ferocious than any in history.*

"Then come," Phillipus said. "Ariadne will take you to suitable quarters." One of the other women stepped forward, herself beautiful beyond measure. She took Morris's arm and started to lead him away. He turned.

"Wonder Woman?"

"I shall join you shortly," Diana said. "I have matters I must now discuss with Phillipus."

"Ah. Yes." Morris allowed himself to be led away. The terrain rose slowly from the point of landing, terraced hills climbing to a tall mountain that was the centerpiece of the island. He reviewed in his mind what little he knew of Themyscira. The Amazons had been sent here by Athena, so the story went, to act as guardians over an unspeakable evil buried deep beneath the island's rocks and hills. So long as they remained there, and so long as no man set foot on the island, a ban which was recently lifted, they were free to live happy and contented lives, for all intents immortal. They had created for themselves a Greek paradise, all gleaming marble and exquisite craftsmanship, which had endured for nearly three thousand years before some great tragedy befell them.

The details of that tragedy were not widely known, except, Morris recalled, that it had been because of this, whatever it was, that Princess

Diana had left Themyscira and journeyed to his world—what she called "Patriarch's World"—to become Wonder Woman.

"Here," Ariadne said, indicating a small, unadorned building set at the edge of a broad square halfway up the mountainside. Morris was amazed to realize he had climbed that slope without feeling the least bit tired. He turned to look back, seeing the sunlight glint on the elusive edges of Wonder Woman's plane, a good mile away down the steep hillside.

"Is there something of a healing nature in this island?" he asked. "Yesterday it would have nearly killed me to climb this high."

"This is a place of peace," Ariadne smiled. "If there is healing in that, then, yes, this is a place of healing. Would you enter and be comfortable, Father Morris?"

He did, finding a small room decked out in rich draperies. A long, low marble bench with plush cushions stood before a table set with all manner of fruits and meats, vegetables, and decanters of a half-dozen liquids of different colors.

"Eat and drink to your fill, sir," Ariadne said. "Diana will come for you when she has finished her business with Phillipus."

"Yes." Morris sat, leaning back. The air was fresh and clean, and a gentle breeze wafted through a broad, open window that looked out across the fields and meadows of Paradise Island, down to the rocky shore and the wide blue-green ocean. "This is very comfortable. Thank you."

The girl—for some reason he could not define, Morris found himself thinking of Ariadne as younger, much younger than he knew she must be—essayed a short bow and left. Morris poured himself a glass of dark red wine and took a bite from a succulent fresh pear.

So, Donald, is this at all what you expected? This time yesterday—could it have been only yesterday? His body told him it was almost midnight, but his eyes told him it was noon—he was no closer to meeting Wonder Woman than he had been as he sat in the bus riding in toward Gateway, or so he had thought. Now, in less than twenty-four hours, he had not only met her, talked to her, but had found himself transported to Paradise Island for a meeting with the gods of Olympus.

"Yes, I am Wonder Woman. How may I help you, Father Morris?" He remembered being surprised that she would use the proper form of address. He had thought, even though he had introduced himself to her as "Father Donald Morris" that she, as an Amazon, a creature without any male parent, might have some other term, or might simply call him "Mister."

They had been in the living room of her small apartment on the top floor of Helena Sandsmark's house. He had introduced himself to the woman who came to the door and been allowed entry. Morris was not quite sure why this had been so, but he had begun to formulate a notion. *Because I am a priest, and because I came saying I needed Wonder Woman's help. With certain forces rallying against her on ostensibly religious grounds, to have a priest come knocking at the door, asking for help, that must have seemed like, well, something of a godsend. One of the "enemy camp" coming in search of aid.*

He recalled his surprise to discover Wonder Woman actually lived in Helena Sandsmark's house. He had hoped Helena would be a link, but this came as a total shock, to have Diana herself open the door.

Of course her friends, Helena and the young policeman called Mike Schorr, had been suspicious of Morris's motives. He wore his clerical collar for the visit, to lend, he hoped, some credibility to his story, but he realized almost at once that to them it would be a danger sign, a red flag.

"I'm not here to attack you in any way, Wonder Woman," he had said, taking the chair Helena Sandsmark had vacated for him. He hesitated to do so, since she appeared to be in greater need of it than he, but she had insisted.

"Please call me Diana," the Amazon Princess said, her voice calm and soft, and, yes, he had noticed a slight accent, as he had read reported in the earliest stories of her arrival on these shores.

"Diana. Thank you. I came in the hope that you could be of some help to me." He had paused then, wondering just how he would proceed, realizing that, after all these days to think about it, he had not come up with a clear and cohesive manner in which to state the problem. Still, he tried. He spoke calmly, with as little emotion as he could. He talked of his years in the seminary, learning the intricacies of his vocation. He spoke of his decision to work with children, to seek a posting with a children's aid organization, then with hospitals all across America, as he moved up through the ranks and became better and better equipped to handle the needs of these blighted and tormented souls.

He drew a deep breath to go on, to talk at last of the wearing down of his own spirit, of the terrible daily burden that ground away at him, watching children come in, sick, dying, as if cursed and forgotten by the God who was supposed to love them.

At first he had found solace in the words of the Bible, in this as in all facets of his life, but as the years went on, as he grew older and the suffering seemed not to diminish, he found less and less comfort there, and only greater hypocrisy.

"I tried to understand," he had said. "I believed that everything in the Universe happens because it is part of some overall plan. I genuinely believed in a benevolent, loving God who concerned Himself with all the workings of His creation, who truly saw the falling of the least sparrow. But I watched these children suffering, dying, snuffed out before they had the chance to truly begin living, and over and over I found myself asking 'Why?'—why did they suffer, what possible purpose was achieved by their pain? I looked into their faces, I sat with them at the moment of death, so many of them, and I saw nothing in their eyes but pain and fear. There was nothing gained by their suffering. Nothing."

He had leaned back heavily in the chair, the three others looking on, silent, compassionate. After a moment Diana had put a hand on his shoulder. "Go on when you are ready, Father Morris," she had told him softly. "There is no need to hurry yourself."

"Thank you," he said, gaining strength from her own. "I'm fine. I can do this."

So he had gone on, speaking of how he had at first come to resent God, to hate Him as a callous, uncaring deity more concerned with instilling fear and garnering worship than with the needs of His "flock." For several years Donald Morris had moved through a black fog, ministering to the needy who came into his care, yet totally unconnected to it all, separated from the words he spoke, the clichés assembled and repeated so many times they had no meaning for him any more.

And then, one day, he had read a story about Wonder Woman, how she came from a hidden island where a race of surviving Amazons still worshiped the gods of Olympus—and not merely because they had been isolated, cut off from the changes that had come to the world in the years since Themyscira had been set apart from it. No, they worshiped the gods of ancient Greece because they knew them to be real, because they had met them. *Talked* to them.

It had all seemed the most outrageous fantasy, of course. Donald Morris, who had lately come to doubt the reality of his own God, was not likely to take at face value tales of gods who had fallen out of favor thousands of years ago. But the more he read, the more he learned of Wonder Woman, the more he came to think she was sincere, that the stories she told of Zeus and Athena, of the six gods who had officiated at her birth, who granted her a portion of their powers—the stories were all true, and the gods of myth were much, much more than that.

Then had come the true turmoil. If he had thought himself confused and separated from his faith before, that was as nothing compared to what he found himself facing now. Here, in the stories, he had been confronted with a kind of truth such as he had never known before. All his life he had accepted Jehovah, *YHVH*, the God of the Bible, the God of the Old and New Testaments; he had taken all the stories and lessons on faith, understanding that the time when God spoke through mortals, the time of Prophets and divine intervention, was long past, and understanding, too, why this was so.

God had spoken through the Prophets. He had laid out, through them, the pattern of His plan, in detail, and that done He had withdrawn from intimate involvement with the daily lives of Man. He had left it for the sages, the wise men, the rabbis to interpret and teach, to keep alive what the Prophets had spoken, saying to the people, "Here, this is what Ezekiel said, and this is how it relates to your life, your time." So the God who had once moved freely among men, who had acted to bring personal vengeance and personal reward to those who defied and those who served Him, this God now asked of his children that they accept Him on faith, that they no longer require miracles and visions as a confirmation of His existence. That, in fact, to prove that He existed would be contrary to faith.

"And then I was confronted with gods, real gods, who made no such demands," Morris said. "Gods who still acted and interacted with humans, who were just as the legends described them, and who still walked the Earth when it pleased them to do so, today."

"Yes," Diana had said, "I have mentioned before how the single most confusing thing, to me, about the many religions I encountered in Patriarch's World, was that so many people accepted the existence of their gods with no physical proof. But, then, it is difficult for me to divorce myself from my own beginnings; if my gods did not exist, neither would I. Hippolyta alone could never have summoned me to life from the clay of Themyscira."

"That's really true, then?" Morris looked up at the woman. Her beauty was absolutely incredible. As a priest he had taken a vow of chastity, of course, but that did not interfere with his ability to appreciate a beautiful female face and form. *I would need to be dead not to appreciate this woman,* he had thought. *It's more than physical beauty. It's in the way she stands, the way she moves. It's something that seems to radiate from the very center of her being.*

"Yes," Diana had said. "At the time I was created the gods looked down and determined that I should be in every way human, and yet much more. Demeter granted me the power and strength of the very Earth itself, Aphrodite gave me beauty and compassion for all things, Athena gave me wisdom, Artemis the eye and skills of the greatest hunter, Hestia granted me the ability to compel truth in those I speak to, and Hermes gave me flight and his own immeasurable speed. And from Gaea herself came the greatest of all gifts, life."

"I still remember the first time Diana told me that story," Mike Schorr had said. "It was when I took her home to meet my mother." Despite himself, Morris thought, Mike allowed a small smile to play around his lips. "It might not have been the best timing. I was trying to get Ma to understand that there was nothing wrong in my seeing Diana, even though she was a gentile. I'd done pretty well, I thought, until Ma asked about Diana's own mother, about her upbringing, and Diana told how she was molded from clay and brought to life. And Ma slapped her forehead just like in a movie and said, 'Oy! On top of everything else, she's a golem!'"

"Amazing," Morris said at last. "Astonishing. And so, you see, this is why I came to you, Diana. I need to understand what is really happening in the Universe. I need to know if any part of what I have believed all my life is true, or if it's all just lies and fairy tales."

"And you think Diana can help you do this, Father?" Helena Sandsmark stood next to her famous friend, her brow knotted, her eyes shadowed.

She doesn't trust me yet, Morris remembered thinking. *She's looking for signs of a trap. And with her own daughter having turned on her like she has, how can I blame her for not trusting a stranger?*

"I don't know, Professor. I realize it's asking a great deal, but . . . well, I just don't know. I thought, perhaps, if I could just talk to you, Diana. If I could ask you some questions."

"Of course." Diana had asked her two friends to excuse them, and Helena Sandsmark and Mike Schorr had departed—reluctantly—leaving Morris and Diana to talk alone until the first light of the morning sun had begun to pink the sky beyond the windows of Diana's small apartment.

"I think there may be something that can solve both our dilemmas to some extent, Father Morris," Diana had said, and Morris had noticed, at last, that the way she seemed to be dealing with his title was to treat it as part of his name. Unlike Professor Sandsmark and Officer Schorr, Diana never addressed him simply as "Father."

"And what might that be?" he had asked, never for a moment guessing what her answer would be.

Cassie Sandsmark was eating breakfast with Rebecca Chandler when the news arrived about Rebecca's personal secretary.

Cassie was already deeply troubled. The morning news, which they had watched while they ate, had revealed the names of those arrested and injured in the skirmish in Parkertown, and Cassie knew the name of the police officer who lay in guarded condition at Beth Israel Hospital—Michael Schorr.

Her first instinct was to call her mother, to call Diana, find out what Mike's condition was. The news people always exaggerated, she knew, always made a story bigger than it really was. But she could not call Helena, or Diana. Not yet. Not until she was free to tell them what was happening, why she had turned Benedict Arnold. Not, she knew, until she had the goods on Rebecca Chandler.

And that was proving more difficult than Cassie had anticipated. It had all seemed so simple, when her mysterious ally had explained it to her—*And where the heck is he, anyway? I haven't seen, like, sign one of him in days, not since the first time*—but now Cassie was not so sure. She had come in fully expecting to catch Rebecca in lies and hypocrisies at every turn, but the truth was proving far more difficult to deal with.

Who figured she'd be so nice? I mean, she cares about all this stuff. Really cares! I never thought she'd take such a personal interest in me, worrying all the time that I'm okay. Okay, so at first I thought maybe she was queer for me, but it's nothing like that. She's just this really, really nice lady . . . oh yeah, who happens to be trying to destroy my best friend.

Not for the first time since this adventure had begun, Cassie found herself remembering her mother's words in another context:

"Very few things in life are as simple and straightforward as they seem, Cassie. The best thing you can ever do—and the hardest, I'll grant you—is not to form opinions before you go into anything. Go in blank and open, and let the information come to you without prior coloring."

Guess I never really got that until now. I wish I had. Maybe I wouldn't have agreed to this crazy scheme if I had. I might have wanted to know more about Rebecca before I set out to sabotage her.

And, even with that, how was she supposed to achieve that sabotage, Cassie asked herself. If she flat out lied, Rebecca would protest and perhaps even come to suspect the stories Cassie had told about Diana. Of course, at the point where Cassie would be prepared to lie in order to bring Rebecca down, it would not really matter if she believed the other stuff, would it?

Cassie slathered more strawberry jam on her toast and scowled into her plate. *This is way harder than I thought.*

"Miss Chandler?"

Cassie turned to find Mrs. King had entered silently and approached to within a few feet of the table.

"Yes, Agatha?" Rebecca picked up the television remote control from its place by her plate and muted the news broadcast.

"We just received this fax," Mrs. King said, extending the shiny, flimsy paper in such a way, Cassie noted, that it seemed almost to be painful to her hand.

Rebecca took the fax sheet and Cassie saw all the color drain from her face. "What is it, Rebecca?"

"Alyce . . ." The word was a croak. Rebecca crumpled the fax sheet, rose, and rushed from the room as tears exploded from her eyes.

Cassie was on her feet to follow, but Mrs. King restrained her with a hand to her arm. "Not now, dear. Leave her be."

Cassie turned. "Mrs. King . . . what's going on?"

"Her secretary, back at the Crystal Tower. Alyce Ruste. She took an overdose of sleeping pills last night. Killed herself."

•   •   •

Mike Schorr had always thought the term "a world of hurt" was a hackneyed cliché. Now he understood otherwise.

He swam up out of black molasses, struggling toward light and life, and every breath was agony. Even opening his eyes was painful, and he sensed without seeing his reflection that both were swollen nearly shut, his whole face puffy and painful. He could only guess at the color.

A shadow moved at the edge of his vision, and he turned his head, discovering new pains. "Hi, Ma," he said, and the movement of his jaw was agony. "I must look a picture, huh?"

"Mike! Oh, thank God! I thought—"

"You shouldn't think, Ma," Mike said, finding that a smile was no less painful than any other movement. "It only gets you in trouble." He looked around, determining that he was in a hospital room and, from the amount of equipment wired into him, probably in Intensive Care. "Last thing I remember was getting the crap kicked out of me," he said. "How long ago was that?"

"Nearly two days, Officer Schorr." A doctor had entered by the door to Mike's left, and Mike realized his mother must have buzzed as soon as he showed signs of consciousness. "How do you feel?"

"They may have to invent new words to cover that," Mike said. "How am I? How badly did they mess me up?"

"It could have been a lot worse. Somebody called 911, and the police arrived in time to break up the mob and save you from any permanent damage. As it is, though, I'd say you'll be with us for a while."

"I feel like Dick van Dyke in that episode where he had the skiing accident. Somebody asked him where it hurt and he pointed to a little place on his lip and said that was the only place that *didn't* hurt."

The doctor laughed. She was a middle-aged woman with silver showing in her dark hair. Her eyes were dark and friendly, and when she took Mike's wrist to feel for his pulse, her touch was cool. "I'm glad they didn't break your sense of humor, Officer Schorr. Your mother has been telling us all kinds of stories about how funny you are."

"I'm a laugh a minute, Doc." Mike frowned. "How are things outside? Diana?"

"It's still pretty crazy," the doctor said. "There have been full-blown riots in Washington, Metropolis, Gotham, Chicago. There's even a movement started to get all super heroes banned. Some people seem to think if Wonder Woman is rotten, they all are."

Mike stiffened, hurting as he did so. "You think Wonder Woman is rotten, Doctor?"

Satisfied that Mike's pulse was normal, the doctor released his wrist. "I don't know, to be frank, Officer Schorr. I know you and Wonder Woman have some kind of special relationship—"

"That's beside the point." Mike shot a look at his mother, scolding her without words for having said too much while he lay unconscious. "Why would you think anything bad of Wonder Woman? What has she done that's been wrong? She's done nothing but help people since she came here."

"True enough," the doctor nodded. "But there are a lot of people who wonder what it would be like if these super heroes didn't exist. If there was no Superman, would the menaces he battles show up to bother us? If there was no Wonder Woman, would Gateway City have been attacked by some of the people, the things she's fought? It's a hard call."

"And the religious aspect," Mike pressed. "Do you think Diana is here to pull down our temples and churches and put the Greek gods back on top?"

"Well . . . that does sound a bit silly, I'll admit. But who knows?"

"I know," Mike bristled, and his pain was, for the moment, forgotten. "I know Diana, and I know who she is and what she stands for. And that has nothing to do with tearing down anything." He turned. "Ma. You tell her. You know Diana."

Esther Schorr struggled for a moment with the words she wanted to say. "I . . . I don't know, Mike. Since you've been seeing Diana, how many times have you been to temple?"

"Oh, for cryin' out loud, Ma! It's not like I ever went regularly before!"

Esther shrugged. "Still, since you ask me I would have to say, yes, I think Diana has had an effect on you and, no, I don't think it's been altogether a good one."

Mike opened his mouth, but words would not come. *This is insane,* he thought. *The whole bloody world has gone completely insane!*

INTERLUDE
IN METROPOLIS

THE crowd began to pray just after dark. They had begun drifting toward the massive stone Saint Bartholomew's Cathedral on Metropolis's Fifth Avenue in the early afternoon, gathering around its steps, milling about the sidewalk, soon, well before dusk, blocking the sidewalk and street with their numbers.

The Metropolis P.D. at first attempted to move the shifting, shapeless crowd along, but for every person who was directed away from the steps of the cathedral, three more would join the growing mass of humanity, pushing those in the forefront up onto the stairs. The police next tried invoking the need for permits for this rally, but quickly learned it was no organized effort, that there were no leaders, no individual the authorities could hold responsible for the organizational oversight. It was, the police found to their dismay, a spontaneous gathering, a grassroots protest whose time and location had spread by word of mouth. The best they could hope to achieve was a maintenance of some semblance of order while keeping Metropolis's infamous evening midtown rush hour traffic flowing as best as they could around the human roadblock.

As the crowd grew larger and the hour later, the first signs began to rise above the heads of the gathered throng. Crude, hand-lettered affairs they were, proclaiming messages of love for God and Jesus, and of condemnation and hatred for Wonder Woman. Some participants had come prepared with candles, which they lighted and held aloft, the cumulative effect of the many small flames combining to create a subtle, hauntingly flickering light over the scene.

Patrolman Howard Burke watched the multitude grow from his vantage point at the top of the cathedral steps. In six years on the job, Burke had done his share of crowd control, having been assigned to situations ranging from planned political rallies to loud mobs of protesters angry about everything from civil rights to abortion rights, both pro and con. Sometimes the job required little more than keeping people off the grass or on the sidewalk. Other times he'd had to get between the disparate sides of whatever issue it was that was being protested or supported. At times things had gotten loud, or rowdy, or outright violent. But no matter the situation, Burke had learned one thing early on, that every crowd, every mob had a life of its own. It was up to the cops to assess that life and handle the situation accordingly.

But this crowd was unlike any Howard Burke had ever handled. Not for its size, or even for the ridiculousness of its purpose—in his estimation at any rate, since Wonder Woman rated high in his book, and what the hell did religion have to do with super heroes anyway? No, this crowd was too still, too quiet. There had to be five thousand people present, maybe more; they filled the avenue from one side to the other, spreading out for a span of at least four blocks in either direction. In any such gathering, even those with the most peaceful of purposes, one expected a fair amount of noise, if only from the combined murmur of that many voices. But there was hardly a sound here, and in that silence Officer Burke found something strange, unsettling.

And then the praying began.

A man, perhaps twenty-five years old, sporting a conservative haircut and clad in a dark suit, seemed to rise above the heads of the people around him at the top of the steps—standing too tall, Burke thought, to be on a box, but he could be perched on the shoulders of his fellow fanatics for all Burke knew—and began to recite, not twenty feet from where Burke stood. "Our Father, who art in Heaven . . ."

The crowd joined in almost immediately, their voices a rolling wave of sound that spread rapidly across the assemblage. "Here we go," Burke breathed to himself and started to move across the steps toward the man. When the officers first deployed around the area, the sergeant had made one thing perfectly clear: "They got the right to assemble till the cows come home, but without a permit, they ain't supposed to have speakers. Anybody starts making speeches, keep it cool, but shut them down before things get out of hand."

Burke was not sure the Lord's Prayer, now rumbling through the crowd, counted as a speech, but he decided to opt for safe over sorry. He shouldered his way through the crush of people, until he stood beside the man leading the crowd in prayer. A wire trash can—*city property,* Burke told himself, *that's got to be a violation right there*—had been overturned to make an impromptu speaker's platform. The officer decided to wait at least until the prayer was concluded before hauling the speaker down.

But as he waited, Burke noticed the man wore an armband, a blue strip emblazoned with the emblem of the Soldiers of Salvation. That, he knew, was the organization of Rebecca Chandler, the woman who had started all these protests against Wonder Woman. And that made it look to Burke as though this "spontaneous" gathering was actually anything but. More like an organized rally, but without the headaches and bother of obtaining the requisite permits.

Self-righteous idiots, Burke thought, the realization making him suddenly angry. *Bad enough they're giving Wonder Woman a hard time, but now they're above the law, too good to bother following the rules while they bust her chops. This Chandler babe thinks because she invokes the name of God, she doesn't have to bother with City Hall.* He shook his head, eyes narrowing as he scanned the immediate crowd, spotting here and there more blue armbands scattered among the throng. "Soldiers," they called themselves. *Jackasses can call themselves soldiers all they want, that doesn't make it so—or make them too good to obey the law*. The law Burke had sworn to uphold as a member of the Metropolis police.

"Okay, pal," Burke said, fighting to retain his composure as he tapped the man's thigh with his nightstick. "Unless you can show me a permit, you're gonna have to get down from there."

The self-proclaimed Soldier looked down at the officer, stopping in midword while the crowd around them continued in prayer. "Excuse me?"

"I said, get down from there. Now!" Burke repeated.

The man smiled, and for some reason, that irritated Burke even more. "All we are doing is praying. I believe the Constitution guarantees us that right, officer, with both freedom of religion and speech."

"Thanks for the civics lesson," Burke sneered, "but this party's over. Now do you climb down from there, or do I take you down?"

"Leave him alone," someone cried from nearby. "He's not bothering anybody!" Other voices joined in to protest the policeman's orders, and the more people spoke up, the louder they became, the greater the anger Burke felt rising within himself. It was far from rational, he knew. He was not one to lose his temper so easily, but he found it impossible to rein in his emotions. His hand went up to grab hold of the man's sleeve. "Let's go, mister."

Burke started pulling to bring the man down from his perch atop the overturned trash can.

And all hell broke loose.

An object, Burke would never be sure what, flew out of the crowd, striking him in the head, knocking his peaked duty cap askew and stunning him enough to send him staggering back several steps. The other man's sleeve was still caught, and he was yanked off balance by the inadvertent tug. The two fell together in a heap of tangled limbs upon the cathedral steps as screaming and shouting erupted all around them. Like the beginning of the prayer only moments before, the shouts and screams spread out from the epicenter at the top of the stairs across the entire crowd. All that most of those gathered had seen was the man who had been leading them in prayer suddenly start to gyrate wildly and then fall from sight. Screams of police brutality were heard, and people began pushing and shoving forward in an attempt to see what had happened or to help defend the man against the over-zealous police.

The rest of the police officers situated around and through the crowd began pushing back in an attempt to maintain order, but they were vastly outnumbered and unprepared for the trouble that was erupting all around them. Within minutes of Howard Burke's fall, the peaceful crowd of worshipers had been transformed—against all logic, as though a switch had been flipped—into a seething mob.

Screams filled the evening air, surging bodies fell against the store windows that lined the avenue opposite the cathedral, crashing through glass, sending men and women falling to the ground under churning legs and pounding feet. The relatively few police tried des-perately to subdue the hysterical crowd, but the situation had exploded so swiftly there was no time to analyze it, much less deal with it effec-tively. But they tried, against men and women fighting them—and each other—in sudden, almost blind panic, with swinging fists and kicking feet, with whatever came to hand as weapons. There seemed no rhyme or reason to the violence, but every cop knew that mobs, like the crowds that spawned them, were living, mindless things dangerous to everyone and everything around them.

But this being Metropolis, they knew something else as well, some-thing that ensured this riot would not last long.

That something arrived ahead of a sonic boom, an ear-shattering burst of sound that exploded overhead. The tidal wave of violence paused for a fraction of a second as questioning eyes turned to the sky, before emotions, running too high to be easily dissuaded, returned to the violence at hand.

From out of the night sky, a blurred streak of crimson and blue dove almost to street level, sweeping over the heads of the rioters on Fifth Avenue. A wind stronger than anything nature could have produced on this otherwise clear, calm night—calm, at least, as far as the weather was concerned—whipped across them, staggering them, and they had to fight to remain on their feet.

The wind picked up, like a hurricane born out of their own turmoil, and people found themselves losing the battle to remain upright. They began to topple, falling against one another, tumbling head over heels across the pavement like flimsy sheets of newspaper in the breeze. The screams and shouts of violence were replaced by the banshee howl of the wind as people tried desperately to run, crawl, or roll to the side streets that intersected Fifth Avenue.

Officer Howard Burke huddled in the doorway of the cathedral, out of the wind, dazed but far from confused by the events transpiring in the street below. He would never be able to say quite why he had lost his temper the way he had, why the smug certainty of the young man wearing the SoS armband had driven him to act as he had, but he knew as sure as night followed day what was the source of this unnatural wind.

"Superman," he whispered in awe.

That was confirmed in the next instant as the wind ceased as abruptly as it had begun, and the familiar caped figure could be seen hovering over the street. The Man of Steel, cape whipping about him, peered down at the crowd, as though daring them to continue their mindless rampage. The reaction to his appearance was immediate, although far from universal, as most of the crowd looked up in the sky, and in response to Superman's presence, immediately broke off and, though unable to tear their gaze from him, began to flee, funneling down the side streets as fast as their legs could carry them. No matter what the provocation, no matter how great the anger that had ignited the blaze of their emotions, there was nothing worth incurring *his* wrath.

Those remaining, those few not intimidated by the hovering hero or too caught up in the violence to care, were quickly shown the error of their ways. The Kryptonian seemed to disappear from sight, then reappeared there, a split second later, whisking a woman wounded by broken glass to the hospital, then here, to separate two combatants smashing at one another with their fists, then over there, two blocks away, to toss three men ganging up on a downed police officer like rag dolls in three different directions. On it went, a flash of blue and red up and down Fifth Avenue that paused only long enough to right what was wrong, to send the last remaining rioters fleeing, or into the arms of waiting police.

Then it was over, and with a last glance back over his shoulder, Superman sped away into the evening sky. Still on the top step of the cathedral, Officer Burke watched him disappear into the heavens, unable to believe that in less than three minutes, the Man of Steel had cleared the entire area of protesters. *With a police force full of the likes of him,* Burke thought wistfully, *Metropolis would be a paradise.* He shook his head, wondering for not the first time how anyone could believe there was anything evil about super heroes. Especially Wonder Woman. Wasn't she a friend and colleague of Superman? If ever there were good guys in the world, the Amazon had to be one of them.

The officer started down the steps of the cathedral. *Whatever Rebecca Chandler believed, she couldn't be more wrong.* He stopped, looking down at a torn cardboard sign that had been dropped by one of the demonstrators. WONDER WOMAN: HERO OR HELLSPAWN?

Rebecca Chandler may be full of it, he realized, *but who is going to convince the thousands who follow her of that?*

CHAPTER TEN

HE immediately thought of it as a temple, though there was nothing about it to suggest anything particularly special or holy about it. It was set into the side of the mountain that was the central core of the island of Themyscira. Had it not been pointed out to him, Donald Morris was quite sure he would have walked past the structure without noticing it at all, and he suspected that the effect was deliberate. It was smaller than the house in which he had spent the afternoon—time did pass on Paradise Island, it seemed; in the west, the sky was aflame with the most spectacular sunset he had ever seen—and the front was plain and largely unadorned. There was a single small door, just barely taller and wider than he—Diana had to bend to enter ahead of him—and a subtle glyph above the door suggested without actually describing the form of a mountain rising from clouds. That was the only marking of any sort on the otherwise smooth dark marble.

"I learned of this place only recently," Diana said, as Morris stepped into the shadowed interior. The doorway provided the only light within, and that seemed to fall off, he thought, rather more rapidly than he would have expected it to. "It is the most secret place on all Themyscira. Only those who have a valid reason to be here can even see it."

"Fascinating. Do I take that to mean my needs have passed some kind of magical test?"

"Yours or mine, Father Morris. Since we journey together, we are judged by the same enchantment."

"Ah, yes." He reached out a hand to probe the enfolding darkness. The temple must be the opening of a tunnel or cavern of some kind, he decided, since there was no trace of a wall where logic told him a wall should be. "How far do we have to go?"

"Not far at all," Diana said, stepping back through the same door by which they had just entered. "Come along, Father Morris."

Hoping his confusion did not show on his face, Morris followed, then stopped dead in his tracks one pace beyond the door.

The world had turned sideways. More, it had folded and bent upon itself, up and down, left and right suddenly devoid of all meaning.

Around him was a scene of truly Olympian splendor—marble columns, floors, steps, statues, as far as the eye could see, all larger than life, more impressive, more magnificent than anything his imagination could have conceived.

White, he thought. *I'd been led to believe the ancient Greeks decorated and gilded with paint and gold leaf to make their columns look like the trees that were their inspiration. That Athens in its glory, like Rome, was not the stark, brilliant white that ruins and Hollywood have taught us to think it was. But here, everything is white.*

But there was more to confuse him than that. Nowhere in his line of sight was there anything approximating a true perspective. It was as if he had stepped through the temple door into an Escher etching brought to three-dimensional life—buildings sprouted from other buildings without the least regard for logic or gravity. Immediately before him a massive temple jutted edgewise from the vast floor on which he stood, its columns parallel to his horizon, yet within its columned halls he could clearly see people—if "people" was the word—walking casually about, pausing in conversation, as if there were nothing at all odd in the fact that their floor was at ninety degrees to his. And to the sides, behind, all around, this confusion was continued, no single building, be it temple, palace, house, or shrine, standing on quite the same plane as any other. And, perhaps most disturbing of all, no matter what direction he looked—up, down, left, right—he saw blue sky shot through with white clouds, as though they stood on the jumbled surface of some bizarre planetoid, floating in an infinite ocean of sky.

Morris was aware that Wonder Woman had stepped to his side and slipped a strong hand under his arm. "Thank you," he said, realizing at that moment how unsteady he felt on his feet. "The effect is . . . most unsettling."

"You will get used to it," Diana smiled. "Hard as that may seem to believe, at first. Now, come, Athena awaits."

Athena. Morris allowed himself to be led, following Diana as she stepped easily, nimbly from one skewed plane to the next, and he found, as she had predicted, that it became easier as he went, that the twisted perspectives and impossible angles became, slowly, more and more natural, even soothing to the eye.

I'm like Fred Astaire, he thought. *Fred Astaire in* Royal Wedding, *dancing around the walls and ceiling of his room. Only this isn't some Hollywood trick photography. This is real. This is Olympus, and I am on my way to meet Athena.*

He was determined not to let preconceptions fog his mind—and his first glimpse of Olympus had demonstrated the wisdom of his choice. He had no idea what to expect of Athena, what she would look like, how she would sound. The natural instinct was to think of a woman of mature years, tall and regal, her beauty somewhat faded, wisdom etched on her face in place of glamour. *But who knows?* he thought. *She could be a three-foot crone with eyes like a bullfrog and skin like an alligator. There's no way to know until I'm actually there, actually talking to her. To Athena.*

There was no possibility of making an accurate judgment, of course, given the shape of the places they passed through, but Morris had the impression they were moving upward. Somehow, though, he felt that passage in any direction through Olympus would be upward, like the Escher etchings the place most resembled, staircases that looped around to touch end to end and yet, somehow, managed—impossibly—to climb and keep on climbing.

"Wait here a moment, Father Morris." Diana released his arm and started up a long, broad flight of white marble steps toward a temple more magnificent than any he had ever seen. *Fatuous thought, really. Somehow each building here manages to be more magnificent than the one next to it, as if there is some enchantment in the stone that makes the one you're looking straight at automatically the biggest, the brightest, the best.* "I shall be only a moment."

"Of course." Morris turned to look back in the direction from which they had come. All around him Olympus fell away in tiers and terraces, and he was sure that any other vantage point would seem equally at the top of this strange world. All around him people moved, walking, gliding, passing by with no notice of him at all, as if, he thought, there were nothing more natural to them than to see an old man in a clerical collar and frayed coat standing on the steps of the Palace Athene.

And maybe there is nothing more natural. These are gods, after all. All of them, from the highest to the lowest, gods in the true sense. Far beyond anything we mortals can comprehend. Maybe for them seeing me here is perfectly natural. Maybe they see through time and space, so that all moments are the same moment, and as far as they are concerned I've always been standing here, and I always will be.

What must it be like to be a god? He found it impossible to even begin to comprehend. *We toss off that word so easily, "god," without giving any thought to what it means. According to Diana these beings were created out of events not mentioned in the Bible. Nowhere does it say "And God created the One World, and set upon it beings of great power, and they were gods."*

He shook his head. He was far past any point at which he could truly say he understood what was happening. *That's why I'm here, after all. I want to understand. I want to know what the Universe is all about.* A small smile found its way to his thin lips. *Not so very much to ask, after all, is it?*

"Father Morris?"

He turned at his name. Diana emerged from the palace, temple, house, to stand a few steps above him. "Diana?"

"You may come in. Athena bids you welcome."

"I think you'll appreciate, Mr. Mayor, that it has fallen to you to take the necessary steps. You are the highest local authority. Since the President and the governor are determined to sit on the fence, only you can do what is necessary."

Benjamin Garrison stood with his back to the speaker, looking out the window at his city. He found himself doing that a lot of late, staring down through the tall glass, watching the people move along the sidewalks, the traffic flow. *When Hardiman Crane proposed the new City Hall should be the top of a skyscraper, back in the Thirties, everyone thought he was mad,* Garrison thought. *They didn't like the expense, at the height of the Depression, or the implication of a civic employee—the mayor—setting himself up on the top of his own man-made Olympus. They didn't like much of anything about it, in fact. But Crane wasn't a man to be argued with. He'd been mayor for thirty years at that point, and he was mayor for another fifteen after that. He died in office, literally in this office, and I've always thought his spirit just left his body, stepped out this window, and caught a cab for Heaven.* Garrison chuckled. *If there was ever a man who could deal his way past the Pearly Gates, it was Hardiman Crane.*

"Do you think this is funny, Mr. Mayor?"

Garrison turned from the window. The man speaking was tall, blond, altogether too Aryan, Garrison thought. He had remained standing, despite having been offered a chair, and behind him stood two associates Garrison had immediately thought of as goons. All three wore plain, dark gray business suits, yet there was something in their posture, the way they held themselves, in the directness of their gaze and the firmness of the set of their jaws, that made the simple suits look too much like uniforms. The Soldiers of Salvation armbands only added to the effect.

"No, Mr. Caldwell, I do not," Garrison said. "I understand perhaps even better than you how serious a situation this is." At the edge of his peripheral vision Garrison saw Sheldon Minsky fidgeting, uncomfortable with seeing the mayor in any sort of confrontation. *These men could be voters, after all.*

"Then you *do* intend to do something, Mr. Mayor? Miss Chandler would be most pleased to hear you had elected to take proper steps."

Garrison frowned, lowering himself into the massive oak and leather chair behind his desk. He hoped it had never looked so throne-like as it did at this moment. "You will appreciate, Mr. Caldwell, that while I have the utmost respect for Miss Chandler and her works, I do not feel especially beholden to her on any level. If I act, it will be because I have judged that action to be to the greater good of Gateway City, not because Rebecca Chandler has a particular bee in her bonnet."

Caldwell's too-handsome face darkened. "You would be well advised to guard such talk, Mr. Garrison." The deliberate deletion of the proper honorific did not go unnoticed by the mayor. "Miss Chandler has great worldly power. You would be better served to be her friend than her enemy."

"Is that the only choice, Mr. Caldwell?" Minsky stepped away from his place by the wall, setting himself not quite directly on the line between Garrison and Caldwell. "Surely there must be room for neutral ground?"

"No, Mr. Minsky," Caldwell said, "there is not. Since Rebecca Chandler does the work of our Savior Jesus Christ, to reject her is to reject *Him*." Caldwell's pale blue eyes narrowed. "But, then, you have already done that, haven't you?"

Minsky felt heat flash in his face. "That's hardly an argument worthy of the last years of the twentieth century, Mr. Caldwell," he said, his voice icy calm. "It belongs more in the 1940s, wouldn't you say? In Germany, perhaps?"

"Mr. Minsky—"

"Now, now, gentlemen." Garrison raised his hands, ever the peacemaker, ever the politician. "Let's not get sidetracked, shall we? Mr. Caldwell, you're here as an emissary of Rebecca Chandler, and I understand and respect her concerns. I shall look into the matter and make the necessary decisions."

"There is nothing to 'look into,' Mr. Mayor," Caldwell said. "This so-called Wonder Woman has proven herself time and again to be a menace to decent, God-fearing Christian society. As long as you encourage her to make Gateway City her home, you are giving aid and comfort to the worst kind of enemy."

Garrison shook his head. "I'm afraid I don't see it quite that clean and simple, Mr. Caldwell. Wonder Woman has done many good things since she arrived in Gateway. And before. I don't find myself inclined to see plots quite so quickly and easily as you do."

Caldwell took a step back, his associates falling in beside him to form a dark gray wall. "I hope you will not have occasion to regret your indecisiveness, Mr. Mayor," Caldwell said. "Her time of reckoning is close. You would be well advised to be prepared for it."

And with that, all three turned in unison and marched from the office, looking more like uniformed soldiers—*storm troopers?*— than ever.

Minsky moved to secure the door behind them. He turned back to face the mayor, twenty feet away across the width of the office. "Well, that was unpleasant."

"It was more than that, Shel," Garrison said. "This is turning into a real mess. He wasn't exaggerating when he said Chandler has power. She's a force in this country. There's not a politician born who doesn't envy the loyalty she commands in her followers."

"She'll fall," Minsky said. "They all do. Swaggert. Bakker. Now Chandler. She's got feet of clay, and if I can mix my metaphors, she'll set one of them wrong sooner or later, and down she'll go."

Garrison rubbed his eyes with the heels of his hands. "I'm not so sure. I would have said, if you'd asked, that she was crazy to attack Wonder Woman. I mean, *Wonder Woman!* Someone who's never been seen or heard to have done or said a wrong thing in all the years since she came here, and yet—bang!—Chandler starts in on this nonsense and all of a sudden it's like people were just waiting for an excuse to start tearing Wonder Woman down. Tearing them all down. Larry Pearson's column in this morning's *Guardian* was all about Superman, and how little we really know about him."

Minsky nodded. "I read it. It was kind of spooky, the way it made a weird sort of sense."

Garrison leaned back, deflated in his big chair. "I'd give a lot to be the mayor of Gateway City when this is all done and finished, when the decisions have been made, and if they're the wrong decisions, the heads have already fallen."

"But you're not. You're the mayor *now*."

"I'm the mayor now." Garrison shook his head. "And the damnable thing of it is, I have to think if I do what they want, if I put out some kind of ban on Wonder Woman, even order her to leave town, I'll still come off better in the next election than if I do nothing."

"Then? . . ."

"Then . . . nothing. I don't know. Another twenty-four hours. I have to think. But, Shel . . ."

"Yeah, Benny?"

"This really sucks, you know?"

Cassie Sandsmark had never flown in a private plane before—and certainly not a private plane this size.

Rebecca Chandler's personal aircraft—the *Bird of Pray* as some wise-ass in the press had dubbed it—was a converted 727, old but maintained in perfect condition. The interior had been gutted of anything and everything that might evoke a conventional aircraft, and as she sat sipping a Cherry Coke, Cassie could not help but think she was in some strange extension of her hotel suite—as if that suite had been magically shaped into a tube without losing any of its splendor and luxury.

Cassie was alone for the moment—alone in this cabin, at least. She knew there were four people in the cockpit and perhaps a dozen or so of Rebecca's associates scattered through the rest of the plane. Rebecca was in her bedroom in the back, sedated and, Cassie hoped, finally sleeping.

It's too weird that I care about this woman. I really want to hate her, I really, really should hate her, but I just can't. She's too nice. It troubled Cassie greatly that she was now on a razor's edge, and, she realized, no matter which way she turned, she would find herself betraying someone she considered a friend.

I mean, I can't betray Diana . . . well, okay, I've sort of already done that, but it's all part of the plan. But that plan is to bring down Rebecca, and I don't want to do that now, either. Cassie felt tears hot on her cheeks. *It was supposed to be easier than this. It was supposed to be so simple to make Rebecca out to be this complete idiot. All my stories were set up just for that purpose, but now. . . .* She shuddered, sobbing. *I don't want to hurt her, but I don't want to hurt Diana, either.*

She pulled her knees up to her chest, hugging them and folding in on herself as the tears flowed faster. *There must be some way I can get out of this mess without hurting Rebecca. I can't just go up to her and say, "By the way, I've been lying to you all along." That would break her heart, and it's the last thing she needs after this thing with her secretary.*

That was still the strangest thing. Cassie had spoken to several of Rebecca's closest confidants, and none of them could recall ever seeing anything like suicidal tendencies in Alyce Ruste. She was, they all said, a simple, plain woman, utterly and completely devoted to Rebecca Chandler and the Soldiers of Salvation. She was not known to have much of a life outside her work—never married, no living family, few friends—but she never demonstrated any need for one, either. Her universe was centered on Rebecca, and as long as Rebecca did nothing to disillusion or betray Alyce—and as far as anyone could determine, she had not—it seemed to all that Alyce Ruste would have been perfectly content to continue in her role as Rebecca's personal secretary until the day she died.

Which is pretty much what she did. But why'd she kill herself? What could've been so terrible? Cassie had experienced suicide before. A young friend of hers—more of an acquaintance, really, than a friend—had killed herself last year, and Cassie and her classmates had been devastated. Cassie could not conceive of anything in life that would be so awful, so devastating that it would inspire her to kill herself. That, she thought, was too final, too complete. There was no way to change your mind once you were dead.

And in the case of Marion, the girl who had killed herself, there had been clues. She had been depressed, drifting from class to class without focus, without purpose. She had said on many occasions that there was nothing in her life that had any value—although, in the central tragedy of the episode, no one had really taken her seriously until it was too late and she was dead.

Why did Alyce kill herself? If she was as devoted to Rebecca as everyone says, you'd think she wouldn't've wanted to do it just because she knew how much it would hurt Rebecca. And nobody seems to think she had any reason to hurt Rebecca.

Cassie took the TV remote from the holster on the side of her chair and clicked on the big screen at the other end of the cabin. She flipped down the dial to CNN and watched for a while, hoping there might be something on Alyce Ruste's death, something that might possibly give her insight and understanding.

There was nothing. The Soldiers of Salvation had closed an impenetrable gauntlet about the incident. Cassie began to suspect no one outside Rebecca's immediate circle—*which now includes me!*—even knew Alyce was dead. Cassie found that a little frightening. She was, after all, more or less at the center of the web, and if Rebecca decided, suddenly, that Cassie Sandsmark should be made to vanish without a trace, it could be accomplished with only the smallest expenditure of energy.

But Rebecca would never do that. I might've thought she could have, but not any more. I wish I still thought so. It would make my life easier. Make my decisions easier.

CNN was nothing but stories about the Wonder Woman riots. Cassie was disturbed to learn these protests—increasingly large and unfailingly violent—had not only been given a name, but that it was Diana's name. "The worst thing you can do with fanatics of any kind is give them a title, a buzzword they can hang on to," Cassie remembered her mother saying.

Mom. Cassie had been so busy worrying about Diana and Rebecca that she had given little thought to Helena. She knew her mother was strong, cool, calm. She was sure she was dealing with all this in her usual competent manner. She was even sure, deep down, that Helena had figured out that her daughter was up to something and was not worried that Cassie had truly betrayed her.

Cassie watched the television for a while, numbed by what she saw. All across the country—and even in three or four cities overseas—these massive protests were springing up. Hundreds, thousands of people turning up at arenas, ballparks, parking lots, malls, school auditoriums, anywhere people could gather in large numbers. And at each of the gatherings, whether calm and reasonable or—as with most of the ones covered by the cameras—wild and violent, the theme was the same: Wonder Woman must be destroyed.

Not just sent away. Not just put in prison or something. They want her destroyed. They want to burn her at the stake or something.

And as Cassie watched the flickering video images on the forty-inch screen, she was overwhelmingly aware of one thing: at each of these rallies, no matter where, no matter what time of the day or night, the blue armbands of the SoS were there, more and more of them, scattered through the crowds, on the stages and podiums, leading, inciting, driving the flood of hatred.

Oh God, what a mess I'm in! What a godawful mess I'm in!

"What do you mean she's left? When did she go? Who authorized it?"

Helena would have said, had she been asked, that she had reached the absolute pinnacle of her rage, and yet, it seemed, there were new levels yet to be achieved. As she stood before the desk of Martin Lieber, she felt herself coiling into a tight spring, as though the least prodding could send her across the cluttered desktop and straight at the man's throat.

"The authorization came from the highest levels," Lieber said. "When Miss Chandler expressed an interest in having Cassandra accompany her back to Chicago, we saw no reason to block her."

Helena was seething. She was already past any tolerable level of infuriation from just the proprietorial tone Lieber got in his voice when he said Cassie's name. To have him then inform her, as casually as he might have revealed the loaning out of a library book, that her only child had been taken to another city, half a continent away, by a woman Helena had never met and did not like—Helena was far along in convincing herself there were few juries that would convict her if she indeed strangled Lieber then and there.

"No reason," she said, summoning her very best, her very coolest professorial intonations. "Look, you may have taken my child from me, but you certainly have no right to take her out of the city; I don't care who wanted to do so. Now, I suggest you get in touch with Miss Rebecca Chandler and tell her to bring Cassandra back to Gateway City, immediately, before I take this to higher authorities."

Lieber snorted. "You'd have trouble finding any. This authorization comes from the governor herself."

Helena blinked. *The governor? But she hasn't made any statement at all in this business about Diana.* "Why should she be involved with Cassie and Rebecca Chandler?"

"Governor McBride has supported Miss Chandler for a long time now, Professor Sandsmark. I'm surprised you didn't know that." Lieber's face twisted into a sneer. "Of course, if you were the kind of person who had any interest in what Rebecca Chandler has to say, you would know that, wouldn't you?"

"And what exactly is that supposed to mean?" Helena knew, but she wanted to hear it said aloud, to confirm what she could barely bring herself to believe.

"You know as well as I do," Lieber said. "If you were the kind of person who followed the path Miss Chandler lays down, who put her trust in God above all else, you would never have gotten into this trouble in the first place, would you? You would have treated your daughter with the respect and dignity she deserves."

"You can't be serious! What I choose to consider as the basics for my ethics and morality has nothing to do with this, or with you. The Constitution of this country guarantees freedom of religion. I interpret that to mean freedom *from* religion, too."

Lieber shook his head. "And you see where that has brought you?" His face assumed a more reasonable configuration, his voice a gentler tone. "Look, Professor Sandsmark, I don't want to be your enemy. Sure, you've made some mistakes, and some of them were bad, but you still have a chance to redeem yourself."

"Redeem? . . ."

"Certainly. We haven't even had a hearing on this case, remember. All you need to do is show a genuine, honest intent to mend your ways, and—"

"I don't need to hear this!" Helena snapped to her feet, snatching her jacket from the back of the chair. "I have done nothing, nothing that I am ashamed of or that has been in any way detrimental to my daughter's well-being. I don't know why Cassie has said the things she's said but—" She stopped, a sudden thought slicing off the train of her words like the sharp edge of a blade.

"But? . . ."

"Nothing." Helena turned to the door. "I'll finish this business with you later, Mr. Lieber. And I can promise you, you will not like the end result."

She stepped out of the office and closed the door without a sound.

It's a plan, she thought, her heart pounding in her chest. *It has to be! Just the kind of crazy plan, in fact, that Cassie would cook up if I wasn't around to suggest something else. She hates Rebecca Chandler. She must have cooked up all this nonsense just to get close to her, so she could spy or some such foolishness.*

Her spirits rising, Helena strode down the hall, out of the building. The air outside seemed less heavy, less oppressive than when she had entered.

That must be it. That has to be it.

She hurried down the steps toward the street and her car, a spring in her step, a new focus in her life. But she stopped as suddenly as she had stopped her words, another thought crowding in to darken her mood.

Only . . . it doesn't make sense, does it? How could Cassie possibly know her story would bring her to the personal attention of Rebecca Chandler? I only found out Chandler was behind Cassie being taken after the fact. Did someone tell her? Someone inside Chandler's organization, or someone here at Child Welfare? And if they did, who was it? A friend? A foe? Someone with an agenda that has nothing to do with this business?

It was too much for her to fathom. She had built a career, a life out of assembling the broken pieces of antiquity into pictures that told whole stories of the life and times of ages past, but that had done nothing to prepare her for the kind of detective work demanded by her present situation.

It's all insane. Oh, God, I wish Diana would come back from Olympus! I need to talk to her! I need to know what she thinks about all this madness!

"How the devil did you get in here?" William Winget was not used to looking up from his lunch to find strangers in his private dining room. Especially not strangers who had not only managed to penetrate the security around his office, but somehow managed to reach the center of the room, not three feet from Winget's elbow, without so much as stirring the air.

"That is of no consequence, Mr. Winget," the intruder smiled. "My name is Stephen Ramsey. I am an associate of Rebecca Chandler. I wish to discuss some important business with you."

"Miss Chandler sent you? She didn't inform me—"

"Rebecca did not 'send' me," Ramsey said, taking the only other chair in the room, at the other end of the short table where Winget was dining. His smile did not waver, but it did seem to darken, Winget thought, as though he were holding back a great anger behind those even, white teeth. "No one 'sends' me anywhere."

"Very well, then," Winget said. "A minor point at best. If you work with Rebecca, if you have something to tell me on her behalf, I suggest you get to the point without any further dramatics."

Winget felt a shudder run through him as Ramsey laughed. The sound seemed to come from deep, deep below, rumbling up through the old brick and steel of the *Guardian* building, vibrating through the oak floor and the Persian rug beneath his chair.

"I like your spirit, Winget," he said, and Winget suddenly felt hesitant to admonish him for omitting a "mister." "You are very much a man after my own heart. Strong. Self-reliant. You build the things you want built, and it matters little to you if others are crushed in the process."

"People have said that of me," Winget said. "I have always demanded they produce proof. More than one I have sued into oblivion for his effrontery."

Ramsey laughed again. He reached down the table to take a dark red apple from the bowl of fresh fruit set there for Winget's dessert. The crunch as he bit through the firm skin was louder than the acoustics of the room should allow. Winget had spent a great deal of money shielding himself from inappropriate sound, with curtains, carpets, and carefully sculpted walls all lending to the muffling effect. "I'm sure there is no one who has ever crossed you who has endured to enjoy the experience," Ramsey said. "But, then, I am not here to 'cross' you. I am here to tell you what must be done next."

"Well then?" Winget saw his visitor's nostrils flare for a moment. He was pushing this man to the very limit, he knew. This was one who was in no way used to dealing with anyone on an equal footing. *Who is he? I've never seen him, not in my paper, not on television. Someone who seems as confident as he does, someone who is so used to command-*

ing respect and wielding power—surely I would have come across that face before now.

"Well, then," Ramsey said, "what I have in mind is that you—you and several other equally powerful men across this country—will organize rallies, meetings. Calls to arms, as it were."

"Rallies?" Winget did not like the word. It conjured to mind thoughts of Nuremberg and times best forgotten. "What sort of 'rallies'?"

"Meetings to gather together people of this city and others to hear the words of Rebecca Chandler in person. Where she can tell them why Wonder Woman is a menace, and tell them how to deal with the problem."

Winget dabbed the corner of his mouth with a freshly laundered cloth napkin. He took up his glass and sipped the sherry he always had with his midday meal. Over the crystal rim of the glass he studied Stephen Ramsey, measuring his power, his confidence. There was no lack of either in the man's demeanor. And yet, as much as Winget wished to take umbrage at Ramsey's effrontery, as much as he detested his arrogance for presuming to speak to him as few men had ever dared, the logic of his plan was clear, in fact, overwhelming. "Yes," Winget said at last. "That . . . seems reasonable. The other media are taking up the call I started in the *Guardian*, but there is nothing quite so effective as personal interaction. I've seen Rebecca on television. The way she can move and control a crowd is quite amazing."

"I gave her that," Ramsey said, and there was something in the way he said it that made Winget feel he meant it literally, that he had actually given Rebecca Chandler the ability to manipulate crowds, as a gift in the way a genie might grant a wish.

"Did you indeed?" Winget flicked a nail on the edge of his glass. The crystal *pinged*, but the sound was instantly muted by the clever configurations of the room. It made the loud crunching of Ramsey's apple seem all the stranger to Winget's ears. "It was my understanding that Rebecca was something of a self-made woman. She appeared from nowhere and, by the power of her words and her conviction, made this Holy Empire for herself."

Ramsey sneered. "In two years? Do you honestly believe anyone could accomplish what she has in two years? Do you think that Crystal Tower of hers could even be built in two years, never mind the ten months it took?" He shook his dark head. "You are not the brilliant man I had been led to believe, Winget."

"Perhaps. Are you now going to tell me you are some kind of magician, Ramsey? That you worked all this for her with your magic?" Winget felt a strange twisting in the pit of his stomach. As he spoke them, his words took on a sudden, strong sense of credibility, as if he was looking through the keyhole of a locked door and discovering some long-hidden secret.

"I would never say such a thing," Ramsey smiled, and the moment was broken. Winget realized his heart had been pounding, his breath short. He forced himself to relax.

"What, then? I have no time for games, Ramsey."

"Of course you do," Ramsey said. He rose and rounded the table to stand, looming, close by Winget's elbow where he had first appeared. "It is all a game, Winget. Every moment of your puny little lives is a game, all of you, down to the last man and woman. You cheat, you connive, you work your little schemes to make things better or worse, as if anything a human being does has the least effect on the great pattern of the Universe."

"And what of you, Ramsey? You seem confident you can make a difference in things. You seem to think you already have."

Ramsey smiled. "I have. And that is not at variance with what I have said." He turned and stepped a few paces away from the table. He seemed to Winget to be larger, more angular, less human. He turned back to face the publisher, and for a moment Winget thought the face he saw was not the bearded, handsome face he had first looked at, but something shadowed, black, like peering into an abyss, a Stygian darkness that somehow wore the shape of a grinning skull. That moment too passed, but its effect gnawed at Winget's guts with teeth of ice and steel.

"Do what I suggest," Ramsey said, and there was irony to spare in his choice of words. "Do what I suggest, and quickly, and I promise you, in the order that will come from this chaos, you will have a special place."

A shadow passed over the broad windows to Winget's right. Instinctively he turned to look, but he saw nothing. When he brought his eyes back to the spot where Stephen Ramsey had been standing, there was only empty air. That, and a strange conviction in Winget's mind that the spot on the rug where Ramsey had stood was somehow several shades darker than it had been a few minutes past.

CHAPTER ELEVEN

T HIS *is truly a temple*, Donald
Morris found himself thinking. *Like no church I have ever been in, I feel
the presence of godly power in this place.*

He could not begin to measure the degree to which this thought disturbed him. It burrowed down into the very core of his being, rooting
about in the most sacred, central parts of whatever might be left of his
soul. It was a bull, a juggernaut. There was nothing small, nothing delicate about the thought. It tore through the fabric of his mind, his reason. It pummeled him as if with fists of stone.

"Diana. . . ." It was only a whisper, but it echoed between the
columns, the tall, white columns that seemed to stretch out beyond
infinity above him.

"Are you all right, Father Morris?" Diana was at his side at once,
supporting him again.

"No. Not at all. I feel . . . quite faint." His cheeks colored. "And also
very foolish. I don't know what I expected, how I thought I was going
to react to all this . . . I'm sorry, Diana. I guess I expected some kind
of Hollywood version of Olympus. Something comprehensible, with
normal horizons and Laurence Olivier as Zeus."

Diana smiled. "Come, sit for a while. Athena has infinite patience.
She will understand."

Morris allowed himself to be led to a low marble bench. It was cool and somehow soft beneath him when he sat. It seemed to yield, not hard stone at all, though beneath his fingertips he could find nothing to suggest it was other than the marble it appeared to be.

"Athena," he said as his breathing eased and his heart slowed a little. "The real Athena. It's all too much to take in, Diana."

She sat beside him. "I can imagine. When I came to Patriarch's World there was much I did not understand, much I had to encompass in a short time. Nothing on the scale to which you are now struggling to adjust, but still enough to make it seem as though my whole existence had been turned inside out."

"Why did you ever leave Paradise Island, Diana? Surely it would have been better for you to have lived out your life there, without involving yourself in the affairs of the outside world."

She nodded, and he saw a deep sadness in her bright blue eyes. "I left because a god had chosen to interfere in the lives of humans, Father Morris. You know of Ares, the god the Romans called Mars?"

"Yes."

"He had become interested anew in the arts of human warfare. I fear that much of the terror that has vexed your world in recent times was his doing. He is a careless and unfeeling god, concerned only with death and destruction, and the intricacies of mad schemes to foster them."

"You left Paradise Island to fight Ares?" The words seemed almost to belong to another language. "Is this the battle you mentioned before, when you said you've fought many gods?"

"It is. I battled Ares and defeated him only by using the gift of Hestia to compel him to see the ultimate truth of his madness—to see a future where the world was laid bare by nuclear fire, with no humans left to fear and worship him."

"And that stopped him?"

Diana smiled. "We live now, do we not, Father Morris? Yes, that stopped him. Like all the gods, Ares is nothing if not vain. He needs to be worshiped. He cannot survive if there are no humans to raise temples in his name."

"But, surely, even if the Earth was destroyed, somewhere out there in the cosmos . . . I mean, Superman comes from another planet. Surely there are others where a god like Ares could find worshipers?"

Diana shook her head. "The gods are bound to the worlds where they sprang into being, Father Morris. The gods who came to life in the cradle of the Mediterranean are Earthly gods. Though they may journey to other planes, other dimensions, they cannot leave this world too far behind, or they will fade away and die."

"You mean . . . a god can die?"

"A god can die. All things can die. That is the one truth of all the Universe." Diana looked away, through the tall columns to the blue of the surrounding sky. "Even the Universe itself will end, some day, perhaps finally, perhaps to begin again. I do not know."

"That no one knows," said a voice behind them. Morris turned. A woman had stepped into the small area defined by the columns surrounding the bench on which he sat. She was tall and brown-haired, and her face was at once young and infinitely old. Her eyes were what he most noticed, though—large and dark, kind.

"My lady," Diana said, springing to her feet and inclining her head in a modest bow.

Morris swallowed hard. "Athena? . . ."

The goddess extended her hand to him, lifting him from where he sat. "Yes, Father Morris. I am Athena. Welcome to Olympus."

They passed through the middle of O'Hare International Airport like Moses crossing the dry floor of the Red Sea. Surrounded by her people—the blue armbands seemed brighter than they actually were, Cassie thought, in the fluorescent lighting of the terminal—Rebecca and her young charge moved unhampered by the throng, oblivious to the press of travelers around them.

They moved quickly, but not so fast that Cassie did not have time to note a distinct change in the traffic of the airport. She had traveled enough with her mother to assume that most large airports were essentially the same, and therefore there should be Hare Krishnas, Moonies, Jews for Jesus—all the little groups of subcults and sects milling about the doors, offering their pins, their flowers, their pamphlets. Helena had taught Cassie to ignore them, to pass them without notice, but what she noticed that day was that they were gone.

In their place were more of the Soldiers of Salvation, hundreds of them, Cassie thought, all with their plain suits and their blue armbands—and now with their banners and signs, their badges, their own pamphlets, each and every one with the same message, over and over: Put an end to Wonder Woman. Bring her down. Destroy her before she destroys you!

Frightening. But even more disturbing, Cassie thought, were the people who stopped to talk to the Soldiers. The busy, hurrying travelers who were pausing to take buttons, leaflets. To read, to listen. To nod. They were not bustling past, as they would brush by the bald heads and saffron robes of the followers of Krishna. There were no sneers as greeted the disciples of Reverend Moon, no outright hostility as Cassie had so often seen directed to the Jews who put their faith in the Christian Messiah. There was calm, reason. There was attention being paid.

How can everyone be turning on Diana like this? How could it've happened so fast? Rebecca's good, she's persuasive, but not this good. Not nearly this good.

They came out of the airport and stepped into a waiting limousine, pale blue with the SoS white and gold emblem on the side. The windows were smoked glass, and inside it was warm and lit only by slender lightstrips in the floor. Cassie sat with her back to the driver and looked at Rebecca. She looked drawn, Cassie thought. In the past few days she had seen Rebecca's face in most of its forms, but never like this. It was as though the life had been emptied from her. Since the news of Alyce Ruste's suicide, Rebecca had made no public appearances, given no statements to the press. She had pulled deep inside herself, and the eyes through which she looked out into the world were dull, clouded, no longer burning with seemingly unquenchable fire.

Cassie had been searching for something to say, but words failed her. She had never had to deal with the kind of loss Rebecca was clearly feeling. Her youth and the smallness of her family unit—only herself and Helena—had served to protect Cassie from some of the harsher truths of the world. Even the suicide in school had been detached, a separate entity that she came to realize had not been something she— as Cassie or as Wonder Girl—could have done anything about.

She felt a mounting frustration, looking at Rebecca as she stared out at the shadows of Chicago's suburbs beyond the dark glass. *I oughta be able to do something for her. Say something that'd help. I'll bet Diana would have something to say. Something from the Wisdom of Athena.*

Once again, Cassie was surprised to find herself caring about Rebecca, worrying that she would be all right, that she would find a way out of this darkness.

"I keep thinking there should be something I can say," Cassie offered at last, hesitantly, disturbed by the silence stretching between them. "I wish there was something."

Rebecca turned to look at Cassie. "There isn't. But thank you. I appreciate the thought."

"You and Miss Ruste were good friends, I guess, huh?" Cassie was not sure this was a good time to ask, but she was curious. She needed to understand the depth of Rebecca's grief.

"Not really," Rebecca said, and the answer was not at all what Cassie had expected. "She was my personal secretary, and she was very, very good at her job. A good right hand. But I would not have called us friends. By her choice. She worked for me, and she wanted to keep the relationship on that level, very professional, very sound and secure. I think she had been hurt by letting people inside her life, before. She was so much in awe of me—I could feel it, even when she did her best to cover it—that I think she was afraid of an even greater hurt if I became her friend." Rebecca shook her head. "But I have to wonder if I could have spared her this, if we had been friends. Close friends. To be so sad, so hopeless, that she would kill herself, choosing eternal damnation. I might have sensed whatever was wrong, whatever led her to take her own life."

Cassie leaned forward to put her hand on Rebecca's, where they rested folded in the older woman's lap. "I bet you wouldn't have, though, Rebecca. I mean, you're real good at that sort of thing. You can read people—" *except me* "—and just being around her at work you would've been able to pick up what was wrong, if there was anything to pick up."

Rebecca nodded. "That's part of what makes it so hard. I didn't see anything. Not the least indication. No one did. I called the Tower as soon as we got the news, and no one there had seen anything wrong with Alyce at all. Nothing. It's as if. . . ." She paused, shaking her head.

"What?"

"I was going to say it's as if something . . . some outside force suddenly compelled her to kill herself. But what? And why?" She turned to look out the window again. "None of it makes any sense."

Donald Morris returned to consciousness in a small room lit by subtle, elusive phosphors that danced at the corners of his vision. He did not remember having passed out, but he realized that was the only explanation for what was, to him, a sudden shift of scene.

Old fool, he thought, pushing himself up on his elbows. He was lying on a loose pile of cushions—like the marble bench, they seemed somehow to arrange themselves for his maximum comfort—and as he looked around he determined he was on a couch to one side of the room. The room itself was not more than twelve feet on a side, and the ceiling was only about nine feet above the scattered rugs and carpets on the floor. There were no windows, and the light that floated about the room had no source that he could see. Delicate mosaics covered the walls. A table stood at the center of the room, upon it a large bowl of fruit, a plate of breads of different sizes and shapes, and several ornate wine decanters.

"Welcome back, Donald Morris."

He looked to his right, to the head of the couch, and saw her, the Goddess Athena seated on a small, simple chair—*yet just by being in it, she somehow makes it a throne*—Wonder Woman on a similar chair beside her. It was Athena who had spoken.

"Are you all right, Father Morris?" The concern in Diana's voice was genuine. "You gave us quite a fright."

"I feared the journey had proven too much for you," Athena said, "and that we might have to summon you back from death's dominion."

Morris struggled to speak around a suddenly uncooperative tongue. "You . . . could do that?"

Athena smiled. "It is the least gift of a god, Donald Morris. Perhaps it is even what defines us as gods. But I suspect it would not have helped you in your quest here. It would have only served to create greater confusion and fear."

If I had really died, he thought, *if I had really dropped dead of a heart attack—not such an outrageous speculation—and gone on to . . . what? Heaven? Hell? Limbo? Would she really have been able to "summon" me back? A doctor can bring a patient back from death. I've seen them do it. But that's not what she's talking about here. She's talking about the literal power of life and death. She could kill me and bring me back to life as many times as she pleased. Just by thinking about it.*

"My quest," Morris said at last, forcing words to form between mouth and brain. "Diana—Princess Diana—Wonder Woman—" *What the devil do I call her, here?*

"Yes," Athena said, "Diana has told me of your needs. I am not certain I can be of very much help to you in this matter."

Morris sat up, carefully. Couch and floor seemed solid enough. The room showed no sign of suddenly tipping or inverting itself. "If you can't," he said, mind still reeling as he struggled to come to terms with the precise nature of the conversation—*I am talking to the Goddess Athena. The* real *Goddess Athena*—"I don't imagine there is anyone who can. You are the living embodiment of wisdom, after all."

"So I have been called. But not all things are knowable, Donald Morris."

"I suppose not. Um . . . Is there a proper way to proceed with this? Do I . . . ask questions, or would that be presumptuous? I mean, I suppose you know my questions before I even ask them."

"No," Athena said, "I am not omniscient. I can read your face, I can interpret the emotions you project, but your mind is closed to me. As it is to all gods."

"Really? Jesus said God knew all our thoughts. He cautioned against public prayer, because it was for personal glory, not the glorification of God."

"And yet you are a representative of a church that revels in public prayer, are you not? And we enjoy the public displays of devotion our worshipers grant to us."

"It's true the Catholic Church is fond of pomp and pageantry," Morris said. "But that's never been part of my job. I was always at a lower level, a more intimate level with the public."

"I see. Diana has told me that you worked with children, sick children. This is a noble cause, Donald Morris. Children are the future, the legacy of all Humankind."

"The children I worked with had precious little chance to be anyone's legacy . . . my lady." He recalled Diana using that term and tendered it carefully, fearful of causing offense. When none appeared, he went on. "They were all dying, mostly in pain, some before they even understood what it was like to be alive. Children born with cancer, my lady. With AIDS. Children born addicted to drugs. Does your wisdom extend to a comprehension of what it must be like for them? I've often tried to understand it, myself. To be thrust into the world, uncomprehending, no real mind yet, no real personality, and yet immediately at the center of pain, of infinite suffering. And to have no way to understand that it might pass, or that it could pass. To have no memories of a time when there was not pain." He felt the tears on his cheeks and was surprised by them. *Well. I can still cry, after all.*

"I understand," Athena said. He was impressed by her command of English, the smooth, unaccented way in which she formed words. Though, he supposed, she would probably be as comfortable were he speaking French, German, Italian, Swahili. *It might not even be speech, as I understand it. I can see her lips moving, but that doesn't mean anything. I'm not prepared, entirely, to believe anything I see is really as it appears. There's no reason to assume Athena really looks like this, like a beautiful woman of indeterminate age. Or that she is speaking. She might be pure energy, and what I think is speech might be some kind of telepathy.*

"It is my curse," Athena said, "to comprehend all things. Wisdom does not come without its price, after all."

"Then you understand why I have lost my faith? Why I can't believe there is really a benevolent god who looks down on all this and allows it—even causes it? A god who would have children born with such afflictions—why? To punish the parents? To test them? I was taught that God does not act directly in the affairs of men nearly as much as He used to. There have been no Prophets in more than two thousand years. But if that is so, where does this pain come from? And why does it come? Is there a purpose? Is there a higher reason? I can't believe it. Not any more."

"You seek order out of chaos," Athena said. "This has always been the central quest of Humanity. The need to understand. And when there is insufficient knowledge to form true understanding, Mankind invents its own truths. For some, we gods are such truths. Our beginnings are shrouded in mystery even we cannot penetrate. Diana, I know, has told you one version. There are others. Let me ask you this, Donald Morris, to begin with—do you believe I am a god?"

"I'm . . . not sure." *There's not much else she can be, is there? There's small likelihood that this is something other than Olympus—unless it really is that dream on the bus I keep thinking it might be.* "We've tried a lot, in this century, to reconcile all the different gods and goddesses

Humanity has worshiped, and still does," he said. He struggled to find a place to begin, a place where he could start his line of questioning, but now, sitting across from Athena, he felt foolish trying to find the words for questions which, to her, he was sure must be the smallest and least significant of all. *I am a mortal man. I can't begin to think in the same manner she does, let alone put my thoughts into words that won't seem astonishingly trivial to her.* But he reminded himself that Athena, perhaps because of her wisdom, was known also for her compassion. She was ever patient, ever tolerant. Looking into her eyes he saw no suggestion that she might be bored or eager to be done with the audience. He found solace in that, the assurance that she would sit and listen to him for all Eternity—if Eternity were what he required to have his answers.

"I am aware of this curious habit mortals have lately developed," Athena smiled. "It has always seemed strange to me that the path that carried them away from us has taken them to a place where they seek ever to reduce their gods."

"Reduce?" There was still enough of the Catholic priest in Donald Morris that he was not quick to accept the notion that God was somehow a reduction of the old gods, the other gods men worshiped.

"To turn from pantheons to single gods is an act of reduction, Father Morris, would you not agree? When your ancestors worshiped my brethren and myself, they created about us huge tapestries of tales, vast and intricate. They took the truth of our existence and wove into it the fables of their own imagining. They were not content to have us as we are, but made us even greater, even more magnificent. It was their need to make us incomprehensible, you see. In order to comprehend." She smiled. "A uniquely human dichotomy."

"And I am seeking my own kind of comprehension," Morris nodded.

"Your God has always been a puzzlement to me, Father Morris." Athena leaned back in her chair, and for a moment Morris felt a kind of whirling vertigo, as though the floor had dropped away. *She's going to talk about God,* he thought, trembling, though whether in fear or anticipation, he could not say. *My God, the God of the Bible, the God of Abraham and Jesus. And if she now says she has met Him, that she has spoken with Him, discussed the workings of the Universe with Him. . . . Diana told me that she offered to bring Rebecca Chandler here, to Olympus, to see if Zeus could arrange an audience with Jehovah for her. Chandler thought Diana was mocking her, but now here I sit, and that has to be the unspoken center of my quest, doesn't it? I want to find out if these gods know my God, if they can say, "Oh, yes, He lives in the third temple from the end, down that avenue over there."*

"Are you all right, Father Morris?" Diana left her place in the chair by Athena's right hand, crossing to kneel beside him. "You're shaking."

"I'm . . . afraid." He said the words carefully, not wanting to lose control of his voice. He felt as though he might begin sobbing uncontrollably at any moment, as the enormity of all that was happening continued to pound down upon him, wave upon wave. "It's something like the Moon landing," he said, knowing his words would make no sense, but pressing on, needing to verbalize the emotions, the turmoil in his soul. "I watched for three days without a break when Armstrong, Aldrin, and Collins went to the Moon. I watched as Neil Armstrong stepped out onto the Moon's surface, and I thought 'This is the most important thing you will ever see in your life. Maybe the most important thing in the whole history of Humankind!' But it didn't seem real to me. Even now, almost thirty years later, it doesn't seem real. I'd seen so many movies and TV shows, I'd read so many books about space travel, about going to the Moon. The fact that I was seeing it on television didn't make it more real for me, it made it less."

"And this is somehow a similar experience, Father Morris?" Athena remained seated, her bare arms draped loosely across the cushioned arms of the chair, her feet together, the satin-smooth fabric of her gown falling about her in gentle waves that the best sculptor on Earth would fail to capture. "The reality somehow makes belief all the harder?"

"Yes. I guess that's it. I'm here. I'm sitting talking to the Goddess Athena, on Olympus, asking about God. And when you said He has always puzzled you—there was something in the way you said it. Something that suggested . . . I'm afraid even to say the words."

Athena nodded. "You are afraid I am now going to tell you of a meeting I had with your God. A discussion that perhaps He and Zeus and I had, concerning the workings of the Universe."

Morris swallowed in a dry throat. "Yes."

Athena shook her head, the subtle highlights floating through her umber curls. "No, Father Morris. I have not met your God. None here on Olympus have met Him."

"Why?" *Because He doesn't exist?*

"That is difficult to explain. There are many pantheons of gods we have met. Diana has told you of the gods of Apokolips and New Genesis. And I suppose, from what she has told you, you will have deduced that there are other gods who are just as real as we—Odin, for instance. Thor. Balder. Loki. These I have met. Zeus and Odin have discussed the future of Humankind many times, especially as they fell from favor in the houses of your different faiths. But this God of yours, this Jehovah, YHVH, whatever name you choose to call Him . . . none of us have ever seen or spoken to Him. He is beyond us, perhaps above us. Has Diana told you of the Source?"

"No? . . ."

"When the One World was destroyed there survived a single artifact. It stands on the surface of New Genesis. I have been to that world, and I have seen it. It is a wall, or more exactly a fraction, a broken segment of a wall. Occasionally, when dire times threaten the gods of New Genesis, their leader, Izaya, their Highfather, will go to the wall to commune with the Source. A moving hand appears, and writes in words of fire upon the wall messages that are sometimes . . . cryptic. That hand, that writing is a manifestation of the Source. The Source is all that remains of whatever existed before the One World was destroyed. When the gods of Apokolips and New Genesis die, they become one with the Source. I am inclined to believe a similar fate awaits the gods of Olympus, of Asgard, of all the pantheons of Earth and beyond."

"The Source is . . . God?"

"Perhaps it is a piece of your God. Perhaps He, like us, is a piece of the Source. Do you know that there are tales older than your Bible that speak of your God as a lesser deity? One who committed some unspecified mistake, and so for His punishment was assigned to oversee a small and unimportant world—Earth?"

"I've . . . heard such things. They are in the Gnostic Gospels, I know. And some suggest that there are hints of this surviving even in the Old Testament. That when God speaks in the plural He refers not to Himself in a 'royal we,' or to Himself and the Heavenly Hosts, but to the higher pantheon of which He is but a small part."

"But you do not believe this?"

Morris sighed. "The Bible might be said to take its authority from the fact that it is the transcribed Word of God—the Old Testament, at least. And if those words are not true, if they have been altered by careless scribes and people with their own agendas—well, then, how much of the book can we accept as valid?"

"Bold words. Do you seek from me, then, the assurance that the story you know from your Bible is true and perfect?"

"I suppose I do. It's a crazy sort of irony, to ask Athena if God is real. But, yes, I suppose that's the reason I'm here. Tell me God is real, and I might, perhaps, be on my way to understanding why He allows or even causes suffering in the world."

"I cannot say what you need to hear," Athena said. "You seek knowledge of something that, if it is real, lies beyond the beginning of the Universe. I can confirm that such a thing exists, that there is a power greater than ours, older and far beyond ours. But I cannot say its name, for I do not know it."

"Then . . . my coming here was for nothing?"

"Perhaps not. You have looked upon Olympus, Donald Morris. What will you take with you from that?"

"Well, if nothing else, I guess I know now that what Diana says is true. That she's talking about the gods she worships not because she wants to destroy the Christian faith, or any other. She's just reporting what she knows is real."

"And you believe this? There is no portion of your heart that fears all this—" Athena waved her hand and the room dissolved around them. Father Morris looked again upon the mind-twisting face of Olympus—"might be some manner of trick?"

"No," he said. "For one thing, I can feel, somehow, that it's all real. It's nothing like what I would have expected it to be—maybe that's part of what makes it seem real. If it was what I expected, I might be more suspicious. But I feel in my heart that this place is real. And that you are real. And, anyway—" He turned his eyes toward Wonder Woman. "I trust Diana."

Athena rose, tall, beautiful, yet somehow human in a way Morris found impossible to describe or understand. "Good. Now, come. This matter that vexes Diana is of great concern to the gods. Zeus has called an assembly. Though you will not be allowed to participate, it might be enlightening for you to witness it, at least."

The telephone was ringing when Helena Sandsmark returned to her house in the hills overlooking Gateway City. For a moment she had the crazy thought that it was Diana, somehow calling from Olympus. She shook that foolishness from her head and raced across the living room to snatch up the phone.

"Hello?" The buzz of the carrier wave was loud in her ear. "Damn." She pressed a button on the answering machine beside the phone, and one by one the numbers of the previous callers were printed out on the liquid crystal screen. There had been ten calls, and seven of them showed only the word PRIVATE, indicating an unlisted number, or someone calling from a number that blocked call monitoring. The last call had been one of those. She checked the message tape and heard three messages of no consequence and seven clicks.

Cassie. But if it had been, why? And why no message?

Knowing it would not work, but feeling she had to try, Helena pressed the buttons on the phone that should, under most circumstances, connect her with the last number to have called. The phone rang and clicked, and then a mechanical voice informed her that the call could not be completed as dialed.

She cradled the handset and stepped away from the phone. She turned on the television, cycled through the dial to CNN. Of course the first story she saw was about Wonder Woman, about the increasing bile and hatred being spewed out from all corners against her friend.

Like Cassie, Helena found herself having no small amount of difficulty understanding how this matter could have ballooned to such proportions so fast. Were people always ready to turn on Diana? Had there always been a hatred of the Amazon Princess boiling and festering just below the surface, needing only someone to come along and spear it, lance it, open it up to spill out and poison the whole country?

The newscaster spoke in a calm, steady voice, assuring viewers that what they were seeing, the violence in the streets of New Orleans that had accompanied the latest anti–Wonder Woman protest, was not the norm. Most people still trusted Wonder Woman, he reported, rattling off numbers, a poll, a graph, demographics. It seemed that the greatest concentrations of hatred were not at all where Helena might have expected, had she thought in terms of conventional clichés. There was a strong anti–Wonder Woman sentiment in the Deep South, which did not surprise Helena, but the figures were even higher in the Pacific Northwest, and for reasons she could not quite understand, lowest through the middle of the Bible Belt.

This thing is hitting people in places they didn't realize they had. It's bringing out a kind of insanity and hatred that has nothing to do with race or education, with politics or even religion. It starts as a religious argument—Rebecca Chandler started with that—but it turns into something else. Some kind of primitive thing, jealousy, fear. Xenophobia.

Helena was convinced that all irrational hatreds began there, with an ingrained, instinctive fear of the unknown. *It's where racism, where anti-Semitism, comes from. Whenever we encounter something different from us, whenever the larger number are confronted with the smaller, it inspires fear. If it is another color, we turn it into something less than us, something inferior, so we can justify enslaving it. And religion? Yes, if there is a reason I'm not at all religious, it is because I have seen what that power does in the world. More harm than good. More chances for persecution and murder than salvation.*

She watched the broadcast for a few minutes longer, until the phone rang again. She glanced at the LED screen before she picked up the handset. PRIVATE again.

Cassie. Please be Cassie. For whatever reason. Just so I know you're all right. . . .

"Helena Sandsmark."

"Mom . . ."

"Cassie! It is you! Oh, baby, where are you? What have they done with you?"

"I can't talk long, Mom. But I had to call you. I'm at the Crystal Tower. With Rebecca."

"Rebecca?? You mean—?"

"Chandler. Yes. Listen, Mom, please, I don't have a lot of time. I just wanted to tell you there's a reason for what I've been saying. I know it sounds crazy, but I'm doing it to help Diana."

"Help. Yes, I thought that might be it. Listen, honey, whatever it is you're doing, it's probably dangerous. Please, let me—"

"I'm sorry, Mom. I can't say more right now. For all I know, they're tapping this phone. That's not really Rebecca's style, but some of her people—"

"Rebecca's style? Cassie, what's going on? You're talking as if this woman is your friend?"

"She is. Mom, it's hard to explain. Just trust me, okay? And tell Diana to trust me. It's gonna turn out. . . . Mom? Mom?"

There was the sound of a telephone being returned to its cradle and the line going dead. Rebecca Chandler pushed the rewind button again. She had heard this telephone conversation, taped less than an hour earlier, several times already, yet no matter how many times she listened to it, the words did not seem to sink in, to make any sense to her.

"How many times do you need to hear it?"

Rebecca looked up into the lean, hard face of Davis Kavanagh, her chief of security. He stood before her desk, feet apart, hands clasped behind his back, and Rebecca found herself thinking for the first time that the uniforms Stephen Ramsey had issued to her security people had become more and more militaristic as the months had gone by. Small changes, subtle, but enough that when she looked at Kavanagh she saw a man in something altogether too much like a soldier's uniform.

She recalled now, too, that she had resisted the name "Soldiers of Salvation" when Ramsey had given it to her—*not suggested. There was never any sense that I had a choice*—because she did not want to think of her followers as an army so much as a family. She would have preferred something with "brethren" in the title, or perhaps something less gender-specific.

"I'll listen to it as many times as I need to, Kavanagh," Rebecca said, pressing "play" again. The short exchange repeated.

She means to betray *me*, Rebecca thought. *All along, if this is what it sounds like, Cassie has been plotting against me.*

She shook her head, turning her chair so that her back faced her desk and Kavanagh. *Am I being paranoid? Am I reading too much into this. When Cassie says "there's a reason for what I've been saying," what can she possibly mean other than that there is some reason beyond what her words appear to mean. Ramsey told me of her horrible home life, counseled me to make the moves that led to Cassie being taken from Helena Sandsmark. Cassie's stories—the way she implicated her mother and Wonder Woman in all sorts of unsavory things—seemed almost too good to be true. Were they? Did I accept them so easily because they were what I wanted to hear? Did I take them all on faith because there was nothing I needed so much as the absolute confirmation that I was right about Diana?*

The night sky was gray and featureless over the lake, low clouds forming a solid mass, a ceiling that bounced back the city lights in a pearly glow that faded slowly into distant darkness. No stars, no hint of a moon.

I am at the center of a great darkness, Rebecca thought. *It's where I have always been. Sometimes I think I have managed to climb out, when I see the smiles on the faces of my followers, when I hear their voices raised in song, in tribute to the Lord Jesus and the Heavenly Father . . . but the darkness is always there. I feel it as a part of my life, moving around the edges. I've pushed it back as far as it will go, but when something like this happens. . . .*

She struggled to choke back the sobs that threatened at any moment to break her reserve and set her weeping uncontrollably before the chief of her security force. *Why did it have to happen now, right on the heels of Alyce's suicide? Why do I have to have these barbs hurled at me, just when it seemed like things were turning, finally, down the right path? The television and the newspapers are full of stories of people coming to my cause. They are seeing Wonder Woman for the evil thing she really is, and they are rallying behind that revelation, just as Ramsey said they would.*

Ramsey. She frowned. *What is his part in this, really?* He had provided her with money, made things happen around her at a pace she would not have thought possible—the building of the extraordinary skyscraper was only a single example—and yet he still stood as distant from her as he ever had, as the day he had introduced himself.

Who is he? she asked herself for the hundredth time. *Where did he come from? What is his real motive for wanting to destroy Wonder Woman?*

This was the first time she had allowed herself to form that particular question. She had skirted around it in the past, but she had never taken out the words and looked closely at them. *Why is Stephen Ramsey doing this?* Does he have some secret agenda of his own? When he had made her aware of the insidiousness inherent in Diana's very existence, Rebecca had seen it and agreed. And when he had told her that this should be the focus of her energies, the core around which she should construct her holy campaign, she had seen the wisdom in that, too. *And it's not as if it hasn't worked. I've risen higher and faster than I would ever have dared dream, and my followers all see the world now as I see it.*

It was the purity of the vision, she thought, that gave it its power. Unlike so many Evangelicals, Rebecca Chandler had no hidden agendas, no motives beyond those she stated openly. As Cassie had learned, Rebecca was, indeed, completely sincere.

Maybe that's why I feel so uncomfortable with Ramsey. It's not so much that I doubt his sincerity, it's more that I think he's focused on a purpose other than mine. I want to spread the Word, I want to bring the Holy Gospel into every corner of the world. He wants to destroy Wonder Woman.

"Will you be needing me any further, Miss Chandler?"

She turned to face Kavanagh again. "No. Leave the tape. I will let you know what I want done in this matter."

Kavanagh frowned. "I remind you, Miss Chandler, that if the child is some kind of spy, if she is working at cross-purposes with what she claims, it could be extremely damaging."

"I am well aware of that," Rebecca said. "We will therefore limit Cassandra's access to the outside world. Have only your people near her, from now on, and cut off all her telephone privileges. She is not to have access to her mother, the press, or anyone else without my specific instruction."

"Do you wish her confined?"

"Not in any overt manner. I want her to be unaware of this change in her status, if that can be managed."

"Of course it can." Kavanagh smiled. "That's why you hired me, isn't it? To manage just this sort of thing."

As a matter of fact, I did not hire you, Rebecca thought. *That, like most things, was Ramsey's doing. You were presented to me as a done deal.* Looking at Kavanagh, Rebecca thought that she would not have hired him, had it in fact been her choice. He was not at all the kind of man she liked to have around, felt the need to have in her organization in any capacity. He was too cold, too calculating. . . . *Too much like Stephen Ramsey.*

"You may go." She waved her hand, dismissing him.

His expression indicated quite clearly that he did not like being sent from the room with such a tone and gesture, but Kavanagh departed. Rebecca waited until he was gone, the door closed behind him, before she flicked the hidden switch under her desk to lock her outer doors. She needed to be alone, to think. She had a sense, an undercurrent really, but distinct and disturbing, that she was losing control of this business.

She looked again at the fax received that morning from William Winget. Under the gothic logo of the *Gateway Guardian*, his hand-written note informed her that the plans for the large rally were proceeding apace, and everything would be ready for her when she arrived in Gateway three days hence.

Odd that I did not know I was going to be in Gateway this weekend, Rebecca thought. She exhaled heavily through widened nostrils, drawing her lips into a thin, tight line. *I will have to have words with Mr. Stephen Ramsey. It is time he understood he is not the master here, time he understood I serve only God and Jesus, and no small, secret schemes of his are going to get in the way of my performing that service!*

"Officer Schorr! What in the world do you think you're doing?"

"Leaving." Mike leaned heavily on the edge of the tall bed. No part of him did not ache, and in more than one place the ache was elevated to the level of sharp, intense pain. He gritted his teeth until he feared they would shatter, edging his way along the bed toward the door. He had disconnected himself from the monitor leads and probes—itself a most painful procedure—causing the sudden loss of signal from the monitors that had brought the duty nurse running to his room.

"Don't be insane, Officer!" She was a small woman, compact, but Mike felt the strength in her hands and arms as she moved to stop him. "You've got broken bones, internal injuries, a concussion. You could be dead in a matter of hours, even minutes, if you leave."

If I leave. Mike was beginning to believe his brave show was just that, a show. Too many of his parts did not want to behave as he wished them to. Too much hurt.

With mingled reluctance and relief, he allowed the nurse to steer him back onto the bed, waiting patiently while she summoned others to reattach the octopus of wires and tubing that linked him physically to the bed, the room, the hospital.

As he lay there, frustrated and helpless, Mike Schorr had the distinct image of himself as some tiny part of a larger organism, some small, relatively insignificant part, deep inside the greater beast. *If I were to die it would diminish this place not at all,* he thought, and in so thinking found a greater resolution. He would get out of there. Soon. He would leave the hospital, get out onto the streets of Gateway City once again, and confront head-on this monster that had taken over the hearts and minds of the people.

"There now, Officer." The small squad of nurses and orderlies stepped back, proud of their work. "You be a good boy," said the nurse who first discovered his abortive escape attempt, "and try not to overtax yourself again. Here—" she handed him the remote control for the small television set mounted on a steel arm over the door. "Watch some soaps. Get your mind off things."

They left, and Mike bounced the remote in his hand, not interested in soap operas, not interested in anything beyond his concern for Diana. They had been through so much together in the months since they first met out there on the violent night streets. At her side he had seen gods, demons, wizards and witches, aliens, resurrections, and death and destruction on a vast scale. And he had seen courage, the native courage that was Wonder Woman's heritage, her whole being, born of her Amazon background, of the warrior training that was central to her life and her existence.

"You love this girl?" he remembered his mother asking, when the two of them found a moment together, alone, after Esther first met Diana.

"Love her?" Mike remembered shaking his head, amazed, astounded at the power of the emotions he felt then and, even after all that had happened since, still felt. "How could I do anything else?"

CHAPTER TWELVE

Helena parked her car in the big lot in the shadow of Beth Israel Hospital. She hit the alarm button on her key chain and crossed toward the main lobby. The building rose like a solid glass block before her, the smooth sides reflecting the older, more elaborate forms of the buildings surrounding it. Toward the top, the glass reflected the sky and clouds, and the building seemed, in Helena's eyes, on the verge of blending into its surroundings so completely as to vanish altogether.

She crossed the lobby to the elevators and took one up to the fourteenth floor, one level below the ICU. There she slowed her pace, stepping off the elevator cautiously, butterflies fluttering in her stomach. The small tote bag she carried suddenly seemed the size of a steamer trunk, and all her movements seemed exaggerated, blown far out of proportion by the very fact that she wished them to be small and discreet, to not draw attention to herself in any way.

This is so utterly ridiculous, she thought. *I'm not some kind of secret agent, skulking about on a mission.* But she was on a mission at the hospital, and it did require a degree of stealth.

The phone had rung a second time right after the connection with Cassie broke.

"Cassandra?"

"No. It's Mike. You okay, Helena?"

"I'm all right. How are you? Or is that a foolish question?"

"I hurt all over," Mike Schorr had told her, "but mostly I'm frustrated. I keep watching the news, and I know I need to get out of here, to do something."

"That doesn't sound very wise, Mike. Even if there was something to do."

"Wisdom isn't at the top of my list of priorities right now, Helena. And that's why I'm calling. I need a favor. A big one."

Helena had paused before answering. She had known Mike Schorr only a few short months. He had been introduced to her by Diana, and while she liked and trusted him—he seemed an honest, upright fellow, and in Gateway, especially on the police force, that was something rare and special—she did not consider him one of her most intimate friends. "You need a favor from me? Why me?"

"Because I think you, of all people, will understand why I need it. Because of your own relationship with Diana."

"Yes? . . ." Still cautious, not wanting to commit herself just yet. *It's not like I don't have enough on my plate already.*

"I need you to go to my apartment for me," Mike said, lowering his voice to a stage whisper. "There are some things I need. Clothes and . . . things. I want you to go there, get them, and bring them to me here."

"Isn't your apartment locked?"

"Yes, but I've got a spare key hidden."

Helena considered. "Why do you need these things, Mike?"

And he had told her, and now Helena moved down the hall, conscious as she always was in hospitals of the smell of ether and disinfectant, of bleach and medications. A smell that made her always feel unwell, reminding her of her own times in places like this, as a child, when she seemed to be sick more often than not.

Following Mike's instructions, she walked calmly past the reception desk, a circular counter in the center of the foyer onto which the elevators opened. Three nurses were there, but as Mike predicted, they paid no attention to Helena and were not likely to provided she did not draw unnecessary attention to herself. Beyond the reception desk— Mike had described it as being "at twelve o'clock," and Helena made herself think in the same way as she walked toward it—was a hallway, and just past the hallway entrance Helena saw a green door exactly where Mike had told her it would be.

Helena tested the knob and, finding the door unlocked, stepped inside. It was a large closet, almost more a small room, and, again as Mike had predicted, down one wall hung the white smocks the doctors wore when making their rounds. Helena took one, slipping it on. It was too large for her narrow frame, but she did not think she had the time to search for one closer to her size. She went back to the door, checked to be sure the corridor was empty, and stepped out, once again carrying the satchel. She walked down the hall away from the reception foyer, following Mike's instructions to find a fire door.

"Now, this'll be the tricky part," Mike had said on the phone. "That door will have a sign on it that says 'Emergency Exit—Alarm Will Sound,' but I'm betting it won't. Funding has been so tight on the city hospitals they've been forced to cut corners, and the last time I was here on official business, I was able to go from floor to floor by the stairwell without setting off any alarms. That was almost five months ago, but I'm betting it hasn't been fixed since."

Helena stood before the door, breathing hard, waiting for someone to stop her. *It would have been so much easier to just walk into ICU and hand Mike the bag, without all this subterfuge.* But, as he had pointed out, the staff would want to check the bag for contraband—the patient in the room next to him had been busted the day before for a corned beef sandwich being smuggled in by his wife—before they let it through into the Intensive Care Unit, and when they opened it, they would find Mike's Service Model .45.

I hate guns, Helena thought, and opened the fire door. The alarm did not sound. Breathing a sigh of relief, she went up the stairs one flight to the ICU level and confronted a second door, also with a warning sign. She pushed through, and again there was silence.

Greater silence, in fact, since ICU did not share the normal hospital noises of the floor she just passed through. There were no patients walking and wheeling about here, no nurses chatting. This was, she thought, as close to a morgue as it was possible to get with the occupants still alive—albeit some barely so.

She made her way down the corridor, past narrow private wards all fronted with glass. Inside were the ragged remains of human beings who, Helena thought, might well have been leading normal, ordinary lives, quiet and content, oblivious to what the Fates held in store for them, until the awful moment when everything turned awry and they woke—if they woke—to find themselves here, their bodies if not their lives in ruins.

We walk such a fragile tightrope, she thought, *always a single step away from disaster. An automobile accident, a slip on the stairs, a stupid blunder by someone else, and we're ripped out of the pattern of our lives and thrown into something else. And sometimes we're not even aware of it until weeks have gone by, months.* She looked at some of the people as she passed. Many were old, kept alive a few long moments more by the machines that surrounded them, sucking out their blood, cleaning it, processing it, squirting it back. Dripping nutrients into them, breathing for them, living for them.

Not for me. Not ever for me.

Some were young, victims of accidents. A shape that was roughly female was swathed in bandages from head to toe, suspended in a curious cat's cradle of cables and pulleys. Another was a boy, not more than eleven or twelve, Helena thought, staring blankly into space as machines at his bedside counted his heartbeats and a slender trickle of drool drew a wavering line from the corner of his mouth to his chin. A woman sat with him—his mother?—reaching out with a towelette to wipe away the drool. *How many times can you do that in a day,* Helena thought. *How many times will you do it, before he dies?*

She thought of the story Donald Morris had to tell. She understood completely, as she walked through that horrible place, what it was that had ground the faith in God and heavenly justice out of the old priest. *I was never religious to begin with, and I think this might be at least part of the reason. I could never believe in a god—any god—that allowed this kind of senseless suffering in the world. A god that allowed pain and crippling afflictions, war, torture. All those things we do to ourselves. What's the point? What purpose is served?*

She found Mike's room and entered. He was right where she expected to find him, lying in bed amid a tangle of wires and tubes, an impatient frown creasing his forehead. He looked at her when she slipped through the door.

"Helena! Wow, thanks! I really owe you one."

"I think you owe me more than one," Helena said grimly. "I don't like handling or carrying guns, Mike." She thrust the tote bag toward him as though it contained badly soiled underwear.

Mike smiled, shuffling himself to the edge of the bed. "Hopefully I won't need it." He grinned at her. "At least, not to get out of here."

"Which is insane, I remind you."

"I know." Mike was sitting now on the edge of the bed, legs dangling, head forward and down. Even at that angle, Helena could tell his face was contorted with pain. "Every part of me knows. And the biggest problem is gonna happen the moment I unplug myself from this stuff. That'll bring them running from the nurse's station again."

"Then what are we going to do? You don't look like you can run out of here."

"No. I think the appropriate word is *hobble*." He slid off the bed, testing his footing, the leads and tubing trailing behind him like a surreal bridal train. "Help me get dressed, would you? I need to have as much clothing on as I can before I start popping these wires."

Helena blushed, hoping Mike would not notice, and pulled a pair of jockey shorts from the bag. "Lift your feet," she said, and bent to the task of dressing Mike Schorr.

•　　•　　•

Donald Morris was running out of words, running out of adjectives and superlatives to describe, even within his own thoughts, all that was happening around him.

He sat on the outer edge of a vast spherical amphitheater, easily more than a hundred miles across, he thought, yet crammed with bright, shining beings. No matter which way he looked, up, down, left, right, Morris saw gods and goddesses arrayed before him, nearby, or across the great globe, far to the other side of the floating platform on which Zeus and his fellow rulers of Olympus—Apollo, Aphrodite, Athena, Hera, others Morris couldn't name—sat and stood.

All were roughly humanoid, all had what he supposed would be considered classic Greek features, and all wore variations on the same simple toga—only their ornamentation, their jewelry, their girdles, staffs, and scepters distinguishing one costume from the next. And yet, within all those hundreds of thousands of beings, Donald Morris could find no two who were in any way alike.

I never knew there were so many gods. I knew Zeus, Apollo, Athena, Aphrodite, Hermes, all the ones of classical myth—no, not myth after all!—but this is more than I ever imagined. This is truly a race, a whole species of beings.

At the center of it all, Zeus commanded the attention of the crowd. Though Morris was, it appeared, a great distance from the King of the Gods, he found he could see every feature of Zeus's face, hear the Lord of Olympus's least whisper, as if Zeus sat at his elbow, speaking directly to him.

Morris could not explain how this was so. It was not like watching the proceedings on some huge screen, not like a baseball game. There was no projection, no enlarged image of Zeus and his attendant gods projected into the air above the center of the hippodrome. He did not even feel the need to incline his head, although every bit of reason told him that if he were seated squarely on the inner surface of a sphere—as he clearly was—anything at the center must be up from his position. It was, instead, as if every seat in the deep, broad bowl was at the center, as if all places within this structure were the same place, and it mattered not at all that Father Morris was miles from the debate. He was as deeply involved in it as he had been in his private audience with Athena.

Still trying to understand that one. Still trying to understand all of it. I'm not sure how I got here, to this seat. Diana led me, but the path was through the topsy-turvy architecture of Olympus. I don't know if I went up or down. I might have been going backward, for all I know. It seemed as though we walked for a while, and sometimes the horizon was in one place and sometimes it was in another, and then she was settling me in this seat. I don't remember coming through any sort of door. It was just that we were not in this arena, and then we were.

He listened quietly to what Zeus was saying. The King of the Gods was something of a surprise himself. He was every bit as magnificent as Morris had expected him to be, but, like Athena, he was also completely human. There was petulance in his tone when anyone interrupted him—especially Athena—and there was boredom on his face when the other gods took their turns at speaking. Morris watched, enraptured, quite oblivious to the passage of time.

And in this place, how much time has passed, I wonder? When we return to Earth, will it be a week, a month, a year? Or will we return at the precise moment we left, as if we had never been away? From what Diana had told him of Paradise Island, the point was moot. Themyscira itself was not bound by the rules of conventional chronology; as Morris understood it, the island not only touched all points on the Earth's surface, so that anyone leaving could go to whatever place they chose, but it touched also all times in history. It would be quite possible, he accepted without quite understanding, to arrive on Themyscira on, say, Tuesday of one week, and leave to arrive back in the world of Man on the previous Wednesday—or a Wednesday of another year entirely.

For some reason the god Apollo had chosen to launch into a long and rambling speech, and Morris found his attention drifting. The intent of the convocation was to discuss Rebecca Chandler and the effect her message was having on the people of America and the world. Diana was a direct representative of the gods; she had journeyed as much on their mission as on her own, and they were rightly concerned that this disturbance might seriously damage her status and credibility. What that had to do with Apollo's ramblings about green fields and simple shepherds, though, Morris could scarcely imagine.

Perhaps he just likes the sound of his own voice. He was supposed to be the most vain of the gods, as I recall. The son of Zeus and a mortal woman named Leto—he did not wish to consider the implications inherent in the parallels of this God of Light and his mortal mother with another Son of God—*he is the twin brother of Artemis, and Diana takes some of her skills from the gift of that particular goddess.*

Morris realized, with considerable surprise—*it's all surprises, these days*—that he was actually growing bored. He had expected to be riveted by every word exchanged between the gods, but as Apollo sermonized, seeming never quite to reach any sort of significant point, Morris found himself losing interest.

Astonishing, that I should be bored by the discourse of the gods! And yet, perhaps this is at the center of the whole matter—after a while, one becomes used to these gods. It's like some of the children I've worked with, burned in fires, their flesh melted and roasted from them, so they had to be patched together like tattered garments. No matter how horrible the results, no matter how hideously twisted their bodies and faces, I found—we all found—that there came a point when we were used to it, when it would not shock us any more. A self-defense mechanism of sorts, I suppose. The brain has its own ways of dealing with the world around it, and nothing smooths things out so much as familiarity. And here, even though I am continuously overwhelmed by Olympus and all I see and hear, I find I am almost used to being overwhelmed. When being overwhelmed is the constant state, being overwhelmed becomes . . . less overwhelming! Maybe that's why these gods fell from favor. Maybe that's why Jehovah chose to withdraw Himself from quite such intimate dealings with humankind, after the time of the Prophets. Perhaps He understood that, if He continued to interact with mere mortals on a regular basis, we would grow complacent, we would start to look elsewhere for our answers.

He found himself not a little amazed as his line of thinking unfolded. *It is possible, after all, that you could see one too many burning bushes, have one too many Holy Revelations.* The cynicism in his thoughts was disturbing. Donald Morris had come to Olympus— *Yes, Olympus*—seeking answers. These were not quite the ones he expected.

Apollo had stopped talking, finally, and Morris was not quite sure if the god had come to a logical conclusion, run out of steam, or been commanded to silence by his father. In any case, it was Zeus who next spoke, and Morris's senses snapped back to full attention.

"We are ever puzzled by the infinite foolishness of mortals," Zeus said. His voice boomed across the amphitheater, rolling through the inside of the vast globe like the thunder that followed the lightning bolts he hurled in divine retribution. It was a big voice, befitting the King of the Gods—but, Morris noted with a wry smile, despite the testament of a hundred Hollywood epics to the contrary, Zeus did not have an English accent. "We have walked among them in many forms, and never have we come close to understanding why they think as they do, why they act as they do. It is as if their hearts and their minds are set on different paths, and these twain only rarely converge."

"On the other hand. . . ." The voice was cold and cut through to the marrow in Morris's bones. The speaker appeared suddenly at the edge of the stage, dark, swirling, his eyes red fire, his armor burnished steel. His face was largely hidden behind his elaborate helmet, but even so Morris found it difficult to shake the feeling there was very little flesh upon it—were the new arrival to remove his helmet, Morris was sure it would be a blackened skull that peered out on the world.

"Ares!" Aphrodite was on her feet, immediately interposing herself between the black figure and Diana.

Ares! Morris gasped. *The god of war! The one the Romans called Mars. The one Diana fought.*

"On the other hand," Ares repeated, striding past Aphrodite toward the center of the stage, "I have always found humans completely comprehensible. It is simply a matter of understanding how small they are. You, my dear brethren, look for far too much in them."

The arena exploded in sound. All the gathered gods and goddesses were on their feet, straining forward, brandishing fists, swords, daggers at Ares. He looked around him at their anger and smiled, and through the narrow slit that divided his helmet's vertical face, Morris saw the god's teeth bright and sharp.

"You take chances beyond measure coming here, Ares," Zeus thundered. "We have not yet forgiven your previous transgressions."

"No, of course not." Ares chuckled, and Morris felt his blood turn to ice in his veins. "But then, you were never quick to forgive, Father."

Ares moved in a slow circle around the group, and Morris tried to remember what he knew of the relationship between these beings. The legends were confused and often contradictory, but Ares calling Zeus "father" suggested that the War God himself subscribed to the version that had him born of Zeus and Hera. *And Aphrodite loves him, Morris thought, which is why she moved to stand in his way when he arrived. I don't know if the feeling is mutual, but her concern for him is obvious.* He watched as the goddess of love and beauty followed Ares in his path around the stage. All the goddesses of Olympus were beautiful, Morris noted, and Diana seemed, with her own perfect beauty, very much a part of this place, these beings. But Aphrodite, the one the Romans called Venus, was more beautiful than anything Morris could ever have imagined or described. It was a beauty that transcended the physical—though certainly the goddess was in no way lacking in that area—to become a kind of aura, a field of energy that surrounded her, that reached out to touch all who looked upon her and bring to them, if only for a moment, a peace, a tranquillity of soul that was unlike anything Morris had ever experienced. She was, then, the precise antithesis of Ares, bringing joy and peace, a complete and utter sense of order and reason to the Universe, where he brought complete and utter fear and chaos.

"I, likewise, am slow in offering forgiveness," Ares continued, circling, spiraling in toward the place where Diana stood beside Zeus.

"But I have come here this day to offer an olive branch, and, if I may, a promise of assistance."

"Olive branch?" Ares was so close to Diana that there could be no doubt but that he was addressing her directly. "You seek to make peace with me, God of War?"

"A kind of peace." Ares' voice was deep, resonant, but Morris noticed an odd sibilance that seemed to catch some of his words, as if he were always on the verge of hissing. "Peace is not part of my nature, after all. But there is in this business something that seems to threaten the very core of our own existence, and this concerns me."

Morris could tell Diana was unmoved by Ares' words. "It would seem to me, Lord Ares, that you would rather welcome anything that reduced or weakened the power base of your Olympian brethren."

Ares shook his armored head. "How little you know me after all, Princess. I am the God of War, and it is my curse as well as my pleasure that I must always play the games of death and blood. But I am, after all, also of Olympus. This must take precedence."

Zeus scowled from his throne. "Say your piece then, Ares, and be done. We find your presence an irritant as always."

"What I propose is simple," Ares said. "This woman, Rebecca Chandler, has a centralized headquarters near the mortal city of Chicago, the Crystal Tower. I suggest I take a small legion of my more ferocious demons and obliterate that tower." He smiled again. "That should serve to convince the world Princess Diana is not lying when she speaks of our existence."

CHAPTER THIRTEEN

W HAT *I wouldn't give for the Sandals of Hermes right now! I'd fly right outta here and the heck with these bozos.*

But even as the words passed through her mind, Cassie found herself thinking, in a protective, almost sisterly way, about Rebecca. *If I left, who'd take care of her? And she needs somebody to do that. She needs to be straightened out, and nobody around here is gonna do it.*

She tried the phone again, but, as had been the case since speaking to her mother, the only sound she heard was a recorded voice. "We're sorry. Telephone systems are temporarily unavailable. We apologize for—"

Still out. Cassie frowned. Almost half a day since the line went dead while she was talking to her mother. *Way too much of a coincidence. I mean, it seems like it's just too convenient for all the phones to be out right at this time.* And they were out all over the building, at least as far as she had been able to determine. She had wandered through several floors of the Crystal Tower—no one stopped her, no one even asked where she was going, or why—and each phone she picked up had presented her with the same recorded message. *You'd think they'd be quicker than that getting stuff back online. Rebecca's folks live off all the money they pull in over the phone. How can they let the whole system stay down this long?*

With that, Cassie had another, more disturbing thought. *What if the phones aren't down? If it wasn't just coincidence the phone went dead when I was talking to Mom? It'd be so easy for them to watch me on the cameras and shut off any phone I picked up, wouldn't it? And to tell people not to use the phones when I was around, just so I wouldn't see them talking when the whole system was supposed to be down.*

She shook her head, sitting on the foot of her bed in the small suite—a far cry from the Gateway Plaza!—that had been set aside for her on the residential level of the Tower. *Is that too paranoid? Not with all these goons wandering around in their little storm trooper uniforms.*

She wondered about that, too. It seemed to have happened in the time since she had been there—yes, the security people had been in uniforms before, but not so severe, so much like something out of an old movie. And, she thought, there was suddenly something decidedly unpleasant in all these security people. More and more it seemed as though they were turning into pod people, cold, aloof, not at all the friendly—aggressively friendly, she might have said—folk who had formed the security squads before. Now they were more like automatons, marching around the Tower and the grounds, stopping and questioning people. They were far less inclined to be helpful, Cassie thought, and far more inclined to be downright mean.

She had wanted to talk to Rebecca about that, but Rebecca hadn't been around much in the last twelve hours—*Another coincidence?* Cassie had seen her only at a distance, and then moving away.

Cassie drummed her heels on the side of the bed, wishing she could call Helena, wishing she could reach Diana, wishing she could fly away.

But what about Rebecca?

Rebecca Chandler was at that moment in the middle of a most annoying and enlightening telephone call.

At the other end of the phone, William Winget, publisher of the *Gateway Guardian*, was chatting in convivial fashion about the plans he had set in motion for the huge rally to be held in Gateway Park, while on her end Rebecca was striving to maintain her composure and pretend that it was all something about which she had been fully informed.

"We're already anticipating some forty thousand people," Winget said, and Rebecca could see the beaming smile on his cherub face as clearly as if he were seated across the desk from her. "And that's just the first pass. My people are convinced we will be able to at least triple that number. Quite possibly quadruple it."

"And this simply by announcing a rally is to be held? No . . . coercion of any kind was necessary?"

"Coercion? I think, my dear Rebecca, that you do not fully understand yourself the deep core of feeling you've tapped into. I confess I was not aware of it myself, in myself and others, until you brought it to my attention. But there is a tremendous resentment of these so-called 'super heroes' by many of the common people."

Common people. Rebecca wondered just how Winget meant that phrase. *Common people as in "not super heroes"? Or common people as in "not William Winget"?*

"It has been most gratifying to see it manifest itself," Rebecca said, "though I will confess a degree of concern. The reaction is what I had hoped for, but I am not altogether sure of the purity of the motive. I don't want people turning on Wonder Woman simply because they are jealous of her powers. I want them to understand how insidious her presence is, what a threat her very existence is to the central fiber of our Christian society."

"Which I am sure they do," Winget said. "Certainly, that is the emphasis of my paper's pieces. Though, if I may, I have to wonder . . ."

"Yes?"

"Well, what would happen if it turned out that Wonder Woman was not lying? There are so many things in this world, in this Universe that are more than we once understood them to be. I wonder if there might not be gods living on the top of Mount Olympus."

Rebecca felt the blood drain from her face. "You can't be serious!"

"Well, no, not gods as in God, as in Jehovah. But vastly powerful beings that might seem to be gods. Maybe they really exist, and they are what Wonder Woman is talking about."

Rebecca struggled to keep her voice calm. "And if that were so?"

"Well, it seems as though that is something that would need to be addressed, would it not?"

"Why? Do you see this as somehow less evil? If she is telling the truth about the existence of these beings, is that any less a threat to our beliefs? To the souls of our children?" She felt the tears come hot and stinging to her eyes. She felt suddenly alone in the Universe, as she had many times in her life. Alyce's suicide, Cassie's duplicity, Ramsey's scheming behind her back. Now Winget was seeming to slip away, to seek to be "reasonable" in the face of this monstrous threat. *Outside of Ramsey himself, Winget is my most powerful ally. If I lose him, it could take weeks, even months to rebuild the power base necessary for this crusade.*

"There, there, my dear," Winget was saying. "Don't distress yourself. I am in no way altering my position. I agree fully that Wonder Woman's existence is in and of itself a slap in the face of our beloved faith. But that does not keep me from wondering what it would be like if those beings were real. If Zeus and Hera and Athena and all the rest were actual beings—flesh and blood, not divine—that one could meet."

Rebecca calmed down a little, breathing evenly. "Yes," she said, playing along for a moment with Winget's line of thought. "It would be interesting, I am sure, to be able to talk to those beings, if only because they have lived so long and seen so much of our history firsthand."

"Quite so. Quite so. But, now, in any case, I wanted to secure some of the details of your stay here in Gateway. The *Guardian* will, of course, be more than pleased to cover your expenses. . . ."

And Rebecca allowed the conversation to turn back to its original track as she discussed the rally and listened for any further clues to

Stephen Ramsey having exceeded what she considered his authority in this business.

Donald Morris clutched the edge of his seat and tried to hold on to consciousness and sanity.

The God of War just offered to attack Chicago. He just offered to take a legion of demons and launch a full-scale assault on a city in the United States!

"Preposterous!" Diana was standing directly in front of the War God, looking strangely small, Morris thought, before his gleaming armored bulk.

Inside the shadows of his helmet, Ares' eyes flickered red and yellow. "Why so, Princess? Would this not be a quick and easy solution? For once—" his teeth were bared in something Morris could not quite convince himself was a smile "—you and I are on the same side."

"Hardly that," Diana said. "We will never be in agreement on anything, so long as your first solution to a problem involves slaughter."

Ares shrugged, a surprisingly human gesture, Morris thought. "I have rarely seen a situation," the god said, "in which your approach, your pacifistic, talk-first approach has achieved anything I could not have accomplished more quickly by simply eliminating the opposing argument—and those who espouse it."

"In any case," Athena spoke from her place at Zeus's side, "we are not prepared to consider your . . . suggestion, Ares. Diana was sent into the world of men to teach the ways of peace. If she now resorts to war to solve her problem, she will undo all she has accomplished."

Ares' chuckle sent a ripple of revulsion through Morris's belly. "And what," Ares asked, "do you imagine she has accomplished? Is it five years now, as mortals measure time, since Diana left Themyscira? Five years that she has walked among the humans as 'Wonder Woman'? And do they make war any less? Do they kill themselves any less? Slaughter babes, spill blood, destroy their temples and their good works?" He took a deep breath, reminding Morris of nothing so much as a man reveling in the intoxicating effects of some sinister drug. "If they do," Ares continued, "I am unaware of it. The feast they lay at my table seems undiminished."

"Mortals have made war for all the years of their existence," Diana said. "It is for them almost in the nature of a habit. One that is hard to break."

Ares continued to smile. "It is something of their nature, I think, that mortals relish those things that are most destructive to them personally. They glorify war, make heroes and martyrs of the slaughtered, and, behold! I am made stronger." He leaned closer to Diana, and Morris felt a surge of pride that she did not shrink back before Ares. "And try as you might, Princess, you do precious little to diminish me."

Diana's smile was cold. "I do not see in this a reason to stop trying, War God."

Ares stepped back, turning with a flourish of his dark cloak. "No, you do not," he said, "and so you remain a small annoyance, Princess. A flea I must forever scratch." He looked at her, and the fire in his eyes was white hot. "I have offered my solution to the problem. Not surprisingly, it has been rejected. I now return my attention to my own business, and matters of much greater consequence to me than these small things."

And he was gone. Morris was not aware of any movement, of any measurable transition, any change other than the simple fact that Ares had been there, and then he was not. But he left the old priest with the uncomfortable feeling that more had been exchanged here, more had been said than the shape of the spoken words revealed. *He really was prepared to make war on Chicago, maybe even the whole of the United States, the whole of the world. And he is the God of War. He has the power to do it.*

Morris realized he was shaking uncontrollably, trembling from the tension in his old, tired muscles as he gripped his seat. Painfully he unclenched his fingers, released the edge of the chair. Leaning back, he closed his eyes for a moment, forcing his breathing to return to its normal rate. *How many times in the past has Ares moved his forces against Humanity? How much of the suffering of the world is directly a result of his intervention?*

He sighed. He had gone in search of Wonder Woman in the hope that she might provide him with answers to the deepest questions of his soul. In many ways she had. But Donald Morris now discovered those answers were, in the long run, themselves questions of even greater moment.

I came to doubt the God I had served all my life because I could no longer believe I saw His hand in the workings of the world, for good or bad. I could not believe a truly benevolent, loving God would allow war and pestilence and suffering. Now, here, I have seen made real before me a god who not only would allow such things, but who would encourage them, cause them, revel in them.

It was growing clearer to Morris with every passing moment that he had no real definition in his quest. *I didn't really think Wonder Woman would be my conduit to God, but I also did not think she would take me to Olympus and show me all this. I hoped she would answer some questions, let me understand what she understands, perhaps put it into the context I needed to regain my faith—or abandon it completely. Instead I have seen that there are forces in the world that shape the lives of men and women as surely as the God of the Old Testament was said to shape them. Beings who are so close to gods that it makes no difference, and who can stretch out their hands and, on nothing more than a whim, change for all time the face of the world.*

He opened his eyes, looking at the gods and goddesses on the floating platform. *And if the God I served so long truly exists, why would He allow them to do what they do? Why would He allow them to torment and deceive, to stand in constant, living contradiction of His Word, His message?*

He shook his head, and it seemed as though the motion set off a chain reaction in his body, for almost at once he was shaking all over, sobbing, feeling at that moment more empty than he had ever felt, in all the depths of his despair, all the darkest moments of his soul.

•   •   •

"I don't like this," Mayor Benjamin Garrison said to no one in particular. Minsky nodded, resisting the temptation to grip the back of the
mayor's chair. There were nine men and three women in the office
with them. Garrison sat behind his big desk, leaning back in his chair,
feet up on the blotter, his trademark cigar sticking straight up from
his mouth like the periscope of a submarine.

"The mayor is concerned," Minsky said, filling in the blanks as he
had for so many years, "that so many people seem to be turning against
Wonder Woman. You twelve are the borough chairmen. You have your
fingers on the pulses of all the people you represent. We need a defini-
tive notion, a clear view of how the people really feel."

"Would you not be prepared to take a stand that might lead the
people?" Susan Stoga shifted her huge bulk uncomfortably in the confines of the chair across the desk from Garrison.

The mayor's eyes narrowed. *God,* Minsky thought, *let him mind his
tongue. So she's the ugliest woman ever to hold elective office; I've told
him over and over that she's honest and loyal and her people trust her.
They know she's put their concerns before anyone else's—including
her own—for twenty-six years.* He coughed warningly.

"Susan," Garrison said, picking up on the message and giving it his
own spin, "as one who has built a career out of being exactly what her
people needed her to be, I should think you would understand why I
am loath to take a position that might, in the long run, prove detrimental to this city."

"Or to your reelection?" It was Marcus Greenwood's turn to speak,
leaning on the back of Susan Stoga's chair, his bony frame in sharp contrast to hers, his suit hanging as it always did, as though there was not
quite enough body inside it to keep it in shape. "Come on, Benny," he
said, "we're all walking on eggs here. We all want our jobs back, come
next election, and this is exactly the kind of thing that could bump a
whole lot of us back into the real world."

"I agree," said Al Jefferson, small, dark, always seeming to be
bristling with more energy than three men his size could comfortably
contain. "My borough is almost entirely black, as you know, Mr. Mayor,

and blacks are hesitant to point the finger at someone because of their race, or creed, or color. We've been on the receiving end of that much too often. Still, there is a strong sentiment against Wonder Woman. We're overwhelmingly God-fearing Christians in my borough. Mostly Baptist. We believe what Rebecca Chandler has to say."

"We?" Garrison puffed his cigar, causing it to look less like a periscope than the smokestack of a busy factory. "I don't recall you commanding quite enough of a plurality to be able to say you speak for everyone in your borough, Al."

"Maybe I don't," Jefferson said, "but I can still say the same thing— Wonder Woman rubs a lot of people the wrong way. She's too good to be true, and Rebecca Chandler has seen something we mostly overlooked."

"We probably should have reacted when she first turned up in Gateway," Susan Stoga said. "These super people seem to think they can move around like anyone else, picking where they want to live like it has no more consequence than an orthodontist moving into the house next door. But even without all these religious implications, there is an inherent danger in having someone like her here. I mean, look at what's been happening already, with super villains attacking her."

"That didn't seem to worry us too much," Minsky said, "when it was brought up in council. I seem to recall the main thrust of that meeting was along the lines of how soon we could erect signs declaring Gateway to be the 'Home of Wonder Woman.'"

"True enough," said Deborah Farinelli, perching on the credenza in the corner, looking small and vulnerable and not at all like the bird of prey Minsky knew her to be. "We looked at the profit margin, and we saw T-shirts and postcards and posters and videos, all playing up the fact that Gateway now had its very own super hero. Something we all thought would serve us very nicely in the matter of directing public attention away from the crappy reputation G.C. has developed in the last quarter-century or so."

"And so, what?" Minsky wanted to direct this meeting to some kind of solid conclusion, something the mayor could get behind 100 percent, and he knew if he did not shepherd them, these supremely individualistic men and women would spend the whole day bouncing their egos and intellects off one another to no avail. But he needed also to be careful. More than one person in this room suspected he, Sheldon Minsky, was the real power in this office, and they would be happy to make that an issue come the next election. Tall and handsome, Benjamin Garrison looked like the kind of man people wanted for their mayor, but Minsky knew there were very few in Gateway City who would have been happy to learn the highest city official was only marginally more than a puppet to his manager's manipulations. "The mayor called you here to offer him some kind of plan for dealing with this situation," Minsky said. "What do you have to offer?"

"Just this one, off the top of my head," Greenwood said. "I'm sure by now we've all received our invitations to this little shindig Bill Winget is throwing, this rally Rebecca Chandler is supposed to officiate at." He paused as the others nodded and otherwise indicated that they had, in fact, received the elegantly printed cards bearing the *Gateway Guardian* and Soldiers of Salvation logos side by side in gold ink. "Well, fine, then," Greenwood said. "Let's go. All of us. Not as representatives of one point or another, but as the whole city government basically going to check this thing out. If nothing else, it will look good to be seen as being even approximately in the same camp as Rebecca Chandler. She's got a lot of clout at high levels. Being her friend couldn't hurt. We don't have to speak out specifically in favor of this particular crusade of hers."

"I agree." Susan Stoga pushed herself up from her chair, a great tidal wave of moving flesh that made Minsky want to cringe back in spontaneous self-defense. "We can be a presence there without it being a statement one way or the other. In fact, we can even arrange to arrive together."

Minsky blanched. "I don't much care for having to handle the security arrangements, having all thirteen of you arriving in one place at one time. One nut with a gun—"

234 • JOHN BYRNE

"Could do as much damage in the council chambers as he could there," Garrison snapped. He rose, too, managing to make himself taller than Susan Stoga if not more imposing. "I like this. It feels good to me. Shel, set it up. We're all going to this shindig Friday night."

Word had started circulating around the Crystal Tower. Even Cassie, in her strange, detached limbo, was aware of it. *Rebecca is going back to Gateway for some big prayer meeting or something.*

Going back to Gateway.

Cassie was well aware that her plan, so far, had yielded little—in fact, nothing—for her to give Diana to use against Rebecca. She wondered now, in fact, what she really thought she could have found, anyway. Rebecca's sincerity, viewed in the brilliant clarity of hindsight, was so obvious that Cassie wondered how she could have doubted it, ever. That she could think that way at all continued to surprise her, but she was out of time to worry about such things. Her main concern was to find a way to be in the party going back to Gateway. She had given serious consideration to running away and finding her own path back home, and, forced as she had been by circumstance to think long and hard before she acted, she realized there was virtually no way she, alone, could travel across half the continent to reach Gateway. Rebecca had brought her here, and it seemed Rebecca was going to have to take her back.

Big question, how do I get her to do that? It had not escaped Cassie's attention that the cone of silence that had descended around her had coincided exactly with Rebecca suddenly having a schedule so full there was no longer any room in it for Cassandra Sandsmark. *We haven't even eaten together in two days, and I know she's still gotta be eating.*

For a long moment Cassie started playing with more paranoid scenarios. What if all this was not Rebecca's doing? What it there had been some kind of coup within the Soldiers and Rebecca was as much a prisoner in the Tower as Cassie? It seemed unlikely, but Cassie could not help but wonder. So much power was wielded in the name of the SoS, it would not be at all strange for someone to have gone after Rebecca's throne.

Like that Ramsey guy. The way Rebecca talks about him, I know he's gotta be a real mover and shaker in this thing, but I never see him. Is he just a power behind the scenes, or is he trying to take over the whole show for himself? Who is he? Why'd he pick on Rebecca? I know she's wondered about that kind of stuff herself. She's grateful for the big boost Ramsey gave her, but she's not sure of his motives.

Cassie cursed herself for having slipped. She was more certain than ever that her call to her mother—*Why did you do that? Idiot!*—had been monitored, and that it had led to her personal fall from grace. Now, at a time when Rebecca was making her boldest moves, Cassie had blundered in such a way as to ensure her removal from the center, making her useless to Diana or anyone else. *Even Rebecca.*

And Cassie could not shake the conviction that Rebecca, as much as anyone else in all this, needed her help.

Diana stood on the edge of a precipice overlooking infinity. She was on the lip of a balcony set against the side of the highest palace—if it could be said to be truly possible to measure height in the infinite horizons of the home of the gods—looking out into the endless blue ocean of sky and cloud in which the home of the gods swam. Somewhere below, behind the clouds that clustered all around the underside of the mass of temples and palaces, statues, squares, gardens, and boulevards, Diana knew there was a mass of stone, a mountain on top of which all of this could be said to rest, and she knew too that that mountain was linked, across dimensions, with the smaller, earthly mountain bearing its name, Olympus.

This was not the first time she had journeyed to this strange place, and she was sure it would not be the last. For some time, recently, the gods had absented themselves from the world, severed the connection between this Olympus and the one rising in the heart of Greece, but they had reestablished that link, and were as much as ever part of the daily workings of the lives of Men.

Would it have been better, I wonder, if they had not come back? They had their own reasons, Diana knew, for leaving behind the world they once ruled. It had taken a special mission on her part to coax them into returning, bringing back their influence. Had they not, the Amazons discovered, it would have meant a slow and most unpleasant death to all on Themyscira. They were conjured into the world by the will of the gods, and without the gods, they found themselves returning to the dead clay from which all had sprung. Diana, being shaped from the clay of Themyscira itself, had been stronger, and it had taken longer for the gods' departure to affect her, but affect her it had, and she would have died, surely, had they not come back.

And if I had died, if all the Amazons had died, and the gods had remained forever beyond the knowledge of Humankind, would that in the end have been such a bad thing?

"It is not like you to harbor such pessimistic thoughts, Daughter."

Diana turned to find Athena had joined her on the balcony. "You read my thoughts, my lady? I did not know my mind was so open to you."

"It is not. But your face and posture speak as clearly as words. What troubles you, Diana? More than this matter of the Chandler woman, or the concerns of an old priest."

Diana repeated her most recent thought aloud, and saw the bright eyes of the goddess darken.

"It is always easier to run away from a problem than to face it," Athena said. "Had we remained in our self-imposed exile, had we ignored your plea and allowed all on Themyscira to perish, yourself included, this matter would not be of concern to us on Olympus or those below on Earth. Rebecca Chandler would not have taken you as her target if you no longer existed."

Diana stiffened. "You make me feel ashamed, Goddess, when you put it into words like that. I did not think what I considered would be seen as running away."

"And in a sense it would not, since there is no action in . . . no action. And the dead can take no action. Still, Themyscira has stood above the sea for three thousand years, and it is only recently that the world beyond has come to touch her, or she to touch that world. We sent you into the world as a messenger, Diana. If part of that message has proven disquieting to some, it in no way diminishes the importance of the message as a whole."

"I was sent to teach peace, as Ares said," Diana frowned. "I have not accomplished this."

"You haven't been at it very long." There was a hesitance in Donald Morris's voice that made it clear he did not wish to intrude upon the conversation between these women—no, between this woman, and this goddess. "Jesus' message has been in the world two thousand years, and it has had precious little effect."

"Jesus, yes," Athena said. "It was His words more than any other than brought down our temples. You serve Him, do you not?"

"I did." Morris advanced cautiously onto the balcony. It made him nervous, in the midst of all the wildly skewed perspectives, to walk out onto a slippery marble surface with no wall around it. "I'm not so sure any more. That's why I sought out Diana, as you know."

Athena smiled. "Yes, I know everything." But the smile turned bittersweet. "Everything, it seems, but the solution to your problem, Donald Morris. I am . . . sorry to have failed you in this."

"You shouldn't be." *And now I'm in the business of consoling goddesses?* "If there is any sort of answer, I think I will find it only if I look inside myself. That's where my faith came from in the first place, after all. I was taught, yes, and all the knowledge I have came from outside. But the conviction that what I heard and read was real, the conviction that I have lost—that came from in here." He tapped his breastbone with the tips of the fingers of his right hand.

"That is the source of all courage and conviction," Athena said, laying a hand on the old priest's shoulder. He felt a momentary thrill, an electric tingle coursing through him as the power of the goddess flowed through her hand into his body. "We gods, in the end, serve only as a focus for the strength humans have within themselves. Without us, I imagine you would manage, somehow. It is in your nature to survive. To grow. To conquer. That is what brought you up from the slime in the beginning."

"I'm never sure if you're speaking metaphorically," Morris said, finding a smile of his own, "or of something you have seen firsthand. You speak of the whole history of Mankind, and I know that you were there for all of it, somehow. If what Diana has told me is correct."

"We are at least as old as Man," Athena nodded, "whichever version of our beginnings you choose to believe. There were greater powers before us, and perhaps we shall leave lesser powers in our wake, as they did. But if you imagine I watched as the first wriggling protozoa made their way from the oceans to the land. . . . No. I have seen much of the long march humans call evolution, but not that." She turned to Diana. "And now, if you will both excuse me, there are other matters to which I must turn my eyes."

"Of course, my lady." Diana bowed. She turned to Morris. "Well, Father Morris? You still seem greatly troubled."

"That sounded a bit like what the politicians call a *non-denial denial,*" Morris said, cocking his head in the direction of the departed Athena. "I feel as though there is so much she can tell me, but for her own reasons, she won't."

"For her own reasons and yours." Diana moved to stand close by the priest. The absolute perfection of her beauty struck him to the heart. Not enough that she was tall and lithe, with a figure most women would die for, a face any man would sell his soul for, but there was also a beauty beyond the physical, a beauty in her eyes, her voice, in the energy, the power that radiated so easily, so calmly from the center of her being. *Does she have a soul? If there are such things as souls, did the gods manage, somehow, to give her one when they called her to life from the clay her mother sculpted? If she does, if there is some essence beyond the physical, it, too, must be beautiful beyond measure. She is everything a woman should be—everything a* human being *should be. And if these gods created her, what better proof is there of their divinity?*

"Athena could probably open your eyes wide to the knowledge of all the Universe, Father Morris. But if she did, do you think your mortal mind could contain it, comprehend it?" She saw a flicker in his eyes and smiled. "I do not mean to belittle you. There is no mortal mind that could encompass all that Athena knows and understands. It is this, as much as anything, that makes her a goddess."

Morris nodded. "I suppose so. But . . ."

"Yes?"

"There was a question, something that passed through my mind just now. Do you consider yourself to have a soul, Wonder Woman? I mean, as humans understand the term?"

Diana frowned slightly, thinking. "I have told you that I was sculpted from clay by my mother, Hippolyta," she said, "and that the gods, sensing her need for a child, brought that clay to life. But there is more. You have noticed, I am sure, that Paradise Island is populated by women of many races. All the races of Earth, in fact."

"Yes. I was surprised by that. I expected them—you—all to be Greek."

Diana nodded. "All the Amazons of Themyscira, my mother included, are creations of the gods, brought forth from clay, as vessels for the souls of women who, down through the ages, suffered death before their proper time. Some died at the hands of men, others in ways no less tragic for being accidental or even unavoidable. Still, each and every one died before she had completed that which she was set upon earth to do, and all their souls went on in frustration, knowing they were not finished. The gods, when they found a need for such spirits, created Themyscira and placed all those wandering souls into suitable bodies. They could not go back to their broken lives, to complete whatever it was that had left them frustrated, but they could be given a new purpose, perhaps a greater purpose."

"I don't understand. Are you saying you were one of these frustrated souls? Why weren't you put into an Amazon form at the same time as the rest?" *I can't believe I'm asking this, that we're discussing these things so casually.*

"No, I was not a frustrated soul—not in that sense, at least. But when the body in which my mother's soul formerly reposed was slain, that form was with child. It was because of this, because she had been pregnant when she died, that Hippolyta felt such need for a child. My spirit, though the gods had not detected it at first, was interwoven with my mother's. When her longing brought her to the point of crafting an icon from the clay of the lake bed, the gods at last understood and used their skill and power to separate my soul from that of my mother and infuse it into the clay to which they gave life."

"Astonishing! But . . . but, Diana, if your soul existed before the intervention of the gods, if you were conceived in the normal way, and your mother—even in some prior incarnation—carried you as a mother carries her child. . . ." Donald Morris paused, waving his hands helplessly before him.

"You seem to be having difficulty saying what you need to say, Father Morris." Her voice was gentle. "Do not be afraid. Say whatever it is that is on your mind."

"Well, it's just that . . . Diana, don't you see? I'd assumed, as I suppose everyone did, that when the gods made the clay baby come to life, they gave it whatever constituted a soul at that time. Something they created. But now you tell me that your soul was something that came into existence in—well, I hesitate to call it the 'conventional' way. But—but your mother in some prior incarnation was pregnant, and that baby had a soul, and that soul survived along with your mother's soul, to become you."

"Yes."

"And the gods had nothing to do with the creation of that soul?"

"No. The soul, the spirit as I would prefer to call it, is something immortal, eternal. The precise moment at which it is called into being is less important than what happens from that moment onward."

"To you, perhaps," Morris said, and he felt his old heart pounding again. "But to me, this is the core of my dilemma. My faith teaches that all souls come from God, that He creates them, that He shapes them and sends them to Earth. And if you have a soul, an eternal soul, something that clearly survives death, and yet the gods of Olympus had nothing to do with creating it. . . ." He reached out a hand to her, seeking physical support as the power of his realization began to overwhelm him. "Diana, don't you see? That, as much as anything else, is the proof I needed. The proof that my faith is valid and my God truly exists!"

CHAPTER FOURTEEN

C ASSIE had most of the details of her plan worked out when Rebecca walked in, her small, slim form bracketed by a matching pair of brick walls in SoS uniforms.

"I have decided to take you with me to Gateway," Rebecca said. She looked pale and drawn, dark circles under her eyes. Cassie wondered what new troubles had appeared in Rebecca's life.

"Why?" Cassie asked, not quite believing her luck. She had been fairly sure she had worked out how to get out of the Tower and find the limo Rebecca would almost certainly take to O'Hare. She had been a little less sure that she would be able to hide herself in the trunk, and truth to tell, getting from that trunk to the *Bird of Pray* was, at best, a series of ifs, buts, and lucky breaks that Cassandra was not entirely certain she could depend on. Not knowing the layout of the airport, for instance, had forced her to make up some rather important bits, filling in large areas with conjecture. Now, it seemed, that would not be a problem after all.

"I want people to see the viper Wonder Woman sent into my bosom," Rebecca said, sounding more tired even than she looked, Cassie thought.

"Diana didn't send me," Cassie said. She debated telling Rebecca of the mystery man, but, since she still knew nothing at all about him, elected to leave him out of the story for now. "It was my idea. I wanted to spy on you, to find out your weaknesses, stuff Diana could use against you."

"My weaknesses. Such as gullibility and compassion? And what have you discovered, Cassandra? What did you think you were going to be able to give Wonder Woman to use against me?"

Cassie chewed her lower lip for a moment. *How much do I want to say, now? How much do I want to tell her?* "I didn't really get much of anything at all, Rebecca."

"You sound disappointed."

"A little. But mostly I was surprised."

"Surprised?"

"Surprised to see you're not, y'know, an ogre." Cassie felt the tears welling in her eyes. She wanted to run to Rebecca and throw her arms around her, apologize and beg forgiveness. *But that's not what Wonder Girl would do. Be strong, Cassie. Be strong.* "I was surprised to find out you really believe the stuff you say."

Rebecca registered a moment of visible shock. "Of course I do! Why wouldn't I?"

"Well, if you didn't, you wouldn't be the first TV preacher who said one thing in public and did something else in secret. But you really are sincere, Rebecca. You're wrong, but you really mean it. And that's been the hardest thing for me to deal with, I guess."

Rebecca found herself trembling, wanting as Cassie did to reach out to the young girl, to forgive and forget. She had found in Cassandra Sandsmark a strength, a cocky certainty that Rebecca envied, that she wished time and time again she could find in herself. *I never doubt my purpose until that instant before I have to step on stage. Then I am like Jesus at Gethsemane, suddenly confronted with the larger inevitability of His mission, and wondering all at once what He can really do, what He can really accomplish. If I had half the sheer, blind guts this little girl has, I could have done ten times as much in the last two years.*

"I'm pleased to hear you have learned at least a partial truth, Cassandra." Rebecca tried to keep the emotion out of her voice and was largely successful. "I only wish you could see the rest of the truth—the truth about Wonder Woman."

"Diana isn't here to hurt anyone, Rebecca. Heck, if you were in danger, she'd move just as fast to help you as she would anyone else. That's the kind of person she is."

"I doubt that very much," Rebecca said. "And, if everything goes as I expect it to at the Gateway Park rally tonight, I think you will see for yourself, finally, that this is the case."

"I doubt that very much," Cassie said, deliberately mimicking Rebecca's words.

They stepped out of the dim confines of the little temple into the bright afternoon of Paradise Island.

"How long were we on Olympus?" There was no means by which Donald Morris could measure the passage of time while they walked among the gods. They had left Themyscira at just about the same time of day, by the position of the sun in the cloudless sky, but as far as he was able to tell, that could have been weeks, months, even years ago.

"Here on Themyscira some two days have elapsed," Diana said. "It is, unfortunately, impossible to regulate the time one spends on Olympus. The gods do not heed the rule of Chronos as we do on Earth."

"Two days," Morris said, amazed.

"Two days in which there will certainly have been developments in America and the rest of the world," Diana said. "Come, let us return to my aircraft. The journey back to the United States will be shorter by far than the trip here."

"Why is that, again?" Morris followed Diana down the slope toward the place he could see the transparent plane catching the light of the high sun. Diana moved nimbly but slowly, aware that he was not so light or easy on his feet as she was.

"Themyscira touches all parts of the world. To come here requires the following of a specific path. To leave requires only the desire to go from one place to another. The first time Mike Schorr came here, when it was time for us to return to Gateway City, we merely waded ashore, walking from Themyscira to the waterfront of Gateway. The island, for a moment, manifested in Gateway Bay."

"But . . . surely Themyscira is bigger than the bay?"

Diana turned, smiling. "Hardly a problem, all things considered."

Morris reddened. "Er . . . yes. I see what you mean. I'm afraid I have not entirely wrapped my brain around all this magic."

As they approached the landing site, Morris saw the dark-skinned Phillipus waiting.

"Princess," Phillipus inclined her head in a sketch of a bow. "I hoped I would be able to intercept you when the sentries reported your return through the Portal."

"You have word for me, Phillipus?"

"As you requested, we have been monitoring the outside world in the time you were with the gods. I fear the juggernaut you told us of has gained in speed and power."

"Explain, please."

Phillipus lowered her voice as if, Morris thought, the brave soldier were afraid of the words she had to speak. "There is greater violence and rebellion among the people of America. More and more turn against you. In all the larger cities there have been great riots. Thousands have been injured. Many have been killed."

Diana stiffened. "Dying in my name. Or against it. This is most ill, Phillipus."

"There is more. The Soldiers of Salvation have in many places taken on the literal trappings of an army. In several smaller habitations they have actually supplanted the local police authorities. Government officials are hesitant to act against them, but it seems there is a definite militaristic movement gaining popularity and momentum."

Morris was amazed. "I don't believe it! Why would people become so deranged as to join these crackpot militias just to show they disapprove of Diana?"

Phillipus turned her dark gaze toward the old priest. "That is the most troubling element of all, Father." Morris had noticed, even in the short time he had been in contact with her, that Phillipus, of all the Amazons he had met, had the least trouble with his title standing on its own. He suspected it was her own rank that led her to accept the signals of rank in others, and not question their deeper meaning. "We have detected something more than a simple groundswell of sentiment in the people."

"Something more?" Diana was instantly alert, sensing danger, sensing, perhaps, something she could address more directly than a disgruntled mob.

Phillipus nodded. "There is a force working in the ether, Princess," she said. "We have not been able to pinpoint or define it, but I am sure there is something, some energy, some spirit of evil driving the people to act as they do."

"Of course." Diana seemed, Morris thought, actually relieved. "It only makes sense that something is manipulating the emotions of the people on a level beyond mere propaganda. You cannot isolate the force, though?"

"No. But it is there, and it is real." Phillipus looked again at Morris, turning back to Diana. "If we might speak for a moment in private, Princess?"

"Of course. You will excuse me, Father Morris?"

"Certainly." He watched as Diana and Phillipus walked to the far edge of the field, standing where the broken marble sheet dropped off suddenly to the pounding surf, a hundred feet below.

All this was once temples and palaces, he thought, looking up at the rising face of the island, grass and trees mostly, with only the occasional marble structure still standing. *But according to Diana, this evil god, this "Darkseid" came here with his legions and attacked, looking for a way to reach Olympus and steal the power of the Greek gods. He was repulsed in that assault by the sheer courage of the Amazons, but nearly half of them were killed—freed at last of the unfinished business that bound them here, as Diana put it. Now the task of rebuilding Paradise Island is barely a quarter done, and it will be as much as a century before the island is fully restored to its ancient glory.* He breathed deeply of the cool, clean air, watching gulls wheel in the sky above, seeing how the sunlight gleamed on the standing marble. *Not that it is not glorious enough as it is!*

"Father Morris, are you ready?" Diana had returned while he had been lost in thought.

"More ready than I have been in a long time, Princess," Morris said. He accepted her extended hand and let her help him up onto the elusive wing of the phantom plane. "And I'm ready to stand by your side, ready to fight whatever this is with you."

"Good," Diana smiled, slipping into the pilot's seat behind Morris. "I have a feeling about this, call it intuition, if you will. I have a strong suspicion that I know the origin of this force Phillipus describes. And if I am right, I fear America and perhaps the whole world are in for a taxing such as people have not seen in a thousand generations."

Morris sensed there was no point in asking, just now, what Diana meant. He settled back into the gently welcoming seat and watched the lush green hills of Themyscira drop away beneath them. As the plane rose, Phillipus turned and moved quickly toward the edge of the landing field, to a place where, Morris now saw, a dozen or more Amazons stood waiting, their tall, hard bodies sheathed in armor that burned like gold flames in the sun.

"They look as if they are preparing for war," Morris said.

Diana's words sent a chill racing through every cell of Donald Morris's body.

"They are."

"You can't be serious! Getting out of the hospital almost killed you. What do you think you can accomplish at the rally?"

Mike Schorr was leaning heavily on the counter in the small kitchen of Helena Sandsmark's apartment. He knew all too well that Helena's words were true, but he knew, too, that he had to do something. And the rally tonight, in Gateway Park, seemed like the best place for him to discover what that "something" was.

"No one has seen hide nor hair of Diana in almost two days," he said. "The TV goons are starting to say she's run away. I don't believe that, and neither do you. But if something has called her away, someone has to be at that rally to make sure her side of the argument gets proper representation."

"You?"

"Me. You, if you want to come. Anyone else you can think of." He smiled, a small, tight thing without humor. "I don't suppose Diana ever mentioned what Superman's phone number is?"

Helena returned the smile weakly. "No. And if the reports we've been seeing on the TV are accurate, I think Superman will be busy in Metropolis, anyway."

Mike nodded. "It's insane. All this violence. It's like the movement against Diana has given everyone an excuse to let all their stupid prejudices come boiling out. That riot in Metropolis was only the tip of the iceberg."

"Yes. And it's more than that." Helena frowned, rubbing her hands up and down on her arms. "I mean, you feel it too, don't you? I feel like I'm constantly annoyed at the whole world. And every time I see someone who's a different race, or looks like they belong to a different religion. . . ."

Mike nodded again. "I thought it was maybe just me being ticked off at everybody for being such schmucks about Diana, but, yeah, you're right. There's something. Like itching powder all over everything."

Helena took a deep, shuddering breath. "What do you suppose it can be? I thought this whole business was just Rebecca Chandler and her crackpot ideas about Diana, but I'm more and more convinced there's something else to it. Something . . . darker. Oh, god, that sounds so ridiculously melodramatic."

"Melodrama is just day-to-day life for people like Diana," Mike said. "What worries me is what will happen if a hundred thousand people, all feeling this way, get together in Gateway Park. Superman could barely contain the riot in Metropolis, and that was only a few thousand people."

"Well, he was concerned not to hurt anyone, I suppose."

"Maybe. But if something gets going tonight, I don't think anyone is gonna be too concerned about the niceties. And it seems like there's no way something can't get started. Just in the time since I busted out of the hospital we've seen the volume turned up. The whole city feels like it's ready to explode."

"I know. I—Do you hear something?"

Mike hobbled to the nearest window. Above, the sky was deepening toward twilight. The long rays of the sun painted the sides of the houses black, the faces all the shades of orange Mike could imagine, and more. Below, on the procession of hills that marched down from the house to the shore, lights were coming on in the tall towers of Gateway City. The architectural jumble that made the city look so startling, so jarring in the daylight, softened into the night, leaving only the lighted windows to define the shapes of the buildings.

"Sounds like wind across glass or something," Mike said. He craned his neck, searching. "Is it? . . . It is!"

The transparent aircraft circled once more around the block, high above the steepled rooftops, then drew itself to a halt in midair before dropping straight down onto the empty street. In an instant it had disgorged its passengers and folded itself back into a palm-sized, nearly weightless ovoid.

"Diana!"

She raised a hand, waving in response to Mike's call. She and Morris hurried quickly from the middle of the street to the steep steps up to Helena's front door. Helena had already rushed to open it. "What took you so long? We were so worried!"

"On Paradise Island and Olympus," Morris said, hearing himself form the words, and wondering even as he said them if he was about to wake from an overlong dream.

"Did you find what you needed, Father Morris?" Helena stepped back to let the two of them enter her front hall. Morris was amazed by how small it seemed, how close and claustrophobic the normal-sized dwelling had become after he walked in halls that were truly Olympian in proportion.

"I did," he said, "though not at all in the way I expected. I still need to think about it a great deal, but I have a direction at least. A goal."

"What of events here, Helena?" Diana asked. They stepped through the short hall into the living room, where Mike Schorr was waiting for them. "I have been . . . Mike!" Diana crossed the room in a single step. "Mike, what happened to you?"

"I was playing cop when I guess I shouldn't have been," Mike said. "And be careful, would you? I hurt all over."

Diana released her grip on his shoulders. "Shouldn't you be in a hospital?"

"He was," Helena said, and Morris could hear the irony in her tone. "I helped him escape. It was all very *Mission: Impossible.*" She laughed shortly. "I felt a damned fool."

"Well, they would have kept me in there while all this was going on," Mike scowled, "and I'd have been even more useless than I am already."

"We know there's been trouble," Morris said. "How bad has it gotten?"

"As bad as it can, I hope," Helena said. In a few terse sentences she confirmed what Phillipus had told them on Paradise Island.

Morris crossed himself, something he had not done in a long time. "The fools. If there was only some way I could talk to them, tell them what I've learned."

"I'm planning on crashing that little party in the park tonight, Father," Mike said. "You're welcome to tag along."

"Party in the park?"

Mike detailed what was planned for that evening at Gateway Park. "Crowd control is gonna be next to impossible on a scale like that," he said. "I know. I've worked the park when they've had rock concerts.

The crowd might be a little less boisterous than that, but I doubt it. Not after Metropolis."

Morris shook his head. "I must get there, then. Especially if Rebecca Chandler herself is going to be there. If I can talk to her, perhaps she will follow the logic I have seen, and understand that Diana is proof of God's existence, not a denial of it."

"I doubt that Miss Chandler will be in the mood for listening to much," Helena said. "She's made up her mind. People like that—" She caught herself. "My goodness, how amazingly intolerant of me! I don't like Rebecca Chandler, but the thoughts I was thinking just then. . . ."

Mike nodded. "Yeah, we've been noticing that too. Do you feel it at all, Diana? Kind of an itch, something just at the edge of the brain, rubbing you the wrong way."

Diana concentrated for a moment. "No, I feel no such thing. But I am not made as humans are made. If there is an effect of some kind— as we believe there is—it might not affect me in the same way."

"What are you going to do, Diana?" Morris was formulating his own plans, but he wondered what the Amazon Princess was considering as a logical, acceptable course of action.

"First," Diana said, "I am going to seek out Rebecca Chandler one more time. If she is to be speaking at this rally tonight, the likelihood is that she is already in Gateway City,"

"She is," Mike said. "Her arrival was on the news. Her motorcade went directly from GCX to the Plaza."

Diana's chin rose, firm and defiant. "Very well, then. I shall go there and confront her. But not as Diana of Themyscira.

"This time, I shall face her as Wonder Woman."

From her balcony atop the most splendid of Gateway City's many splendid hotels, Rebecca Chandler looked down on the bustling streets, the hurrying cars, the sound and fury of a city at rush hour.

Tonight. It all comes together tonight. I can feel it. Two years of work, two years of ministry, and tonight will be make or break. Make, I think. Tonight is the turning point, and from here a new age of spiritualism and devotion begins in this country. And where America goes, so goes the rest of the world.

She hugged herself against the deepening chill of the night air. Overhead the sky was deep blue, and there were still hours before the stars appeared in the late summer night. By then, she knew, the rally in Gateway Park would be well under way. If previous such meetings—smaller, but with similar intent—were anything to judge by, she should have brought the people to a fever pitch, a high, rolling boil of deeply religious fervor. The same fervor she felt, all the time, burning in her own veins.

"Tonight," she said quietly to the sky. "It all happens tonight."

"Yes, it does."

Rebecca spun. Stephen Ramsey was sitting on the broad stone rail surrounding the balcony. Turning, Rebecca saw that the tall French doors, closed behind her when she stepped out onto the balcony, were still closed. Inside the big living room beyond, she saw half a dozen of her people milling about, pointedly ignoring her in her moment of solitude, and certainly showing no signs of having allowed Ramsey to pass through them to reach the doors.

"How did you get out here?" Rebecca demanded. She felt a flash of anger that bordered on hatred. She had been aware for several days that her emotions had been running at a high pitch, and mostly negative. She had expected this to pass once she reached Gateway and set herself into the pattern of preparation for the night's affair, but it had not. If anything, it had gotten worse.

"I go where I need to go, *when* I want to go," Ramsey said. His smile was particularly annoying tonight, Rebecca found. He rose and crossed the balcony to stand a few paces from Rebecca's side. He looked out over the city, and his cruelly handsome face—Rebecca had not previously noticed just how cruel it was—was lit by the city lights in a manner that made it look nearly satanic.

"No," he said, as if sensing her thought, "I am not Satan, Rebecca. I have been compared to him, and some of my deeds have shaped his stories, but I am not him. I am . . . someone else." His eyes twinkled.

"Enough of your damn games, Ramsey," Rebecca snapped. She was surprised to hear herself curse, surprised, too, that no one had come from inside the suite to see why she was shouting. She realized with a sudden horror that all was still and silent about her. The city, the moment, was frozen. Rebecca was alone at the center of a sliver of time and space cut off from all the rest of the Universe. Her knees weakened, and she put out a hand to the wall to steady herself. "What? . . . Who? . . ."

Ramsey continued to look out across the city. "I gave you a hint when I told you my name, Rebecca. 'Ramsey.' I was so very amused. A play on words, and very nearly an anagram. Ramsey, for the Ram, you see."

He turned and looked into her eyes, and there was white fire around the black infinity of his pupils. "You have served me very well, Rebecca, as a nearly free agent." He stepped closer and Rebecca felt heat and heard screams as if from a vast distance.

"Now," Ramsey smiled, "it is time for me to take a more direct hand."

Diana felt it at once. The tone of the city changed, the shape of reality was bent aside.

She dropped from the sky high over the peak of the Gateway Plaza hotel, and it felt suddenly for all the world as though she were dropping into something thick and clinging, something that wrapped itself around her, impeding her descent, making all the world grow slow and distant.

Someone is affecting the flow of Time, she thought, forcing herself to drop, to continue the sluggish descent. *If I were human I might not even feel it. This is something that would change human perceptions to match what is happening. If a second was an hour, a day, it would still seem only a second.*

She felt a momentary flash of primal fear, deep within her. She had begun to suspect, as she had told Donald Morris, the precise nature and identity of the force behind all this. Once the deduction was made, the answer seemed so clear that she felt like a fool for not having seen it earlier, but that made it no less difficult to face.

Ares, she thought. *It must be Ares. His appearance at Zeus's council was all playacting and subterfuge. He loves the games, the lies and deceptions of warfare. And this has his seal upon it, all of it. It is exactly something he would conceive, if he thought it might be a way to destroy me. That thousands might perish in the process would be only a small bonus, to him. Icing on the cake.*

The balcony of the topmost suite of the Plaza rose toward Wonder Woman as though drifting up from some great ocean depth. Perspectives and the movement of light were skewed by the time-warping effect, but Diana could see the shape of the balcony picked out by the warm illumination spilling through the French doors, and she could see, too, the man and woman who stood facing one another on the balcony. The woman was Rebecca Chandler, of course.

The man, in Diana's eyes, was not a man at all.

"Ares!" The single word seemed to drag on for hours, tumbling from her mouth as thick clay might ooze from a fissure in the Earth's crust.

Ares turned, looking toward the sky. Diana could sense, without seeing it, that he had some manner of projected image around him. Whatever Rebecca Chandler saw, it was not the blue-black cloak and armor of the God of War.

"Princess." He smiled behind his faceplate, the full-toothed grin of a fleshless skull. His eyes burned in the shadows of his helmet, and Diana sensed in him greater power than he had possessed in many a year.

He feeds on the hatred and violence, she thought. *Every hand raised in anger, every voice hurling bile, adds to his strength.*

Rebecca did not react to Wonder Woman's arrival, her slow descent to the balcony, and Diana understood at once that Ares was not allowing the human woman to see what was transpiring between himself and the Amazon.

"Stand away from the woman, Ares," Diana said. She had to force each word from her mouth as though it were a physical object closing her throat, seeking to choke her.

Ares complied, moving a few paces back from Rebecca. "Of course. But surely you do not mean to confront me, Princess? You do not mean to battle me, here, now?"

"Why not?" Diana could think of many reasons, but she wondered if, should he choose to answer her, the War God might expose some weakness she could then exploit. "You are revealed, Ares. Your plan is laid bare for all to see."

"All?" Ares laughed. "You and a handful of mortals I could sweep from existence with no more effort than a man brushing dust from his sleeve. Less effort, in fact. No, Diana, I am not revealed, and if you attack me now, here, all that will be seen, when I let it be seen, is you attacking Rebecca Chandler, revealing yourself to be the monster she claims."

Diana tested her muscles, moving subtly against the restricting forces of Ares' time distortions. "You cannot maintain this effect for long, Ares," she said. "You are warping time across the whole world, the whole of space itself. Easy enough for you, if there is only one person on whom you need to focus the effect, and she without the power to resist it." She took a sudden step forward, nearly as fast as she might have if uninhibited. Ares stepped back in surprise.

"You see?" Diana allowed herself a small chuckle, seeing immediately that it had the desired effect, annoying the god. "You have taxed yourself too much, Ares. Now, release me, and the woman, and the rest of what you control."

"Not yet," Ares said, and the smile returned to his face. "We shall have a confrontation tonight, to be sure, my dear Princess. But it will be on my terms, and at the place of my choosing." He laughed, a slow and subtle thing. "And when that time comes, when that confrontation is set loose upon the world, there shall be violence and bloodshed such as you have never seen. And there is nothing, dear Diana, nothing whatsoever that you can do to alter it in any way."

For Rebecca Chandler the moment was one of sudden, jarring transformation.

One moment she stood facing Stephen Ramsey—a Stephen Ramsey she now saw revealed as something much more than anything she could ever have guessed—and in the next moment, he was gone and Wonder Woman stood before her.

"What in the name of ? . . ."

Diana turned, realizing instantly that the time distortion effect was gone, and Rebecca was free. "Do not be afraid," Diana said. She extended her hand in what she hoped was a comforting gesture, but Rebecca shrank back as if Diana were brandishing a burning torch.

"Security!" Rebecca's voice was shrill with fear, and Diana could only begin to guess how utterly disorienting the moment must have been for her.

Three uniformed security guards burst through the French doors in response to Rebecca's cry. They had machine pistols ready, and as Wonder Woman took a cautious step backward they wheeled to train them on her.

"Don't move," their leader barked. He was tall and black, and against his dark skin the pale gray of the SoS uniform seemed bleached almost to white. His eyes were shadowed by the brim of his cap, but there was no need to see his expression to understand the intensity of his mood.

"Weapons are not necessary," Diana said, but even as she spoke, she was measuring distances, trajectories. If they opened fire, she had no doubt she could deflect the bullets with her bracelets, but she was worried about the limited angles to which she could direct them without risk to human life.

"We'll be the judge of that, lady," the leader said. He gestured, and his companions fanned out, spreading across Diana's field of vision and increasing the difficulty of safely deflecting their fire. "Put your hands behind your head and lace your fingers. Do it."

Diana did not move. "You understand that I could fly away before you could even take aim, do you not? Is my continued presence here not sufficient proof that I come in peace?"

"It's sufficient proof," Rebecca said, finding, after a struggle, control of her voice, "that you are not so sure as you pretend that you can out-fly machine gun fire."

Wonder Woman sighed. "I have come to make an offering, Miss Chandler," she said, choosing her words carefully. "There is no need for us to be enemies. I have recently returned from Paradise Island and Olympus, where I transported a mortal priest who was willing to accept the offer you declined."

"A priest?"

"His name is Father Donald Morris. He came to me in the midst of a crisis of faith, and he has found the answer he sought. If you will permit it, I will arrange for you to speak to him, so that—"

"He found the answer you *wanted* him to find, you mean," Rebecca snapped. "Just as I would have found those same answers! I don't know what kind of brainwashing you perpetrated on that poor, confused man, but I will tell you now you have only added to my arsenal against you."

"You do not understand." Diana found herself losing patience, beginning to worry that there might not be any way to find a reasonable path through the spider's web Ares had woven around Rebecca and the rest of Humankind. "The man who was just here, you understand who and what he is, do you not?"

"What man? What are you talking about? I was alone out here until you arrived." The words did not sound entirely true, even as Rebecca spoke them, but she felt compelled to do so, and the more she said, the more she was convinced of what she said. "Ask any of my people. There is no way anyone could have come through that room, to this balcony, without being seen."

Diana shook her head. "That is what he has done to you, Rebecca.

Please try to understand. All this—" She waved a hand, a gesture to encompass all Rebecca Chandler's works, but it struck instant fear in the security guards. Two opened fire even as the third turned to run.

Wonder Woman moved with all the speed granted her by Hermes. Her bracelets flashed, bright sparks flowering where the bullets struck. She bounced the bullets back, angling them to strike the stone walls above and around the balcony doors. She could as easily have ducked, or flown up out of the path, but she did not dare let the bullets go past her, into the night air. Falling from this height they could do as much damage as if fired directly at their eventual targets.

"Stop!" Rebecca screamed her command, and the firing stopped. She stood, ashen faced, breathing hard. "Idiots. She could have deflected those bullets right back at us!"

"But I did not," Diana said. "I do not desire your death, Rebecca, nor the death of any of your people. I am here to preserve, not to destroy. It is the one who has you under his thrall who is the destroyer."

"What are you talking about?" Rebecca was aware of repeating herself, and aware too that Diana's words were evoking emotions much stronger than she would have expected. She was angry, yes, but as Wonder Woman spoke Rebecca found herself more and more convinced that, given the chance, she could take one of the machine pistols from her guards and, barring the ability to actually shoot Wonder Woman, cheerfully bludgeon her to death.

"The being who was out here, the being I am certain you saw as a mortal man, and whom you no longer seem to remember, was not a man at all. He was the god Ares, called Mars by some. Ares, whose symbol is the Ram."

Ram. The word echoed for a moment in Rebecca's mind. *"A play on words,"* she heard someone say, *"and very nearly an anagram. Ramsey, for the Ram, you see."*

"And 'Ramsey' is almost an anagram of Ares. . . ." Her voice was barely more than a whisper, but the closest of her guards turned.

"Miss Chandler?"

"Nothing." Rebecca stiffened. "I've had enough of this game, Wonder Woman. If you have anything to say to me, you can come to Gateway Park tonight. You can say it in front of a hundred thousand people who will not be taken in by your lies."

At the first sound of gunfire, Cassie bounded from her bed and raced to the nearest window. She pressed her face to the glass, but her room did not command a clear view of the balcony. She could see only shadows and hear nothing but muted voices, distorted by the wind and the shape of the building. The window was locked tight, and she decided against smashing the glass and crawling out on the ledge. That would be too adventurous even for her—and, she thought, too much of a cliché.

What the heck is going on out there? She turned from the window and rushed to the door, but it was locked, as it had been since they'd put her into this stupid cell.

Well, not a cell. Hardly a cell. It was a room very much like the one she had had in this hotel only a few days before. This suite was much larger, provided by Winget of the *Guardian,* but the decor was the same ersatz luxury, enough to leave Cassie impressed despite herself.

She rattled the knob on her door, on the off chance someone might decide to let her out, to see what was happening, but when no one responded she returned to the window. She could still see nothing. *I gotta find out what's happening. Who's out there? And why are they shooting?*

One answer was immediately obvious, of course. Only someone who could fly could approach the balcony from outside, unless it was a particularly determined cat burglar. But Cassie was reasonably sure Rebecca's security people would not open fire—not so much fire anyway—on a mere mortal. Which left very few options.

It's gotta be Diana! The realization sang in Cassie's heart. *But if it is, how do I let her know I'm here?* She thought again about crawling out on the ledge, but that would require smashing through the window, and that would take throwing a chair. Which, she decided, should be enough to get Diana's attention—*It has to be Diana!*—without risking life and limb as well.

She ran across the room to the desk against the far wall, pulling back the big, ornate chair. It was heavier than she expected, and she had no small difficulty lifting it. She managed, however, to get it within striking distance, positioned herself right under it to put the full thrust of her body behind the throw, and hurled the bulky piece of furniture against the wide, unprotected pane of the window.

The chair bounced back from the armored glass with a resounding *thung*.

Forgetting for a moment that she had slipped off her shoes before lying down on the bed, Cassie kicked the fallen chair and yelped in pain and frustration.

CHAPTER FIFTEEN

I N all the books and travel guides he checked before beginning his journey to Gateway City, Donald Morris had found Gateway Park listed as one of the premiere places to see on a visit to the fabled City in the Bay.

Lying at the city end of the Gateway Bridge, it was almost a thousand acres of green meadow and carefully tended trees and shrubs. The park, he recalled reading, had been a gift to the city from an eccentric billionaire, a woman named Nedra Alfreds, who fancied herself a botanist and who, in the vast array of greenhouses behind her mansion, had grown the original plants from which most of this park had been seeded. The park itself had been her private property, and though it was willed to the city—with the instructions that her house be torn down and replaced by a monument to her late father—it was maintained to this day with the interest from the huge allotment left to provide for the care of her dream project.

She never saw the park, of course, since she lived in the old mansion until the day she died, but upon her death her wishes were executed to the letter, and the people of Gateway City received the lasting gift of this most beautiful of parks.

Morris sniffed derisively as he walked with Helena and Mike in the midst of the throng flocking to the park. He knew, from his reading, that the city fathers since Nedra Alfreds's day had spent all manner of time and money trying to break the conditions of her will, so that they could get at the park funds directly, for their own purposes. In 125 years they had been unable to do so, and even the great bridge had to be located fifteen hundred feet south of its ideal location, in order to leave the park inviolate.

The swarm—he could not honestly think of another word—of humanity sweeping down the long hills toward the park seemed to Father Morris to number far in excess of a hundred thousand. From his vantage point, halfway down one of those very hills, he was sure he could see at least that number, and he could not see the whole park, nor the other streets feeding into it.

So many people, he thought. *And so much anger!* It was palpable in the air, like violin strings pulled taut between each and every person, whining softly but insistently as the crowd moved and added to the stress. People shoved, here and there elbowing their way through small knots traveling less quickly than the mass.

Helena, Mike, and Father Morris were just such a knot, jostled from all sides as the swarm flowed around and through them. They were limited by the speed with which Mike Schorr could negotiate his way down the steep hill. And that was not fast.

"I told you we should have abandoned this foolish idea as soon as we saw we couldn't drive right up to the park," Helena shouted to make herself heard above the noise of the crowd. "Mike, this must be killing you."

"It ain't easy," Mike smiled. Morris was not entirely sure that the show of teeth was not a grimace as much as a grin.

"We should get over to the side," Morris said. "Closer to the buildings. The flow seems slower there."

"That'll be a good trick, Father," Mike said. "These idiots are ready to trample us because we're not going forward fast enough. God help us if we try to go sideways!"

"I think we'll be all right if we keep moving forward at the same time," Morris said. He pushed right, into the stream. "I only wish Diana had returned in time to come with us."

"She would have talked us out of this madness," Helena said. "She would have insisted this was her fight, and we should keep out of it."

"Her fight *is* our fight," Mike said, feeling the exertion as a new pain in every part of his body. Still, he was glad he had not taken any painkillers since his exit from the hospital. He wanted his mind sharp and clear, and if nothing else, pain was a great way to focus, he thought.

So they went, making their way down and to the side, as the unending torrent of humanity cascaded down the hill, fusing into the greater mass already filling the park. Craning her neck to look above the crowds, Helena saw the stage set up at the far side of the park, a broad, flat platform with its back to the bay. Lighting and sound towers rose on all four corners, and even at this distance—they were more than a mile away, still—she could see how massive the speakers were. The sound would reach to more than just those in attendance at the park. She could well imagine being able to hear it, at least as a dull rumble, from her own house on the other side of the city.

All over the stage Helena could see a rigging crew at work, black dots scurrying up and down the skeletal framework of the towers. She saw guylines being pulled, tightened, and heard the crack and pop as the speakers were turned on and tested. A banshee wail of feedback shrieked across the park, and everyone in earshot cried out or moaned in discomfort. Helena slapped her palms flat against her ears.

"We're all going to be stone deaf by the end of this," she said.

Mike turned to look at her, and his eyes were harder than Helena had ever seen them. "If we're lucky," he said, "that will be the worst of our troubles."

In the shadows of the long warehouses, ranged in martial order along the stretching fingers of the docks, five hundred warriors gathered, long cloaks drawn about them to shield the polished metal of their armor from the light.

"The enemy is Ares." Princess Diana of Themyscira, Amazon, Wonder Woman, faced her assembled troops and wondered how many more of their ancient race would pass on to the next world before this night was out.

"This is as we feared," Phillipus nodded. She stood at the front of the Amazon army, tall and dark, her face lost in the ebony interior of her helmet. "Is there any way, Princess, to know what he means to unleash against these mortals?"

"No." Diana frowned, angry that she had no solid information, no tactical data to give these brave soldiers. "He is working some kind of magic, I know that, and it is stripping these mortals of their reason, slowly but surely. I believe, too, that he is exerting a greater influence over Rebecca Chandler than ever before. She may, at this point, be nothing more than his puppet. Therefore we can expect anything she might say to be inflammatory. If it is Ares' intent to foster a holy war— and I believe it is—he has already lit the fuse. Tonight, if we do not stop him, he will see the explosive fruition of his plans begin in the park."

"What do you want us to do, then, Princess?" Phillipus asked. Diana could see the same question on the faces of all the Amazons around her. *They are prepared to fight and die tonight if that is what is asked of them,* she thought, *but they do not know what they can do against the power of Ares.*

"If this scheme is like others the War God has unleashed," Diana said, "he will hold himself back at first, to let his troops do most of the dirty work. In this case, those troops will be mostly human, the followers of Rebecca Chandler, her Soldiers of Salvation. You must be on your guard against these, but do not move against them directly unless you are forced to defend yourselves. My greater concern is that you be ready to do battle with whatever Ares may unleash if I am able to drive through and reach him directly."

"It is still your intent to seek confrontation with him, Princess?"

"I have no choice. To undo the damage he has done, I must reveal him to the world for what he is. Rebecca Chandler must be shown to be a pawn of Ares, if the spell he has woven through her is to be broken."

Phillipus lowered her eyes, weighing her thick, short sword in one hand. "My Princess. . . ."

"Yes, Phillipus?" Diana had heard this tone before, in the voice of the woman who had taught her all she knew of the arts of war. "Do not be afraid to speak your mind."

"We are all prepared to fight and die, on your command," Phillipus said, "but I worry that this will not accomplish anything. You say you are certain the recent madness in the populace is a result of Ares' intervention, the spell he works on the minds of men."

"Yes. He does not create the need to kill and make war, but he is the master of exploiting it."

"But . . ." Phillipus hesitated again, as if afraid speaking the words aloud would make them true. "But, Princess, what will happen if it is not all the work of Ares? It is the nature of mortals to be petty and jealous. Suppose, when a victory over Ares is won, some large portion of the populace still stands against you?"

"I have considered this, Captain," Diana said. She rose, lifting herself into the darkening sky. "If that is the case, there will be nothing I can do. Of all my powers, not one extends to the healing of the human spirit."

Stephen Ramsey was known to the followers of Rebecca Chandler, and it was Stephen Ramsey they saw striding through the makeshift command center behind and below the stage. He seemed, some thought, larger and more imposing than they had thought him before, but there was no one present who did not feel expanded by the energy generated by the event. Everything Rebecca had worked for was coming together this night, in this place, and those who had stood beside her, the growing legions that had come to her call over the last two years, felt themselves lifted and carried on a rising tidal wave that must, they were sure, crash down upon and obliterate all the enemies of the cause.

They were pleased to see the smile on Ramsey's face as he passed through them. He was closest to Rebecca, and if he was happy, they could only assume that she was happy as well. There had been some concern, since Rebecca had yet to arrive at the park—normally she preferred to be on site for such occasions at least two hours before commencement, and usually more—and, as was only normal when groups of people gather under pressure, rumors were circulating. Some were small and easily ignored, but others were large and terrifying. The worst had Wonder Woman actually battling Rebecca's security people on the high balcony of her suite at the Plaza. Shots were said to have been fired, and in the worst-case scenarios, Rebecca herself had been mortally wounded.

As Ramsey made his way through the command center, Agatha King detached herself from a clutch of concerned Soldiers, moving quickly to intercept him.

"Mr. Ramsey. Good evening. I'm Agatha King. You remember—"

"Of course, Mrs. King." Ramsey's eyes were bright, almost feral, and Agatha was, for a moment, afraid.

"We . . . we've been hearing all sorts of silly stories here," she said at last, marshaling her courage. "We were wondering . . . have you seen Miss Chandler recently? Is she all right?"

"She was fine when I saw her an hour or so ago," Ramsey said. "She should be arriving here soon, in fact."

Agatha sighed audibly, visibly relieved. "Thank you. We'd heard about Wonder Woman coming to Rebecca's suite at the Plaza. I suppose it was silly to believe such a thing."

"Not silly at all," Ramsey said. "That happened not more than two hours ago. I was there to see it."

Agatha's eyes went wide in her umber face. "Wonder Woman . . . really attacked Miss Chandler?"

"Well, not directly, of course," Ramsey said, and his face was suddenly as cold as frozen steel. "But if the security troops had not inter-vened, I cannot say what might have happened. Wonder Woman was clearly enraged. She might easily have killed Rebecca."

"K-Killed? . . ."

"Had the security troops not intervened," he repeated emphatically.

"Suppose . . ." Agatha lost her voice, and the hands she raised to her face were trembling. She struggled for a moment. "Suppose Wonder Woman comes here? What will we do?"

Ramsey smiled a catlike smile. "Oh, she is almost certain to come here, Mrs. King. And when she does, the Soldiers of Salvation must be prepared to fight, as good soldiers are prepared."

"But . . . we're not *real* soldiers, Mr. Ramsey. That's just a name."

"Not tonight, Mrs. King." Ramsey seemed in her eyes almost to vibrate with anticipation. He raised his hands before his chest, curling his fingers into massive fists. "Tonight we begin a war, Mrs. King. Tonight, here, on this green field, we set about creating the destruc-tion of Wonder Woman and all she represents."

Mayor Benjamin Garrison and the members of his city council sat in a booth set high into the side of the stage. Glass on all sides, illuminated so that the crowd could see them, it presented them as what they were, prize trophies Rebecca Chandler had won for her efforts. Each and every one of them was aware of this simple fact, and, fully professional politicians that they were, each and every one of them was deeply engaged, at that moment, in considering ways this potentially explosive situation could be turned to personal advantage.

"I feel like a damn fool in this box," Susan Stoga said. She sat in the middle of the row of chairs arranged in the booth for their comfort, telling herself again that she had not been shown to this particular chair in order to assure an even distribution of weight.

"Sit back and enjoy the ride, Sue," Marcus Greenwood said. He was pouring himself a Coke from the small wet bar against the solid back wall of the booth. "Anyone else want something to drink?"

"No," Garrison said, and it was clear he meant it as an order. "We shouldn't be sitting here looking like we're having a party. We should be looking like the concerned leaders we're supposed to be."

He was himself bothered by being stuck in that fishbowl, twenty feet above the stage, thirty feet above the grass lawns beneath. He had expected to be able to sit to one side of the front row, present but not insistently so. Discreet enough that those who saw him, and the others, would be able to draw their own conclusions as to why the mayor and the city fathers were there.

"Benny is right," Sheldon Minsky said, hearing Garrison say the words he had already planted in his brain. "We've got to play this carefully. It all happened too fast for any kind of proper choreographing. Okay, fine. We're all good at thinking on our feet. Let's just be sure we're not thinking at cross-purposes." He was very much aware that by speaking frankly like this he risked precisely the opposite result from that which he desired—these rugged individualists, unlike Garrison, did not take kindly to being shepherded, even in a polite and cautious manner. Minsky knew he had to work things very carefully if all—and especially Garrison—were to come out looking their best.

"Mr. Minsky is quite right," said William Winget. He entered by the door in the back of the booth, huffing and puffing from the effort of hauling his bulk up the steep steps from the stage. "We must show ourselves as united behind Rebecca Chandler. It's what the common people expect of us."

Well, you *missed my point entirely,* Minsky thought, but he only nodded. "A single face would be good," he said, spin-doctoring as always. "Just make like Greta Garbo and keep that face blank. We don't want to offend anyone."

Winget drew a large gold pocket watch from his waistcoat. "I wonder where Rebecca is. I'd have expected her to be here by now, but no one down below has seen her."

•   •   •

The limousine nosed into the crowd, the uniformed security forces walking before it, parting the press of men and women, forcing them back rather more roughly than Cassie thought was really necessary.

She sat in the back of the long car, beside Rebecca, and there was considerably more distance between them than the breadth of the seat dictated.

"Have they got to be so rough?" Cassie asked. She had been watching the security force transform itself from grandfathers with armbands to uniformed Gestapo, and tonight she saw the culmination of that metamorphosis. The troops—and there was no other word for them—in front of the car brandished nightsticks and swung fists with the same kind of focused ferocity she had seen in newsreels from the Forties.

"We must get to the back of the stage," Rebecca said, her tone dull, uninterested.

Cassie turned to look at her. The woman had changed, and in more than her dress. She was clad in the long robe she wore on her television hours, pale blue with the gold cross and letters of the SoS on the curve of her left breast. The collar and cuffs were white, and there was a bunch of delicate white lace at her throat. In the past, when Cassie had seen Rebecca on TV, the effect had been to give Rebecca an aura of tranquillity, the cut and colors of the robe combining with Rebecca's demure haircut and makeup, her small, sweet features, to make her seem more like a porcelain doll than a real woman. Cassie had understood, without being able to verbalize the thought, that in this look, in the innocence and serenity of her appearance, lay much of Rebecca's power. She manipulated the minds and hearts of men and women because she projected—quite legitimately, Cassie reminded herself—the image of one who was completely honest and trustworthy.

But not tonight. No, as Cassie looked at her, she saw a transformed Rebecca Chandler. There was no peace in the smooth face now, no serenity in the eyes. Rebecca's brows were knotted, her lips drawn into a tight, white line. Her eyes darted about, seemingly unable to focus on any one point for more than a fraction of a second. In her lap, where they would normally lie intertwined and at rest, her slender hands coiled and writhed about one another, making Cassie think of nothing so much as a pair of pale, furless cats roiling about in some grotesquely silent battle.

"Are you okay?" Cassie was still concerned for Rebecca's well-being, despite herself. She was more and more convinced that the woman who had unexpectedly become her friend, and just as unexpectedly distanced herself, was now in some great distress. Locked in some inner turmoil that had reached out from her center to color and distort her features.

"I am perfectly fine," Rebecca said. *Even her voice is different. She always speaks precisely, but this is like she's spitting out each word as if it tastes bad or something.*

"You don't look fine."

Rebecca turned. In any other situation, Cassie might have said she turned to look at her, but in this as in everything else this evening, Rebecca's eyes did not seem to focus on any single spot. She looked into Cassie's eyes, then away, then back, then at her shoulder, her hand, her eyes, the window, her chin. Cassie wondered how Rebecca could even remain sitting upright, the violent motion of her eyes being sure to induce a terrible dizziness.

"I am perfectly fine," Rebecca said again. "Everything is perfectly fine. This is the greatest night of my life. Everything is coming together at last."

Cassie looked out through the front window again, seeing the SoS troops forcibly parting the crowd still, as the limo rolled on. *Would we stop, I wonder, if someone got right in the way of the car? Or would we just roll on over them?*

"Is this really what you wanted?" Cassie waved a hand toward the front of the car. "I thought you wanted peace and love and all that stuff. Is that peace and love? I mean, look at these people. Your security guys're fighting them back halfway because they have to. The mob would swarm all over us if they didn't. Is this how you want people to act in your name?"

Rebecca's eyes darted from side to side, but Cassie was not sure Rebecca actually saw anything they lighted upon. "Sometimes the true path can only be reached through the thornbush," Rebecca said. "Sometimes violence is the only way to achieve peace."

Cassie gaped. "You don't really believe that?"

Rebecca looked at her again. For a moment her eyes grew still, focused on Cassie's face. For a moment, Cassie had a sense of genuine contact, the first in days.

"I . . ." Rebecca paused. Just in that single syllable her voice sounded more like what Cassie had come to know.

"You don't, do you? You don't believe any of this. Why are you doing it?"

"Because I want her to."

Cassie spun in her seat. "You! How—"

Stephen Ramsey held up a black-gloved hand. "Silence, child. You have played your part, and there will be more for you to do before the night is done."

Cassie choked, her windpipe closing as though squeezed in an invisible grip. Rebecca seemed not to have noticed Ramsey's presence or Cassie's distress. She continued to look straight ahead even as her head twitched, slightly, spastically, as though trying to turn toward them in acknowledgment. *What's the matter with her? This guy's done something to her, that's gotta be it!*

"We all have our parts to play," Ramsey said. "I brought you here to weaken Wonder Woman's circle of friends. Helena Sandsmark is a strong spirit, and she gives much of that strength in her support of Diana. With her mind focused on you, Helena was of diminished value to Diana. Plus, with the tales I encouraged you to tell, you helped sow the further seeds of Wonder Woman's destruction."

"Who . . . are . . . you? . . ." Each word was fire burning in Cassie's throat. She writhed in her seat, feeling herself trapped like a butterfly in a killing jar.

"I am Ares," Ramsey said. "You know the name, I see. Good. Then you understand I have a personal mission against Wonder Woman. Her fall from grace, her obliteration as a force for what she considers good in the world, these are matters of special significance to me. Tonight, with the aid of Rebecca Chandler and yourself, a final series of dominoes will topple, and Wonder Woman will be forever eradicated."

"I . . . won't . . . help . . . you. . . ."

Ramsey smiled and leaned forward. Cassie felt hot air press in against her like ten thousand blazing needles.

"Yes," Ramsey said with utter, icy calm, "you will."

It was not easy to disguise the face and form of the most beautiful woman on Earth, but Diana had done what she could.

As she moved through the crowd she wore a loose trench coat borrowed from Helena's closet, her hair pulled back into a ponytail. The ponytail served a double purpose, altering the shape of her hair and so, to some small extent, her face, and capturing her raven tresses so that, when and if the time came to shed the coat and reveal her familiar garments beneath, she would not have to trouble herself with seating her tiara upon her brow. The tiara usually held back her thick hair in times of battle, but she did not want to waste time putting it on if violence broke out—and clearly she could not walk through the crowd with it already in place.

She kept her face down, avoiding eye contact, making her way slowly and steadily toward the stage. It would have been easier, of course, to simply fly to the stage, to drop from the sky into the middle of the seething assemblage, but she knew only too well that doing so would be playing into the hands of Rebecca Chandler and the War God.

She was troubled by what she had learned. She had seen Rebecca Chandler as a problem to be solved—Diana had not allowed herself to consider Rebecca truly an enemy—but now she wondered if, in the midst of all this, Rebecca might not be, herself, someone in need of help. Someone who had fallen into darkness and needed Diana to show her the way out.

How much is Ares in control of her? How much free will has he allowed her? She seemed much changed at our second meeting from the woman I encountered in her office in the Crystal Tower. Then, I am sure, she was much more a free agent. As we have drawn inexorably closer to this moment, this night, Ares seems to have exerted greater and greater control. That would be like him. Having chosen Rebecca Chandler as his pawn, he would have been content to leave her to her own devices, acting only occasionally to nudge her in this direction or that. I wonder, was this mad scheme to destroy me something he introduced from the beginning? Was Rebecca made aware of this goal from the first contact, or did he drip it into her mind slowly, like a serpent oozing venom into captured prey?

Diana was amazed at the scope and complexity of the plan Ares had set in motion. Assuming that he had been involved from the very inception with Rebecca's elevation—and Diana was sure of that—then this was a scheme he must have set in motion almost immediately following his last defeat at Diana's hands. *Not surprising, I suppose. Ares has always cherished vengeance as much as any other thing. Smarting from his defeat, he would have wanted some way to strike back at once. He may even have had this plan already in motion, as a contingency.*

She shook her head, a barely perceptible movement that went unnoticed by the crowd though which she passed. *Somehow that seems less likely. Ares is the master of planning for every contingency with a battle, but his single greatest weakness is his inability to factor the notion of his own defeat into his plans. All his machinations are directed toward recapturing victory, not beginning anew after a fall.*

By slow and steady forward pressure, Diana had brought herself within a few rows of the front of the stage. Here the crowd was packed so densely she knew she would have to take to the air to make any further progress, and so she stopped, waiting. *Nothing will happen now,* she thought, *until Rebecca Chandler arrives.*

CHAPTER SIXTEEN

It started as a low rumble away to Diana's right. Looking over the heads of the crowd she saw immediately the reason for this new sound. Rebecca Chandler had come onstage, walking slowly, hands raised above her head in a general benediction to the crowd.

Behind her was a clutch of men and women of assorted ages, races, and sizes, linked only by the pale blue SoS armbands they all wore. In the group—held by the people to either side of her—Diana saw Cassandra Sandsmark. Walking just behind Rebecca, smiling, was a dark man Diana recognized at once as Ares in human form.

And so it begins, she thought, and for a moment sealed out the sights, the sounds, the smells of the crowd. She turned herself inward, locating her most quiet center, her warrior's soul. She remembered all the lessons Phillipus had taught her since she was a child, marshaling all the cool, calm power she would need to face this greatest of perils.

She raised her head, looking up to the stage, and waited for Rebecca Chandler to make the first move.

•   •   •

Rebecca stepped up to the cluster of microphones at the center of the stage. She turned back and forth, her hands still raised, her eyes closed as she sent her silent prayers out into the masses.

More than a hundred thousand, she thought. *There must be much, much more than a hundred thousand.*

But it was only a small part of her mind that made this observation. She had, she realized, only a small part of her mind that was truly hers with which to make any kind of judgment. She moved, walked, talked as if dangling at the end of a puppeteer's strings, and the hand that held the other end, she knew, belonged to Stephen Ramsey.

She felt so small, now. A tiny thing lost at the center of some greater darkness, yet that darkness was her own body, and the small thing was her own mind, her own soul, trapped in a form she could no longer fully command.

Yet, neither was it entirely that simple. She heard the words she spoke, and though she was not fully conscious of forming them, pronouncing them, she agreed with them. She watched as her hands moved, to touch, to greet, and she saw herself doing just those things she would do if she were free.

Thus far I have been called upon to do nothing I would not ordinarily do, she thought, considering the implications. *Does this mean Ramsey does not need to exercise too great a degree of control, to get me to do his bidding?* She was still struggling to come to terms with the fact that Ramsey—and it must be Ramsey—was controlling her. In a world replete with super heroes, there were few things left that lay utterly beyond human comprehension, and Rebecca had no real difficulty accepting the notion that one person could be controlled, literally, by another, if that other was powerful enough. She had, after all, exercised a kind of control herself, over the people who served her cause. From that to this more intrusive and total control seemed but a short step.

Why did he leave me to my own free will so long, though, she wondered. *If he could have controlled me like this from the very beginning, why didn't he?*

She wondered if it was unconscionable hubris to think that, perhaps, he needed something only she could bring to the cause. Her own brand of sincerity, perhaps, which had never faltered in all the long days of their two years of uneasy partnership.

I have never doubted the truth of my convictions, she assured herself. *I do not doubt them now. So why, then, has Ramsey chosen now to bring me under such direct control? What does he have planned that he thinks I would not do, if free to do it of my own volition?*

The thought frightened her. *I am alone now. All these people, these thousands upon thousands of people, they are not here to protect me, to save me. They are here to listen to me say only the things they want to hear. If I waver, they will turn on me.* And in that, she suspected, lay the core of why Ramsey now made her his puppet.

But how does he control me? Am I hypnotized? If I was, would I have these sensations, would I be aware that things are anything other than as they should be? Would I be able to have this reasoned, ordered little internal conversation, ask these questions?

Dim and distant memories floated about the edges of her diminished mind. She was at the center of something beyond her comprehension, and here and there, just where that vast, unknowable region touched on her mind, there were flashes of insight, glimmers of intuition, too small and fleeting to grasp. They teased her, like fireflies in a dark wood, now here, now there, real and solid, but elusive.

Wonder Woman said the god Ares was on the balcony with me, earlier this evening. The god Ares. And—is that a fragment? Is that something real? Ramsey appearing as if from nowhere, saying things about rams and plays on words. And . . . he was in the car, wasn't he? He just appeared in the car, with Cassie and me, but somehow prevented me from seeing him. And that was when I started to feel like a puppet.

She was aware of having lowered her hands. She stood for a moment in silence, looking out through her own eyes as a passenger would look out through the windows of a vehicle, inside, but not in control. Before her, close to a hundred thousand lighters waved gently back and forth, a galaxy of yellow points, moving in unison above the heads of the crowd.

"Brothers and sisters," she heard herself say, and immediately the crowd—one hundred thousand voices raised almost as one—let loose a tremendous cheer that very nearly knocked her back from the mike. "Brothers and sisters," she repeated, holding up her hands again, watching them move, fascinated by the motion, the way the bright lights drained color from her already pale skin, the way the highlights flowed and rippled on the silken sleeves of her robe. "Let me say first how gratified I am that you have all come here tonight."

Another cheer, louder if that were possible.

"You are the new vanguard." Rebecca heard her voice boom from the massive sound system, a huge voice. An Olympian voice. She wished she could be even vaguely amused by that irony. "From this place you, my brothers and my sisters, you will go forth to carry into the world the message. You will take to the people the Word, the Truth. And the enemies of the Lord shall be struck down as the lightning strikes the hollow oak."

The crowd responded with appropriate thunder, and the lighters danced, drawing swirling arcs across the darkness, all the way to the edge of the park.

"This evening," Rebecca said when something close to silence returned, "as you may have heard, Wonder Woman came to my suite at the Plaza Hotel." An angry murmur ran through the assemblage. Of course they had heard. Rebecca's people—*Are they my people, still, or do they belong to someone else?*—had been making sure the word circulated. She doubted there was anyone in Gateway City who had not heard their version of the story. "She was driven back by my security staff—" a huge cheer "—but I challenged her to come here tonight and say her own piece to you, in her own words."

The crowd erupted in angry shouts and catcalls. The dancing of the lighters became frenzied, erratic. In a dozen places through the crowd the lighters had been replaced by full-fledged torches, burning hot and bright like closer stars in the vast firmament before the stage.

Rebecca raised her face so that the light caught it fully. She turned her head, looking out from inside as her eyes scanned the crowd, laser beams probing the faces. "Are you here, Wonder Woman?" she heard herself ask, amazed that any human voice, let alone her own, could contain in so few words so much scorn. "If you are here, step forward and show yourself!"

This is it.

Mike Schorr felt the sudden surge of heightened emotion boil through the crowd as Rebecca Chandler appeared on the stage with her entourage.

"Cassie!" Close to Mike's ear, Helena's voice was a choked whisper. "It's Cassie!"

"She looks okay," Mike said, reaching back a hand to press Helena's arm. *She looks dorky in that silly dress, but she looks okay.*

"We've got to get closer." Helena shifted against Mike's back, but the crowd was a solid mass around them. Movement was almost impossible.

"Careful," Mike grunted, as the closest of the press of people responded to their small motion with greater pressure. "If we push the wrong way they'll crush us to death and not even notice."

Helena's fists thumped against Mike's back. "But we've got to do something! Oh, I wish we hadn't lost Father Morris!"

"That was what he intended all along, I think," Mike said, remembering his moment of surprise when he realized the old priest had used the surging currents of the crowd to detach himself from his companions and strike off on his own.

"You don't suppose he means to throw in with Chandler now, do you?" Helena leaned close so her whisper could be heard by Mike and Mike alone. "After all he said about Diana somehow proving to him that God is real. . . ."

"I didn't quite follow his logic," Mike said, "but it seemed to work for him. And, I don't know. He seemed to think Diana had done him a great service. He . . ." Mike paused. Rebecca Chandler had positioned herself behind the microphones on the stage. She lowered her arms and seemed about to speak.

When she did the sound crashed down across the crowd in great, rumbling waves that resonated to the very center of Mike Schorr's bones. *This is it*, he thought again, and slipped his hand inside his jacket, taking comfort from the smooth, cold steel on the butt of his .45.

It's the pod people thing, Cassie thought. *I saw it happening to all her staff, one by one; now it's happened to Rebecca. Big question, is it permanent?*

She looked to her left, to the place where Stephen Ramsey stood, hands clasped behind his back, face in smooth repose. Cassie supposed he would be considered handsome by some, a kind of Sean Connery handsomeness, rugged, rough, with what Cassie had heard her mother call an elfin glint in his eyes.

He did something to me, too, Cassie thought. *In the car. He looked into my eyes, and it was like all the strength just drained right out of me. And he said he's Ares. Ares the War God. Is that for real? I know Diana has fought Ares before, but I never pictured him looking like Sean Connery and sitting in the backs of limos. Of course, I never pictured Wonder Woman living in the apartment at the top of mom's house, either. And he comes and goes in "strange ways"—that's for sure—and that's something a god is supposed to do, I guess.*

Cassie felt frustration bubbling at the edges of her sensibilities. She did not know exactly what Ramsey/Ares had done to her—he had not taken her over completely, as he clearly had Rebecca—but he had turned off some part of her brain. She would have run away before now, if that were not the case. She could almost see herself bolting across the stage and running across the top of the crowd, like Paul

Hogan at the end of *"Crocodile" Dundee.* The masses before the stage were so tightly packed—and Cassie so sure of her own nimbleness—that she was certain she could have run, head to head, shoulder to shoulder, all the way to the gates of the park.

She could do that. She *should* do that. But she stood as though spikes had been driven through her feet. *Just walk over to the edge of the stage,* she told herself. *You don't even have to run. Just walk there. To prove to yourself that you can do it.*

But she could not, and she realized, as she thought about it, that the reason she could not was that the connection between her brain and her limbs, the mysterious passages through her nervous system, up and down which traveled those millions and billions of unconscious signals, all day, every day—those pathways had been closed off, somehow, and it would require a conscious effort to lift one foot and place it in front of the other. A conscious effort to bend her knee, flex her calf, take that single, first step, and the next, and the next. And the simple fact of the matter was, the incredibly complex process involved in taking a step was more than any human brain could handle through conscious effort. There were ten thousand tiny adjustments to be made, balance, stride, speed, all the things that were processed unconsciously, and Stephen Ramsey, or Ares, or Mars—or whatever he wanted to call himself—had, by stripping her of that unconscious ability, paralyzed Cassie more completely than would any action short of encasing her in cement. He had turned the complexity of her own body against her, and all Cassandra Sandsmark could do was stand, watch, listen, and hope Wonder Woman would spring up from the crowd and kick Stephen Ramsey right in his handsome butt.

Father Donald Morris circled left, away from Helena and Mike, edging his way through the crowd. At first there had been resistance to his movement, as he held back a step and then moved to the side, detaching himself from his companions. People did not like to have him pushing by, but at the sight of his clerical collar they relaxed, opening before him.

He had moved with the crowd down the long slope of the street, through the main gates of the park, down across the rolling grass. Beneath his feet, beneath the trampling feet of a hundred thousand people, that grass was rapidly changing from a carefully manicured carpet to a sea of mud and broken sod. The going was treacherous, the ground rising and falling in frozen waves and valleys, all seeming quite determined to trip the unwary, perhaps the lawn seeking to revenge itself for its violation.

While Morris was still more than a hundred yards from the edge of the big stage, the crowd began to pack in tight, making his forward progress more and more difficult until, at last, it became impossible. No one would step aside to let him pass, now, simply because no one had anywhere to move. All were held as in a vice, rooted to the spot they had reached when the crowd achieved maximum compression and all further motion became out of the question.

Seeing it as his only choice, Morris stepped back, circling around the perimeter of the crowd, moving laterally so as to avoid the constant pressure, avoid becoming a tile in that living mosaic.

He needed to get to the stage, and if this path carried him all around the perimeter of the park and forced him to approach his goal from the back, that would, in the end, be more suitable to his needs. He had to get to Rebecca Chandler. He had to speak to her, to explain to her what he had learned on Olympus.

Will she believe me, though? Would I believe it myself, if someone came to me and said, "Father, I went to Olympus and found the proof I need that our God is real"? It makes no sense at all, when you put it into words, and yet I can feel it in my soul as clearly as nothing I've felt since the first moment I understood what was to be my calling in life. There has been no moment of clarity so sharp, so well defined in all my life as those two, the realization that I wanted to serve God, and the reaffirmation that I was right to make that choice.

He was breathing hard as he moved around the thickening edge of the crowd. The effect of the flow of people was frustrating—as they packed themselves in, closer and closer to the stage, the circle marking their boundary expanded, so that Donald Morris found himself moving farther and farther from the center as he rounded the edges and headed for the back. He assumed, though, that there would be some clear space at the rear of the stage, some area defined as a parking lot, a command center. He could see the mayor and the city fathers in the glass booth up on the right side of the stage, and he assumed they must have come in limousines and that those limousines must be parked somewhere, along with all the cars, trucks, and buses that would have been necessary to transport the rest of the people and equipment necessary to make this event occur.

Circling around, farther from the front of the stage but closer with each step to the back, Morris looked over the heads of the crowd and saw what he realized might—most likely would—be the first major obstacle in his path to Rebecca Chandler. There was, indeed, a large open space defined behind the stage, where he saw all the vehicles and equipment he imagined would be there. But the edges of that area were set apart by the uniformed security forces of the SoS, grim-faced men standing shoulder to shoulder, arms linked. A gray wall that Donald Morris suspected would not, like the walls of Jericho, decide at a convenient moment to fall down.

Sheldon Minsky looked down from his seat at the end of the booth. He was positioned to one side of the council and the mayor, at the opposite end from the chair occupied by William Winget. He looked down on Rebecca Chandler and felt what he could only describe as professional admiration.

She's working this crowd like a real pro, he thought. *But, then, she is a pro. And she's got herself a loyal following any politician worthy of the name would sell his soul to get.*

The term seemed uncomfortably appropriate. Minsky was far from what he or anyone else would define as a religious man, but he looked at the way in which Rebecca Chandler manipulated the thousands crushed against the stage, the way she charmed them, stroked them, coaxed and cajoled them, never once losing control of them, never once allowing them to think they, and not she, held the reins—he looked at this and he thought there was something uncomfortably unholy about it all. It seemed absurd to shape the thought in just those words, but they were inescapable.

Minsky had no time for Evangelicals at best, seeing people like Rebecca Chandler only as tools to further his own purposes. He did not trust them, any of them, from the most exalted playing to packed houses in Madison Square Garden to the lowliest Bible-thumper working his way through the tent circuit in the lost reaches of the American hinterland. He supposed his lack of trust was rooted in something very easy to understand—he saw in them kindred spirits, people who knew how to manipulate the minds and hearts of the masses to achieve their own ends. And that end, of course, was power. Always power.

And if Rebecca Chandler seemed more sincere than most, seemed less interested in her own advancement, it was of small consequence. To accomplish what she felt she needed to accomplish she needed to amass great quantities of power, and if she wanted to pretend none of that power was for her own personal glory, so be it. Sheldon Minsky looked down on her, small and slim, quietly beautiful in her pale blue robes, and saw a fellow professional.

You go, girl, he thought, amusing himself with the phrase. *You're damn good at what you do, and you got yourself a fan right here.*

Patrolman Danny Kurtz was very glad, that night, that he had not pulled duty at the park. He had done crowd control before, and it was, in his opinion, the worst job any police officer could get. There was too much sheer, blatant stupidity in people, he had long ago decided—Patrolman Kurtz viewed the world with the crystalline clarity shared by all twenty-two-year-olds—and when you packed all that stupidity together in a small space—or even a large space, like the park—it compounded itself, and the stupid got stupider.

Patrolman Kurtz, therefore, walked his beat as usual along the broad avenue that snaked along the top of the dockyards, on his left the city rising in manmade cliffs and terraces toward a sky turned the color of honey by the mass of streetlights and signs, on his right the warehouses and piers that served as one of the major import centers not only for Gateway, but the whole nation.

He enjoyed this beat. He had walked it for just over a year, and in that time there had been no trouble worth mentioning. It was a long walk, up and down the avenue, and it allowed Danny Kurtz time to reflect on life, time, all the mysteries of the Universe.

He was looking, he thought, at just such a mystery now.

Standing by the low stone wall that bounded this particular section of the raised highway, Kurtz leaned over to look down at the stairway that rose from the dockyards to the street, and blinked to clear his vision and convince himself that what he saw was absolutely real.

A troop of something he could only think of as Roman soldiers— he lacked the necessary training to recognize their accouterments as more Greek than Roman—was marching up the steps, single file, shields raised, swords and spears held loose but ready at their sides. At least five hundred of them, coming in an unending line, up from the docks and on down the street toward the sound and glow of Gateway Park.

At the top of the steps, brandishing a sword in a manner that Patrolman Kurtz realized must be some kind of sign language, a tall, dark figure was clearly the leader of the troop. Drawing a deep breath and hoping this was all some kind of joke, or maybe someone shooting a movie—though he would surely have been informed of that—Kurtz approached this figure.

"Care to tell me what you're doin' here, fella?"

The figure turned, and Kurtz was amazed, as the movement flared the cloak away from the soldier's body, to see that the dark form was a woman, tall and hard-muscled, her ebon skin catching the glow of the streetlights in a pattern of shadows and highlights that Kurtz found simultaneously frightening and erotic.

"You are a representative of the law enforcement for this city," the woman said, and Kurtz was momentarily disoriented by her accent. He had never heard a black person speak with such a voice.

"I'm Patrolman Daniel Kurtz," he said, seeking a center of authority within himself, "and I need to see some kind of permits from you, lady. I don't know what you're doing here, but I'm sure it needs permits."

Inside the elegant sculpting of her helmet the woman smiled. "There is no need to be alarmed, Patrolman Daniel Kurtz." She ran his name together, as a single word, as though she were unfamiliar with its individual parts. "We mean no harm here. We are on our way to Gateway Park and shall cause no disturbance along the way."

Something in her precise choice of phrasing tickled the worry nerves on the back of Kurtz's neck. "And what happens when you get to the park, if I may ask?"

"Nothing, it is to be hoped." The woman turned. "Now, if you will excuse me—"

Kurtz put out a hand to her shoulder. "I don't think so." His other hand was on the walkie-talkie on his belt. He was not sure how quickly backup could get here—especially with what seemed like half the force assigned to the park—but he was beginning to think he would most certainly need some kind of assistance. He was not so foolish as to believe he could detain five hundred female warriors on his own.

The dark woman's free hand snapped up and seized Kurtz's wrist. She twisted over and down and Kurtz found himself spun on one foot, the walkie-talkie flying from his hand.

The woman barked something in a language Kurtz had never heard, and two other women detached themselves from the parade and crossed to take his arms, holding him. The dark woman said something more in her unknown tongue, then smiled at him. "You have nothing to fear, Patrolman Daniel Kurtz. We are here to help. These soldiers of my legion will now restrain you while we continue with our mission. If you do not struggle or resist them unduly, I think you will find it a most pleasant captivity."

Kurtz looked from face to face, studying the women holding him. He had a limited range of experience on which to base any judgment of female pulchritude, but it seemed to him that, armor and swords notwithstanding, these two might easily have stepped from the pages of *Playboy.* They smiled at him, and though the pressure on his upper arms, where they held him, did not diminish, Danny Kurtz decided the dark woman was probably telling the truth, and whatever happened next was highly unlikely to be unpleasant.

CHAPTER SEVENTEEN

DIANA had given much thought to the precise nature of the action she would take. Since Rebecca Chandler challenged her to come here, to face her detractors in person, she had formulated a hundred different speeches she might give to the crowd, if she were truly allowed to do so.

None of them seemed in the least bit satisfying to her. She was sure Ares was working some magic on the people, and it would take more than words—even the most pleasant, reasoned words—to undo that spell. She did not, however, have the least notion of just what it would take to accomplish this end. The people, she thought, needed to find a way to free themselves of Ares' influence, and, since the War God spoke to their most basic, animal instincts, that was something they would not find easy to accomplish.

Diana looked up as Rebecca delivered her challenge once again. "If you are here, step forward and show yourself!"

Rebecca took a single step back from the microphones, folding her arms across her chest, and stood still, waiting.

And so must I act, Diana thought. *I am not truly ready, but if Phillipus taught me nothing else, she taught me to be flexible, to consider all options and improvise.*

She shrugged off the mantle of gravity and let herself rise. The crowd exploded around her, shouting, pointing, even grabbing at her feet.

Wonder Woman shed the trench coat, slipping it from her broad shoulders and catching it in one hand so that it trailed behind her as she floated over the heads of the crowd toward the edge of the stage. She did not assume a conventional flying posture, her body parallel to the ground, but held herself upright, as though standing on the cool evening air itself.

She reached the edge of the stage and lowered herself to its boards outside the reach of the hands that grabbed at her. She walked slowly to Rebecca's position, careful to contain her movements so that no threat would be implied. In the booth above the stage she saw Mayor Garrison and the rest on their feet, pressing against the glass that sheltered them from the growing chill.

"I am here, Rebecca," Diana said.

Helena was literally lifted from her feet by the reaction of the crowd when Wonder Woman floated up out of their midst. She grabbed at Mike Schorr for support and heard him cry out in pain as the bodies surged and pressed around them.

"Mike!"

" 'Mokay." The bright tears in his eyes and the way his flesh was drawn taut across his face told Helena this was far from the truth, but there was nothing she could do either way. "We've gotta get to the stage," Mike said. He shoved at the wall of people in front of him, keeping one hand on the gun under his jacket while he grabbed for Helena with the other.

I can't believe Diana was here and I didn't sense it somehow, he thought. *She couldn't have been more than ten yards away!*

Keeping an eye on Diana as she drifted toward the stage, he used the spasms and surges of the crowd to insinuate himself through their press, pulling Helena with him. He knew he would not be able to keep this up much longer. His grip on Helena was not strong, and if she snagged, if she were unable for even a moment to propel herself after him, their connection would be broken.

It happened sooner than he anticipated. The crowd moved suddenly, two surges that flowed across one another, and like the great tectonic plates shifting down the length of the San Andreas Fault, the separate masses moved in opposite directions and Helena was pulled out of his grip.

Mike gave no thought to going back for her. She could fend for herself, he was sure, and it was Diana who needed his support right now. He was only one man with a gun—a relatively small gun—he knew, and she was a super hero, but Mike Schorr was a firm believer in the old notion that one man in the right place could make a difference.

He wondered for a moment if it would be worth trying to pull himself up on top of the crowd. He might be able to swim, he thought, across the bodies. He was close enough to the stage. But he was also in great pain, and he knew the exertion would be more than he could tolerate. The world was swimming around him already, and he would be no use at all to Diana if he fainted.

So he rode the motion of the crowd, using this surge to carry him to the side, that one to propel himself forward. It was a tricky, complex path, and Mike found himself thinking of one of those sliding tile games, in which the object was to assemble a picture by moving the pieces back and forth within a restricting frame. Here, as in the puzzle, he found it sometimes necessary to relinquish ground so as to ready himself for the surge that would carry him to an even better position.

In this fashion he reached the edge of the stage just as Diana took her place behind the microphones. Her voice boomed from the giant speakers, and Mike noticed at once that Diana's voice did not sound nearly so soft and soothing as Rebecca Chandler's. Someone, he realized, was manipulating the pitch and tone of the speakers to make Wonder Woman's voice sound shrill and piercing.

Mike pushed himself along the front of the stage, looking for something he was almost certain must be there and finding it just as the crowd rose to what he could only hope was the fevered peak of their rage against the woman on the stage.

Mike dropped down and squirmed through the narrow gap between the boards that fronted the stage and the grass of the lawn. Someone saw him, and at the last minute grabbed his foot, but Mike kicked him away and crawled into the darkness under the stage. There was no way he would be able to get up onto the stage from his position pressed against its front, no way his bruised and battered arms and legs could take the strain of hoisting him up, especially since the crowd would almost certainly try to stop him.

But here, under the stage, he could work his way through the support structure and emerge in the rear, where there would be stairs he could use to get to Diana and Rebecca Chandler.

The sound generated by the massive speakers *thrummed* and shuddered through the enclosed space, deafening, and Mike felt for all the world like a small creature swallowed whole by some mythic monster. He only hoped the monster was not preparing itself to consume everything Mike Schorr loved and cared about.

It will end here. Tonight. One way or the other, it must all come to its final conclusion, in this park, before the sun rises on a new day.

The transformation was utter and complete. Diana looked down at the sea of faces spread out as far as she could see, and it was not human beings that looked back up at her, but animals, wild beasts, all flashing eyes and bared teeth.

Her words shrieked from the great speakers—and, like Mike Schorr, she noticed the change in the quality of the sound—but they fell on deaf ears. And even if they had not, Diana realized now, understanding fully what she had feared would be the case, these people were not prepared to believe anything she had to say. It was not within the scope of their experience to even begin to comprehend the truth of her words.

"This man is not a man," she said, pointing at Stephen Ramsey. "He is the god Ares, the War God. You might know him better as Mars. All this is his doing. All this is part of a plan he has set in motion, not only to destroy me, but to inflame in your hearts and minds the violence on which he feeds."

Ramsey's response was merely to raise an eyebrow, smiling and shaking his head as would any rational, normal man when confronted with what were clearly the ravings of a lunatic mind.

"Please," Diana said, struggling to keep herself from shouting, seeking the right modulation in her tone that would defeat the manipulations of the speakers. It was hopeless, of course. Somewhere, she knew, someone was sitting at a control board and pushing sliders and flipping switches, reacting to each change in her pitch, keeping the sound coming from the speakers as unpleasant as it could be. "Please," she pressed on, "try to keep calm! Try to think rationally! Ares has done something to you. He has introduced some manner of magic that is distorting the way you think and feel. Please, try to remember how you felt before the madness was set upon you."

No one wanted to hear. The crowd pressed against the stage, sending waves of vibration through it, making the guywires sing in the tall sound towers. People were scrabbling at the edges of the stage, trying to pull themselves up, to climb on. For the moment, the SoS security people, in uniform, were able to push them back and keep them off the stage, but Diana knew this would not be the case for much longer.

"You must understand," Rebecca said, and the tone of the speakers changed at once, "that you cannot reach these people with more of your lies, Wonder Woman. I have shown them the truth, and what you seek to build up you succeed only in tearing down."

"You do not speak any sort of truth as I understand the word," Diana said. Again the pitch of the speakers changed, so fast she began to doubt there was any mere mortal hand at work on the controls.

It would not have surprised her to learn this was more of the magic of Ares. It was his way, after all, to use the machines of Humankind in ways beyond those for which they had been intended. "You are in the thrall of Ares. You are no longer free to control your own voice and body."

Rebecca laughed, and the sound floated over the crowd like music. "You can end this simply enough, Diana," she said. "Confess to these people! Tell them that everything you have done since you arrived in America was part of some mad scheme to undermine our faith in the One True God, and you will be allowed to leave here—provided you promise never to return."

"No . . ." Diana started a rebuttal, but the crowd had taken up a single word of Rebecca's challenge and transformed it into a chant.

"Confess!" The word erupted from a hundred thousand throats. "Confess! Confess!" The sound pressed on Diana like a physical force.

"Look here," Rebecca said, her amplified voice easily heard over the noise of the mob. She reached out a hand to grab Cassie by the arm and pull her into the center of the semicircle of microphones. "Tell them, child. Tell them of the wickedness Diana has worked on yourself and your poor mother."

Diana saw Cassie stiffen, saw her clearly struggling against Rebecca's command, but it was obvious she, too, was under the spell of Ares, and in the next moment the words came gushing out, the lies, the horrible tales Cassandra had invented when she had yet to realize that she was only a tiny pawn in a game far greater than she could ever understand.

Father Morris had worked his way all around the back of the stage, to the far edge of the secure area. He moved along a hedgerow, the city rising before him, the bay spread out at his back, and in the middle the stage and its towers rose like some insane Hollywood production designer's notion of a city of the future.

Even though the speakers faced away from him, their sound still pounded down on him, and Morris heard the challenge of Rebecca Chandler, and heard too the shrill, distorted voice of Princess Diana as she arrived to take up the gauntlet.

He had surrendered any hope of penetrating the wall of SoS men surrounding the secure area and now searched for some point where they did not form their human chain, arms linked. Some place where a tree, a bush, even a vehicle provided a breach in the barricade.

He saw it. One of the large moving vans that had carried all the equipment to the site. It stood at the edge of the rectangle defined by the SoS men, and, parked further back than any of the other vehicles, it thrust through their ranks and offered a chance. It would all depend, Donald Morris knew, on how much movement and speed he could coax from limbs that were already shrieking in agony.

Sadly, he remembered the hill on Themyscira, and how easily he had mounted its long, steep face. *If I could command a tenth of that strength, a fraction of that painless ease, what I need to do now would be as simple as, well, a walk in this park.*

What he needed to do next! . . . Morris avoided confronting, even in his own mind, the fact that he was not altogether clear on what he would do next. He was working, he knew, on instinct. And faith. God had directed him to Wonder Woman, to find the answers and the reaffirmation he sought. Surely He would guide Donald Morris now. Guide his hand and mind to the right action, the proper goal.

Primarily, he knew he must reach Rebecca Chandler and, if the opportunity would only present itself, address the crowd and tell them what he had learned. If they could be made to understand that Wonder Woman was, after all, a proof of the faith Rebecca claimed she came to destroy, then the whole argument against Diana must surely fall apart, and the madness could be ended.

Morris hung back on the edge of the line of bushes, his dark coat lost, he hoped, against the darkness of the leaves, out here where the pools of light from the stage dwindled and faded away.

His plan from this point—and it beggared the word to call it a "plan," he knew—was to wait until attention was focused inside the

secure area, then hurry from his place of concealment, under the high
bed of the truck and so, he hoped, into the heart of Rebecca Chandler's
operation. To this end he watched the wall of guards closely, more certain with every passing moment that there was a guiding Hand at work
here, that this was the precise course he needed to follow.

The guards at this end of the enclosure were bored, restless. Unlike
those who blocked access from the sides, they did not link arms, and
some even stood in small groups, chatting, leaving the wall broken in
several places. Morris concentrated on their faces, on their eyes, watching for patterns, watching to see if there was any discernible rhythm to
the turning of their heads, the way they looked here and there. Mostly
they seemed to be ignoring the shadowed grasses between the enclosure and the seawall. They looked toward the sides, and inward, toward
the stage itself.

Morris decided the only way he would achieve what he needed was
to simply seize the bull by the horns and stride across the fifty or sixty
feet to the back end of the big hauler. He stepped away from the concealment of the bushes, walked slowly and steadily in a straight line
across the grass. Here, except for a few deep ruts where heavy vehicles had passed, the grass was still smooth and whole. It had not been
torn up by hundreds of thousands of trampling feet, and, once the
enclosure had been defined, no one at all had strayed into this area.
Morris walked carefully, counting the steps to the edge of the light.
His heart pounded, and he felt the ache in his muscles almost as chains,
dragging on him, slowing him down.

He crossed the lawn without incident, glad of his dark clothing,
the wall of dark night behind him. He reached the back of the truck
and stood perfectly still for a moment. He was now almost within the
perimeter, and he would, when he came out from under the truck, be
in the line of sight of several of the guards. He wondered if it would
be possible to crawl the whole length of the truck, to emerge under
the nose, instead of the side, as he had originally planned. Would the
front end be high enough? He knew the engine of a vehicle this size
must surely be huge, and it would hang low, yet he was also sure a considerable amount of ground clearance would be necessary.

He took a deep breath and lowered himself painfully onto one knee. He looked under the long bed of the truck, past the massive rear axles. As far as he could see, so long as he stayed to one side or the other, he would have no difficulty moving the whole length of the truck. The only concern, as he could see it, was when he emerged at the other end and people noticed what would surely be a remarkably muddy old priest walking through their midst.

"You can't possibly prevail, Princess."

The voice was a hiss in her ear. Diana turned her head, but Ares, in his human guise, was still on the other side of Rebecca Chandler. Still, it had been his voice she heard, as though the War God had been standing at her side and pressing his face close to her ear, his breath hot on her skin.

"If you do as Rebecca asks," Ares said, though Ramsey showed no indication of having spoken or moved in any way, "we can spare this city a bloodbath."

Diana tensed. "What do you mean to do?" she asked, concentrating on Ramsey and hoping whatever magic he was working flowed both ways.

"I mean to win," Ares said. "And if, to do so, I must level this habitation and slay all who live here, you know I will not hesitate."

Diana felt darkness press in all around her. There was little she could do, at this point. All her great powers were of no use against a mortal woman and what appeared to be a mortal man. She had not believed that the throng would accept her statement that Ramsey was Ares. It would be asking too much of a people who, by virtue of the seeds Rebecca had planted in their minds, were already resistant to anything Diana might tell them.

She listened as Cassie droned on, the same tales the newspapers and television news programs had taken such delight in reporting, feigning outrage as they had gone into greater and greater detail. Diana wondered where these stories had come from, what part might have been fed into Cassie's mind by Ares. She had guessed, on the basis of the truncated call Helena had reported, that Cassie had gone into the lion's den with the best intentions. But she had no way of knowing—no one did—that the force that lay at the center was beyond anything any mortal could hope to contest.

Cassie finished and turned to look at Diana. In that moment, Diana saw the anguish deep in her young friend's eyes and knew with final certainty that, at least at this point, Cassie, like Rebecca, was being manipulated directly by Ares.

She laid a hand on Cassie's shoulder, stopping her as she stepped away from the microphones. "This is all lies, of course," Diana said.

Rebecca snorted. "Oh, yes, of course! You will insist on continuing to live the lie, won't you, Wonder Woman? You have been exposed now before all the people of this great city. Surrender now, and things will be easier for us all."

"No," Diana said, "I surrender only before the truth, and there is none of that here. However—" she slipped the golden lasso from her girdle "—there is a way to draw the truth out from the places you have hidden it."

Ares took a step forward, sudden concern showing through the mask of Stephen Ramsey. He had seen the power of the magic lasso, the focus of the gift of Hestia, the power to compel the truth in even the most reticent of hearts.

"This is nonsense," Ares said, and Diana wondered if the mortals gathered here heard his voice now as she did, hissing, rasping, like a pit of snakes speaking in human tongues. "You're not going to use your trickery to distort the stories this girl has told," Ramsey said.

"What are you afraid of?" Diana hefted the lasso in one hand. Its slender cord was almost invisible, defined mostly by the subtle luminescence that played around its length. "These people know the power of my lasso. It can only compel the truth. If what Cassandra has said is true, it will confirm, not deny."

"No, Princess," Ramsey said, "we do not know this toy of yours can only compel truth. It may compel whatever you wish from it. And if you wish this child to lie, she will lie."

My second move stymied, then, Diana thought. *I trip up because I cannot think in the constant state of bluff, lies, and counterbluffs that Ares does. I have spent all my life in a society where a statement was not made, but that it was true. Even my mother, in the deception that drove its wedge between us, spoke as much truth as she could. She did not lie so much as fail to say all that was to be said.*

"And what of you, then, Ares?" Diana stepped away from Cassie and Rebecca. "If I now throw this lasso round your shoulders, will you still be able to call yourself 'Stephen Ramsey'? Will you still be able to hold this form that tricks the eyes of mortals?"

"I would appreciate it," Ares smiled, "if you would not call me that name. I am Stephen Ramsey, and I would prefer you address me as such, if you address me at all."

"Then you refuse, also, the test of the lasso?" Diana was aware that a hush had fallen over the crowd. One hundred thousand people stood mesmerized, eyes glued to the scene unfolding before them. There was just enough doubt in their hearts, she realized, just enough of a tiny grain of something that clung to the notion that Wonder Woman was, in fact, all that she had presented herself to be, that they watched the drama spreading out before them with the rapt attention of students awaiting the revelation of a great truth.

"I do, indeed, refuse," Ramsey said. "I will not let you use your Amazon magic to make me lie to these people. You are the liar, Wonder Woman, and you are the one who will fall this day. There is nothing left that you can do about that simple fact."

"Yes, there is!"

The voice came from the back of the stage. Father Donald Morris hobbled up the last few steps to the platform. He looked disheveled and ragged, Diana thought, but there was a fire of great conviction burning in his eyes and coloring his cheeks.

"Do not involve yourself in this, Father Morris," Diana said. "There is great danger."

"Greater still if I do nothing," Morris said. He crossed to the center of the stage, and Diana could see the pain in his every step. The old man had laid a heavy burden on himself, coming here.

"Listen to me, you people," Morris said, standing inside the curve of the microphones. "Listen to me, please. I have something to tell you, and it may be the most important thing you have ever heard." He leaned heavily on the mike stand, breathing hard. "I am Donald Morris. That name won't mean a thing to any of you. I'm not from Gateway City, and even if I was, the work I have done for the past forty years would not have affected you, unless you were terribly, terribly unlucky. You see, I've worked almost all my life with children. Sick children. Children with cancer, with AIDS, with all kinds of horrible diseases you won't even know by name. Children who have been in fires, children who have been deliberately abused, tortured by their parents. I have seen babies born addicted to crack cocaine; over and over I have seen the look in the face of a young mother when she heard that the child growing in her womb already had terminal cancer."

He paused for breath, looking out into the crowd, seeing that his words were reaching them, at least on some level. The distortion effect did not seem to be working in the speakers, either. Because these people did not know what his normal voice sounded like? Because there was a greater power preventing the magic Ares had wrought? Morris did not know. He was merely grateful for what he heard.

"I worked with those children all my life," he repeated, "and it ground down my spirit, it crushed the faith out of me. I found, one day, that I could no longer look into the eyes of a child dying of an inoperable brain tumor and believe there was truly a benign, loving God who would allow such things. My upbringing, my calling, these things all combined to teach me that mortals should not seek to understand why God does what he does, and I had been content with that for a long time. But I found I could be content with it no longer. I found I could no longer accept that this God existed, and if He did not exist, then what was there?"

He turned, extending a hand to Diana, who took it, careful lest her movement break the mood the old priest was so carefully creating.

"And then," Morris said, "one day I heard about Wonder Woman.

I heard that an Amazon Princess had come to America, a real Amazon, right out of legend, bringing with her a faith that had not been active on this planet in almost two thousand years. Bringing back the names of gods and goddesses who lived now only in the dusty corners of museums, and in the special effects of Hollywood movies. But these were not relics and effects, not for her. No. For Diana they were real. They were true. And she knew this because she had met them!"

He paused for a moment, to let the words sink in, wondering if any of this was having the desired effect. "Can you understand what that means? I believed in the Lord, our God, in His son Jesus. I felt Him in my heart, I saw His works every day in the world, but I had never met Him, never thought I would ever have a chance to do so, until I stood before Him at the end of my life. But Diana had met her gods, walked with them, even fought with and against them. And when I came to the moment of my crisis, when my faith deserted me and I could no longer find God in my heart, in my soul—when I began to doubt I even had a soul—I came here, to Gateway, and I found Diana, and she took me to Olympus."

A murmur ran through the crowd. Father Morris was not sure he could properly interpret it. Awe? Disbelief? The two, he knew, were closely akin.

"And even if that were true," Rebecca Chandler said, her voice dripping scorn, "what would it prove? That the demons God warned us against have taken on the form of old gods. Forms we might tend instinctively to fear and respect, even trust, because of all the fairy tales of our childhood."

"These are not demons," Morris said. "I have talked with Athena. I have seen Zeus, and Apollo, and Hera and the rest. I have seen more gods than I could begin to number, and I have sensed the divinity in them, felt it as a living, palpable force."

"Been bewitched, you mean." Rebecca's words rippled out over the crowd, and Morris sensed that whatever good he might have done, whatever small victory he might have won with his words, hers were stripping away, tearing down, bit by bit, faster and faster.

"If they were demons," Morris said, "they were very poor demons. For I went to Olympus seeking some comprehension, some way to make the Universe work without the God I had worshiped and served all my life, and yet, instead, I found confirmation of that God. I found proof that He is real, that He is the Creator and the Prime Mover in the Universe. And I found that proof in Diana, in Wonder Woman. I found that proof in the simple, elegant, indisputable fact that she exists because she has a soul that is eternal. A soul that could have been created only by God Himself."

Morris's pale eyes were filled with tears. His hands shook when he raised them from the mike stand. "Please believe me," he said, extending his hands to the crowd, pleading to the hundred thousand pressing close, rapt, frozen, suddenly seized each and every one by the power and the mystery of the old priest's words. "Wonder Woman is no threat to our faith. She is an affirmation of it!"

"Blasphemy!" The word exploded from Stephen Ramsey. Diana turned to see him advancing on Father Morris, his face contorted by rage, his big hands quivering with emotions quite different from those that made Morris tremble. Diana moved to interpose herself between the old priest and the disguised God of War, but her feet were mired in molasses. *The time distortion! Ares is bending time to his will once again.*

Diana struggled to take a step, succeeded, but felt the weight of time press all the heavier upon her the more she pushed against it. She saw all around her, moving as if on frames of film creeping oh-so-slowly through a projector, flick, flick, flick, so that each moment was an element separate and defined from the one that preceded it, and seeming an age from the one that followed.

Through this Ares/Ramsey moved as if completely unaffected. He seized Morris by the lapels, yanking the old man off his feet. Diana saw the priest's face begin to contort in surprise, moving slowly, like the face of a waxwork dummy left to stand in hot sun.

Ramsey spun Morris across the platform, seeming almost to dance with him, whirling them both around a common center, a grotesque do-si-do that carried them to the lip of the stage. In sudden, searing horror Diana knew what would happen next. She pushed against the constricting field, advancing far too slowly, she knew, to be of any use.

Ramsey spun Morris once more, turning the old man in the air as though he were the single surviving spoke of some broken wheel, with Ramsey the hub. Morris rose from the ground, lifting almost horizontal to the axis of the spin, and as his feet pointed out over the crowd, Ramsey released his hold on Morris's coat, bellowing "Blasphemy!" once more as Donald Morris sailed out over the upturned faces, pinwheeling like a battered kite suddenly torn free of its master's grasp.

CHAPTER EIGHTEEN

BEFORE Diana's eyes, Morris hung in the air like a doll spinning at the end of a single thread. For the longest time—real time, not the distortion effect wrought by Ares—he seemed to defy gravity, turning and turning, a satellite moving around the world in some impossibly low orbit.

Then he fell, and though Diana summoned all her powers and strength to hurl herself after him, he vanished into the crowd before she could move. The mob rippled back from the point where Morris fell, then surged inward, closing over him like an angry tide.

Diana was off the ground, in the air, flying. But it was as though she had hurled herself against the mightiest of all hurricanes, as though a wall of solid air stood before her, and she had to drive through it, knowing that all across the park time was bending and changing, so that here it ran smoothly, as it always did, there it was slowed almost to a stop—and there, where Morris was falling, it was accelerated, sped up in ways that defied both Einstein and common sense.

And then the effect was gone. Like the snapping of a rubber band, the grip on Diana vanished, and she found herself thrown over the heads of the crowd and past the edge of the park at something very close to her top speed. She slammed into the side of one of the venerable old buildings overlooking the park. At the last moment she was able to twist, so that she did not strike headfirst, but the impact sent a great avalanche of pain through her, as she and a shower of broken brickwork tumbled to the street.

She did not stop to assess damage either to the building or herself. Diana threw herself like a living javelin back into the park, hurtling down on the spot where Donald Morris had vanished into the sea of angry faces. She plowed into them, parting them, thrusting them aside, tossing men and women alike aside as though they were rag dolls. Her fury was consuming, for she knew as clearly as though she had already seen it, what must lie at the center of the raging herd.

A circle opened, people pushing back, forcing the crowd to spread away from the horror that they themselves had created in their midst. Diana saw the bright fire of fresh blood on hands and faces, splatters of scarlet staining shirts and jackets, jeans and skirts.

She landed near the center, near the broken, bloody thing that lay on the grass, his own life fluids spilling out to mix and mingle with the torn, sodden grasses.

Diana dropped to her knees in the bloodied mud. "Father Morris . . ."

His eyelids flickered. His limbs were broken and bent at angles that were painful even to behold. His neck was twisted, his collar torn free and poking into the air now like a bloodied rib bone.

"Father . . ." Diana leaned close. She put a hand to the old man's cheek and felt his blood hot against her fingertips.

His eyes opened. They were clear, sharp, and Diana saw no pain in them. He was, at that moment, far beyond pain, and she knew there was nothing in her power that she could do to save him.

His lips moved. Diana brought her face close to his, her hair trailing across his chest, red blood mixing with the strands like the colors on a painter's brush. He said only two words, barely a whisper. Diana was not sure she even heard it properly, but she understood the workings of Donald Morris's mind by now well enough to know what his last words would be.

Tears streaming down her cheeks, Diana lifted the broken, lifeless body in her arms, turning on the crowd a steel gaze that sliced through them sharper than the sharpest blade.

"Fools," she said, choking to make a voice that wanted only to scream in outrage form real words. "This man meant you no harm. He meant you only good. He wanted to give you the message of the God you claim to worship, the God you say I seek to tear down. And this is how you repay him! This is how you show your love and devotion to your God!" She held out the body of Father Donald Morris, Antony showing all Rome the bloodied robes of Caesar.

All around her, in the eyes and faces of those who could see and hear her, Diana saw a change, a light, a dawning of realization. The spell of Ares was broken, she knew, but in how many? And at what terrible cost?

"No!" The voice of Stephen Ramsey boomed across the field without the need of the giant speakers. "You cannot play your tricks on these people, Wonder Woman. Your servant has done his work and failed. You cannot distort the truth any longer. You are finished, and there is nothing more that you can do!"

"Oh, there's one thing," said Mike Schorr, stepping from behind one of the big support struts under the glass booth. Taking one long step, he placed his .45 against Stephen Ramsey's head and fired.

The effect was dramatic.

Rebecca screamed, Cassie staggered. Diana leapt into the air, still carrying the body of Donald Morris. The frozen crowd became an explosion of arms and legs, angry faces, surging and swirling onto the stage. Half a dozen SoS security men drew their weapons and opened fire on Mike. Diana dropped Morris's body as gently as she could to the stage, hurling herself into the path of the bullets, bracelets flashing in the arc lights, yellow fire bursting from their smooth surfaces where the bullets struck.

Stephen Ramsey stood for a moment, not staggering, not swaying, no gore spilling across his shoulders, no wound at all visible on his handsome head.

"Your illusion is good," Mike said from his protected place behind Diana, "but not good enough."

The advancing crowd stopped, frozen again. From the back came cries as people tried to force their way past those in front, attempting to see why the sudden, vengeful surge had stopped. Those in front stood blank faced, wide eyed, and the thought in each mind was etched clearly on their features.

I saw him get shot. I saw that man point a gun at this man's head, and fire. Was he shooting blanks?

"And just to show I'm not shooting blanks—" Mike said, knowing what must be the point to which logic would carry the crowd. He fired into the wood floor of the stage, two quick shots in succession. Wood chips spit up from the point of impact. Then he fired twice more, into Ramsey's chest.

"Something seems to be stopping those slugs," Mike said. "At least, I don't see them hitting anyone in the crowd. But they don't seem to be hitting you, either. Are you gonna fall down dead now, Ramsey? 'Cause if you do, I warn you now you better leave a body the medical examiner can autopsy." Mike summoned a grim smile. "But it's really too late for any of that, isn't it?"

"NO-OOOOOOOHHHHHHH!"

The word erupted from Ramsey as a physical force. Diana felt herself pushed back. Mike staggered and fell. Cassie and Rebecca, hanging on to each other as the controlling power of Ares left them, stumbled back into the leading edges of the crowd as it, too, toppled and fell away.

Stephen Ramsey seemed to split, to rupture like a fruit left too long on the vine. His skin blackened, his form swelling. The bright twinkle in his eyes turned to crimson fire.

"Fools!" Ares stood revealed, his subterfuge undone by the most simple and direct of methods. Mike had guessed and gambled, and his gamble had paid off. Ares could slow and distort the movement of time, but not even he could reverse it. There was no way he could seize the moment and turn it back on itself. "Fools," he bellowed again, and his voice lashed the crowd like burning ice. "Now pay the forfeit of your stupidity. See what a *true* god can unleash upon you!"

The heavens growled. The lightning flashed. All across the crowd the screaming began.

"Oh, my God!"

Sheldon Minsky made it a point never to swear in public—his actions, after all, would reflect back on the man he ostensibly worked for—but as he looked down on the scene below the glass booth the words pushed out of his mouth before he could control them—as much prayer as blasphemy.

He had seen a man shot in the head with one of the most powerful handguns in the world, a shot that should have turned the man's head to shards of spinning bone and sent his brain foaming out of his skull like bright pink soda pop.

But there had been no effect! And Minsky knew—all in the booth knew, as they crowded against the angled glass—that this was no trick of perspective. Stephen Ramsey had taken a shot to the head that no mortal could possibly survive, and he was utterly unharmed by it. They could not imagine anything more outrageous, more astonishing.

Until the next moment, when Stephen Ramsey burst like an egg in a microwave, his own form rupturing as something black and horrible expanded from within.

"Oh, my God!" Minsky groaned again. The stage rocked. The towers from which the booth was suspended turned slowly, twisting and squealing like living things.

Minsky turned, his mouth moving with the beginning of a suggestion that they, first, back away from the glass and, second, get the hell out of the booth. In that moment the whole front wall bent, shattered, and exploded outward like confetti from the hands of a demon bridesmaid.

•　　•　　•

Pinned by the press of bodies sixty feet from the stage, Helena was unable to move, but she could see everything. The whole tableau had unfolded before her horrified eyes, and all she could think of was that she must fight her way through the crowd, over the crowd, and get to Cassie.

She heard the first scream away to her right and turned to look. Fire erupted in the mass of huddled people, and where a moment ago Helena had noticed a woman wearing the pale blue armband of the SoS, she now saw something that was not at all human.

It rose up on legs that bent the wrong way, and from its scaly, scabrous back black wings spread like polished leather. It swiped at the nearest people with hands transformed to clusters of scythelike blades, and where the hands passed, blood spurted as from a dozen geysers.

Another scream and another gout of flame announced the transformation of another of Rebecca Chandler's followers. Then another, and another.

In an instant there were a hundred or more of the demonic things, beating their vast wings, leaping across the crowd to slash and tear.

"Now shall there be payment in blood and broken bone," Ares said, and though his voice was once again calm and measured, it burned across the crowd, and Helena knew that even those in the most distant, hidden corners of Gateway City heard his words.

The mob tore itself apart, people pushing, scrambling, scrabbling, and tearing as they shoved and screamed and hurled themselves away from Ares' unleashed hordes. Ducking and shoving herself, fighting against the flow of the crowd to reach the stage and her daughter, Helena saw the high platform shudder, saw the mighty towers on its corners shake as though the earth itself were trembling at the horror it must bear.

Helena saw the taut guywires snap. In abject terror she looked on as one of the wires whipped out across the crowd, slicing through the neck of a young man just as he leapt from the edge of the stage. Like something from an old cartoon, the body fell and the head, frozen in midscream, seemed to hang in the air, looking lost and confused at the sudden absence of its familiar perch. Then the head fell, bouncing across the shoulders and backs of the stampeding crowd like a child's ball bouncing down a flight of steps.

A sound like ten thousand locomotives piling into one another blasted across the field, and Helena pushed aside the human wave crashing past her to see the closest of the towers twisting. In the middle, strung between the towers, the visitors' booth twisted too, and the sheets of glass on its face and sides transformed themselves in an instant into a swirling snowstorm of bright, sharp shards.

Helena saw a human form flash across the stage, up to the booth, and she knew without seeing clearly that it was Diana. Wonder Woman seized the front of the booth, tipped it back so that its occupants tumbled to the solid rear wall. She ripped the booth from its supports and flew it away from the stage. As she did the front corner tower surrendered its war with gravity and toppled toward the crush of fragile human flesh beneath.

And Wonder Woman was there again, swooping up under the tower to catch it, lift it, bend it back. Helena called out to her, but Diana was too far away to hear.

And then Helena heard something herself, a keening, piercing cry, an ululation rising from hundreds of throats. She turned. It was coming from the rear—now the front—of the mob, and as Helena finally reached the edge of the stage and pulled herself, torn and bloodied, onto the platform, she saw the source of the sound.

Amazons. In full armor. Swords and spears bristling before them. They leapt across the backs of the fleeing crowd, swinging their swords, jabbing their spears, and before them the demon hordes of Ares suddenly changed from aggressors to prey.

Helena felt a new strength born in her, a kindred with those mighty women warriors. She pushed through the last of the crowd on the stage and ran across to the place where she had last seen her daughter.

Cassie was still there. She knelt on the blood-slick boards of the stage, near the toppled mike stand. She huddled herself over the curled, fallen form of Rebecca Chandler, cradling the woman's head in her lap, and Helena saw Cassie's tears fall to splash upon the blood-ied cheek of the woman she had not so long ago mocked and called "bitch."

Ten feet to her left, Cassie saw the man she knew as Davis Kavanagh pull his gun from the holster on his right hip and level it at Mike Schorr.

The phrase "This looks like a job for Wonder Girl" did not quite pass through her mind, but something very close to it did. Cassie threw herself across the stage, everything she had ever learned in gym class summoned to her as she tucked herself into a tight sphere and can-nonballed into Kavanagh's legs. The man toppled, tumbling over to land hard as Cassie unrolled herself and somersaulted to her feet.

She spun, ready to go hand to hand with the larger, likely better-trained security chief. But Kavanagh was no longer there. In his place, rising from the stage in coils of acrid, burning smoke, was some-thing so far from the form of Davis Kavanagh that Cassie's brain for a moment completely refused to accept the image her eyes were trans-mitting to it.

The thing was human shaped, but only in the broadest sense—it had a head, a torso, arms, legs. But the skin was black—not the black of African skin, but coal black and shiny as though made of stone or metal. It was all hard edges and spikes, no point anywhere on the sur-face that did not bristle with blazes and points as sharp as razors. Under a brow like the edge of a sword, eyes like twin firebrands gleamed with hellish light, and when the lipless mouth split in a smile, the teeth were blue steel and fine as needles.

The thing launched itself to its feet, wings as broad as the span of a small aircraft unfolding from its back in a sudden fluid motion that looked for all the world to Cassie as though they were forming out of the air itself. "Kavanagh" laughed, and the sound was every bit as sharp as the creature's appearance. It leapt at Cassie, swiping at her with long nails like samurai blades. For the first time since she had donned it, Cassie was grateful for the foolish, flouncy dress with all its frills and puffiness. The slashing talons ripped through the front of her bodice, missing her flesh by inches.

Cassie ducked under the second swing and rolled across the stage. Too busy avoiding the attack to pay close attention to where she was going, Cassie came up hard against the side of one of the support towers. The back of her head cracked against metal, and the world swam in fire and blood. She tried to push herself up on her hands and knees, but the stage most uncooperatively refused to remain level. A piece of Cassie's mind registered the startling fact that it was not solely due to her having cracked her head. The whole platform was, indeed, rocking and bucking as the crowd surged on and around it.

Cassie fell back on her side, vision blurred, seeing only shadows and fog as the thing that had been Kavanagh loomed over her.

I'm done for, she thought, and a chill such as she had never known ran through her intestines. *I'm sorry, Mom.*

She saw the thing raise a cloudy shape that she could only assume was its arm, its clawed hand, and she wrapped her own arms around her head and waited for the disemboweling blow.

It did not come. Cassie heard a cry, almost a scream, and saw a pale blue blur slam into the demon. *Rebecca!*

It was Rebecca. Heedless of her own danger, she swung at the demon with an improvised club, a length of steel piping wrenched loose from the lighting towers as they twisted and buckled. Cassie looked about to see that one side of the nearest tower was a veritable porcupine of pipes and twisted metal spikes. She had missed impaling herself by only a matter of inches when she slammed into the tower.

Rebecca swung her club without grace, without any sense of fighting skills whatsoever. Cassie, thanks to the self-defense methods Wonder Woman had taught her, knew she could do a better job. Still, the effort was much appreciated, and Cassie seized the time it allowed her to force herself to her feet, shaking her head and blinking to clear her vision.

The demon was laughing again, swiping at Rebecca, ripping at her robe and her flesh, but it was clear to Cassie that he—it?—was putting no real effort into the attack. He was playing with Rebecca, mocking her as he swatted aside her swings.

Suddenly the demon grew tired of its game. It seized the crude weapon, twisting it out of Rebecca's grip with such speed and violence that Cassie heard the bones in Rebecca's wrist snap. Rebecca screamed, and the demon grabbed her and lifted her from the stage, swinging her about his horned head like the victim of a predatory dinosaur in *Jurassic Park*.

Cassie knew in that instant what she had to do. Half crawling, half rolling, she scuttled across the stage, ducking under the wings of the demon and the flailing legs of Rebecca Chandler. Cassie rolled herself to her feet on the other side of the demon, so that the former Davis Kavanagh was between her and the jagged ends of the broken piping.

Cassie ripped off the foolish skirt she still wore, starched petticoats and all, again grateful for the excessive use of cloth in the outfit. She wrapped the torn material around her arms and, holding the improvised ram before her face to afford some small additional protection, she launched herself at the demon's back.

She hit it as hard as she could, and in an instant the cloth around her arms crackled and the outer layers burst into flame. Cassie ignored the fire and pushed, carrying through the arc of her trajectory. From the corner of her eye she saw Rebecca Chandler sail out of the monster's grip, spinning as Father Morris had in Ares' grasp.

Cassie heard a wet *chuk* and felt a shudder run through the demon. He screamed as she impaled him on the ragged ends of the pipe, and she hoped the fact that steel was an iron alloy would be sufficient to provide the necessary magic.

It did. As Cassie fell back, tearing the burning fabric from around her arms, she saw fire of a different kind erupt across the skin of the demon. Each place where a pipe had pierced him became a torrent of blue-white flame, crackling and burning, spreading almost too fast for her eyes to follow. In one instant the thing was gleaming black and writhing on the spikes, in the next it was a fireball, and its scream evaporated as quickly as the flames that consumed it.

Cassie tossed away the last of the cloth—with its progenitor gone, the flame that threatened to engulf her vanished, too—and stumbled across the stage to where Rebecca lay. Her robes were torn and her skin was bloodied, but she was alive.

Cassie dropped to her knees, pulling Rebecca's head into her lap, folding herself over the fallen evangelist. When the tears came, they were due only in small part to the pain she felt in her young body.

From the moment the Amazons arrived, the tide turned so swiftly that what followed could scarcely be called a battle. Ares' demons were terrifying, savage beasts, but they were little more than beasts, and no match despite their wings and claws for warriors trained for three thousand years in their special arts.

Diana knew at once that she did not need to concern herself with the smaller incidentals of the fight. She landed before Ares, facing him as she had before, wondering if this time, for the first time, it would come down to a physical confrontation between them, and wondering if even all her great power would truly be a match for the unleashed fury of a god.

"Well, Ares?" She watched the way he moved, the way he shifted on his feet, ready for anything that was to come.

"Well, Princess?" There was an unexpected smugness in his voice, a mocking tone as he mimicked her.

"Are we to fight? Is that what you desire from this, now?"

"Not in particular," Ares said. "It has never been my desire to prove myself your physical superior. I wish only to destroy the folly of peace you seek to foist upon this foolish populace."

"You will never do that," Diana said. "Even if I die, you can never destroy the message I have brought. It lives through all the voices that spoke it before me, and it will live in all that come after."

"Mmm. Pity." Ares turned with a broad flourish of his cloak. "Then I suppose I shall, in the end, be forced to content myself with your head."

The last word almost caught Diana by surprise. The swirl of the cloak had concealed the drawing of Ares' sword. It flashed across the night air, lightning caught and made solid, and only in the last instant did Diana snap up her crossed arms, blocking the blow. The sound of steel on steel rang and echoed through all the canyon streets of Gateway City.

Ares recovered instantly from his thwarted blow. He ducked back and swung again, blue fire running down his blade like quicksilver. This time Diana leapt, stepping into the air and over the arc of the sword. She kicked and felt the solid satisfaction of her booted heel slamming into the War God's helmet.

Ares staggered back, and Diana dropped to grab his sword arm with both hands. She bent the arm up and back, twisting his wrist so that the sword drew its thin, sharp line across the space immediately before Ares' throat.

"Can you die, War God?" Diana very nearly hissed as she pressed the blade close in under the lip of Ares' helmet. She was at least as strong as he was at that moment, she knew. But what she did not know, what most concerned her, was what forces, what power Ares might be able to summon to aid him now. They stood thus for a long moment, Diana pressing in, Ares precisely matching her strength, so that it seemed they might be a statue, locked in that deadly embrace until the end of time.

"You've lost, War God," Diana said. Donald Morris's blood was still wet and hot on her bare flesh, putting the lie to her words. In the death of that one good man, Diana knew, Ares had won as great a victory as if he had succeeded in his plan to destroy her. Others would come, as they had before and would again, to take up the banner she might have been forced to let fall. But the power of the human spirit was a rare and precious thing, and to see it extinguished, even in the death of one man, was a tragedy as great as if Ares had laid waste to all Diana's works.

"Yes," Ares said, surprising her. He relaxed his resistance and stepped back. Diana did not push the blade to follow, listening to his words. "You have planned your counteroffensive well, Princess," he smiled behind the helmet. "You have caught me in the smallness of my scheme. I focused too much on Rebecca Chandler as my instrument of your destruction, and by revealing me, this mortal—" Ares waved a gauntleted hand in the direction of Michael Schorr "—has revealed Rebecca to be a dupe of the very forces she set herself to oppose."

Diana nodded, feeling a small compassion stirring. "She is the one who has been destroyed. For the rest of her life, her words will be in doubt, even to herself."

Ares laughed. "You say that as if it has consequence, Princess. To the immortal span of a god, what is the breaking of a single human spirit?" He raised his hands in pantomime of the words that followed. "I play with worlds as others play with grains of sand, Diana. My concerns are greater than any you can comprehend. If I lose this day, it means only that I win another. You know this."

"Never."

Ares laughed again, and at once the laughter and his last words were all that remained of him on the cold night air. "Never is a long, long time, Princess. Even for an immortal."

E P I L O G U E
T W O   W E E K S   L A T E R

"ONE hundred and sixteen dead. More than four thousand critically injured. And, of course, that's not counting the people replaced by Ares' demons. We may never know how many of them there were—or are. Oh, and William Winget had a heart attack and died three days after the riot. His doctors said it was the strain, the shock of being in that booth when it exploded and started to fall."

"I read about that in his own paper." Rebecca Chandler sat in the enclosed sunroom high on the side of Mercy General Hospital. After nearly two weeks of unconsciousness, during which she suffered through a lifetime of horrible dreams, she had recovered enough to be allowed visitors, and to sit in the sun without constant attendance. She listened to Mike Schorr and avoided his eyes, as she had avoided the gaze of all her fellow humans in every waking hour since the fateful night. "The poor man," she said. "I shall add his name to the list of those for whose untimely deaths I am responsible."

"You were not responsible," Diana said. She stood by Mike's chair, and beside her, in two other chairs, were Helena and Cassandra Sandsmark.

"What about the demons and the Amazons?" Rebecca pointedly ignored Diana's consoling words.

"No sign of the demons," Mike said. "They just evaporated when Ares disappeared."

"Ares." Rebecca shuddered. "He really was Ares. The God of War." She shook her head. "I've been such a fool." Now she raised her eyes to look directly at Mike Schorr. "And the people who killed Father Morris?"

It was Mike's turn to shake his head. "No way to know who they were. Not even Diana could describe any of them well enough to make any sort of attempt to pick them up. There were probably a hundred people or more who tore into him. Even people who didn't participate, at least didn't do anything hands on, got his blood all over them."

"Then they will get away with it? With murder?"

"They will know what they did," Diana said. "If they are truly the kind of people you think they are, if the madness was only the work of Ares in their minds, they will carry for all their lives the knowledge of what they did."

"Small punishment. Too small. For them. For me." Rebecca looked at Cassie. "It would seem I'm everything you thought I was in the first place, Cassandra. A liar. A charlatan."

Cassie's eyes were bright with starting tears. "You're not any of that," she said. She wanted to run to Rebecca and embrace her, but she held herself back. She was not sure how Helena would respond, and Cassie felt she had done more than enough, even with the best of intentions, to hurt her mother.

"I should have seen through 'Stephen Ramsey' the first day we met. But I let foolish pride get in the way. I wanted to be the one who saved the world, and when he told me I was going to be the one to do it—" Rebecca shuddered and her own tears were flowing fast now. "I'm a small and stupid woman," she said when her voice was her own again.

"No," Diana said. "You were a tool, and because you were, for the most part, a willing tool, you will have some degree of guilt to carry with you. But you have a lifetime in which to undo what the last two years brought." Diana smiled. "And I have seen in you the courage and conviction of one I fully believe can accomplish anything she sets out to do."

"Doubtful," Rebecca said. "The authorities seized our assets—I have no funding. And no followers. I am back to where I was when Ramsey—when Ares found me. Worse, really. At least I had nothing to overcome, then. Now I have the reputation of being a tool of the devil."

"I don't believe in the devil," Mike said. "And believe me, I've seen enough crap in this town to know what the dark side of the human soul looks like. But it's not because of the devil, or Ares, or anyone else. No one except people themselves. Some of them are bad. Ten million reasons why they're bad, but the end is the same. You want to do something worthwhile, Miss Chandler, you get out there and preach the message that people don't have to be bad. Just because you were abused, doesn't mean you have to be abusive, just because you were the victim of violence, doesn't mean you have to be violent."

"Turn the other cheek?" Rebecca found the words comforting, if, at the moment, a little hollow.

"No," Diana said. "It is never good to turn away from evil and let it have its way. It must be fought, and each of us must fight within ourselves that part of our nature that is inclined to follow the darker path. It is difficult, I know, for many times that path is the easier one."

"Nothing easy in what you see for me, ahead," Rebecca said. "I can't even begin to imagine where I might start."

"Then perhaps I can make a suggestion," Diana said. "Father Morris was alive when I reached him, though only for a moment. Long enough to look at me, and say two words. In those words, I think, you might find the focus of your new crusade."

Rebecca raised an eyebrow, curious. "What were his two words, two words that could help smooth over all the ills of the world?"

Wonder Woman smiled a small, quiet smile, remembering the man who had become her friend for a time that was far too short.

"He said, 'Forgive them,'" Diana said.

Lois & Clark
A Superman Novel

C.J. Cherryh

ISBN 0-7615-1169-5 / paperback / 288 pages
U.S. $12.00 / Can. $16.95

As Superman struggles desperately half a world away to save a village threatened by a bursting dam, Lois Lane throws herself into the rescue effort at a collapsed hotel in Metropolis—and emerges a hero. Caught in the glare of national media attention, nothing in her life will ever be the same again . . . including her relationship with Clark Kent. This exciting novel delves deeply into the private lives and thrilling adventures of Superman and Lois Lane.

"Excellent. Hugo Award–winning author C.J. Cherryh uses her vast talents to add to the adventures of two timeless, beloved characters." —Romantic Times

To Order Books

Please send me the following items:

Quantity	Title	Unit Price	Total
_____	**Lois & Clark**	$ **12.00**	$ _____
_____	_____	$ _____	$ _____
_____	_____	$ _____	$ _____
_____	_____	$ _____	$ _____
_____	_____	$ _____	$ _____

Subtotal	$ _____
Deduct 10% when ordering 3-5 books	$ _____
7.25% Sales Tax (CA only)	$ _____
8.25% Sales Tax (TN only)	$ _____
5.0% Sales Tax (MD and IN only)	$ _____
7.0% G.S.T. Tax (Canada only)	$ _____
Shipping and Handling*	$ _____
Total Order	$ _____

*Shipping and Handling depend on Subtotal.

Subtotal	Shipping/Handling
$0.00–$14.99	$3.00
$15.00–$29.99	$4.00
$30.00–$49.99	$6.00
$50.00–$99.99	$10.00
$100.00–$199.99	$13.50
$200.00+	Call for Quote

Foreign and all Priority Request orders:
Call Order Entry department
for price quote at 916-632-4400

This chart represents the total retail price of books only (before applicable discounts are taken).

By Telephone: With MC or Visa, call 800-632-8676 or 916-632-4400.
Mon–Fri, 8:30-4:30.

WWW: http://www.primapublishing.com

By Internet E-mail: sales@primapub.com

By Mail: Just fill out the information below and send with your remittance to:

**Prima Publishing
P.O. Box 1260BK
Rocklin, CA 95677**

My name is _____

I live at _____

City _____ State _____ ZIP_____

MC/Visa#_____ Exp. _____

Check/money order enclosed for $ _____ Payable to Prima Publishing

Daytime telephone _____

Signature _____